COMMON MOSSES OF THE NORTHEAST AND APPALACHIANS

PRINCETON FIELD GUIDES

Rooted in field experience and scientific study, Princeton's guides to animals and plants are the authority for professional scientists and amateur naturalists alike. **Princeton Field Guides** present this information in a compact format carefully designed for easy use in the field. The guides illustrate every species in color and provide detailed information on identification, distribution, and biology.

COMMON *MOSSES*

OF THE NORTHEAST
AND APPALACHIANS

KARL B MCKNIGHT ❧ JOSEPH R. ROHRER
KIRSTEN MCKNIGHT WARD ❧ WARREN J. PERDRIZET

PRINCETON UNIVERSITY PRESS
PRINCETON AND OXFORD

Copyright © 2013 by Princeton University Press

Published by Princeton University Press, 41 William Street, Princeton,
New Jersey 08540

In the United Kingdom: Princeton University Press, 6 Oxford Street,
Woodstock, Oxfordshire OX20 1TW

press.princeton.edu

Library of Congress Cataloging-in-Publication Data

Common Mosses of the Northeast and Appalachians / Karl B McKnight ... [et al.].
    p. cm. -- (Princeton field guides)

    Includes index.

    ISBN 978-0-691-15696-5 (pbk. : alk. paper)   1. Mosses—Appalachian
    Mountains—Identification.   2. Mosses—Northeastern States—
    Identification.   I. McKnight, Karl B.   II. Series: Princeton field guides.
    QK541.5.A67C66 2013
    588′.2—dc23   2012032069

British Library Cataloging-in-Publication Data is available

The publisher would like to acknowledge the authors of this volume for
providing the camera-ready copy from which this book was printed

This book was designed by Kirsten McKnight Ward and is composed in
Chaparral Pro and Calibri

Printed on acid-free paper ∞

Printed in Singapore

10 9 8 7 6

To *J*erry *J*enkins,

The brilliant and creative naturalist without whom
this book would have been unimagined and impossible.

And to *H*oward *C*rum and *L*ewis *A*nderson,

Inspirational teachers and authors of *Mosses of
Eastern North America*, the source of our line drawings
and authoritative reference on the mosses of the region
covered by this field guide.

Acknowledgments

The beautiful illustrations of Marilou Florian, Lynn Bartosch, Phyllis Pollard, Shirley Watkins, and Karen Teramura found in *Mosses of Eastern North America* by Crum and Anderson add immeasurable grace and usefulness to this guide. We thank Columbia University Press for granting permission to use these drawings and species measurements.

Financial support including equipment was provided to Dr. McKnight by St. Lawrence University and the Alcoa Foundation and to Dr. Rohrer by the University of Wisconsin-Eau Claire Faculty Sabbatical Leave Program and a UWEC University Research and Creative Activity grant. Additional timely and generous financial support was provided by Alma Z. Boyce.

We are grateful for permission to photograph mosses granted by the University of Michigan Biological Station, The Chewonki Foundation, and The Trustees of Reservations (MA). We acknowledge the outstanding network of state and national forests and parks that protect moss habitats and provided access to photograph species.

We are appreciative of the helpful, shaping influences of Lyle Mumford, Jerry Jenkins and two anonymous reviewers. We thank Heidi Lovette at Cornell University Press. We were delighted by our supportive and extremely competent editors at Princeton University Press: Robert Kirk, Mark Bellis, and Dimitri Karetnikov. Dr. Rohrer's early interest in mosses was encouraged by his parents, Tom Daggy, and Bob Solberg. Dr. Rohrer credits Susan Moyle Studlar, Lewis Anderson, and Howard Crum with his formal training in bryology. Dr. Rohrer's wife, Evelyn, was a constant source of encouragement. She cheerfully allowed him to study mosses while others had "real jobs," and she improved our book by testing keys and making suggestions for revising the text. We thank Marshall Ward for computer technology support, text editing and a constant supply of dark chocolate and good humor. We thank Closey and Whit Dickey for granting Kirsten the peaceful space to write and for hosting the research team in their home on numerous occasions. Warren Perdrizet thanks George and JoAnn Perdrizet for their continued support in all his endeavors. Dr. McKnight recognizes and is grateful to Joan McKnight for scanning most of the line drawings and for her consistent and patient support. Dr. McKnight learned much of what he knows from his parents Kent and Vera McKnight.

We are thankful to our field testers for their feedback and enthusiasm, starting with three-year-old Julia who reminds us it is never too early, or too late, to fall in love with mosses.

CONTENTS

A SAMPLE PAGE

Pay particular attention to notes and arrows highlighting essential characters of a moss.

If your specimen fits the **Key Features** of a pleurocarp with lance-shaped leaves without a midrib, for example, flip to the pages with these tabs along the edge.

Is your moss wet or dry? It can look quite different.

Wet **|** Wiry, thread-like mats are formed from creeping shoots covered in tiny leaves **|** Dry

P. subtilis upright capsule; with lid

P. confervoides bent capsule, with lid

Platydictya confervoides

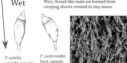

Platydictya subtilis
ALGAL THREAD MOSS

APPEARANCE: Small creeping moss that forms patches of stiff, thin threads with tiny green leaves. When wet, they appear dull green and flare out at 75 degrees, when dry they are slightly shiny and pressed to stems except for their wispy tips.

LEAVES: Tiny lances, ¼–⅓ mm long with narrow tips. Midrib is lacking, but too small to verify with hand lens. Edges are smooth.

CAPSULES: Short-cylindrical, about 1 mm long, upright, with a conical lid. Stalk 7–12 mm tall.

HABITAT: Tree trunk bases and bare roots, sometimes on fallen logs.

SIMILAR SPECIES

Platydictya confervoides, ALGAL ROCK MOSS: Grows on calcareous rocks rather than tree bark. Capsules are bent or curved.

Hygroamblystegium varium (p. 213) Is a similarly stringy, small, creeping moss but its leaves have a midrib and are about twice the size, 1–2 mm long.

Leskea gracilescens (p. 263) Leaves are pointed egg-shaped without a drawn out narrow tip. They also have a midrib.

MICROSCOPIC FEATURES

Leaf edges are free of even minute teeth. Cells near tip of leaf in *P. subtilis* are relatively long, being 3-5× longer than wide versus at most 2-3× in *P. confervoides*.

Compare your capsules to those illustrated, but remember: they might be at different developmental stages, with or without their lid or hood.

Check the information regarding the general appearance, leaves, capsules, and typical habitat.

How to Use this Book

1. Determine the three **Key Features** of your moss (pp. 10–15).

   Apply these Key Features to one or both of the following methods to identify your specimen:

   a. Find the section of the book where the colored side tabs match the Key Features of your moss. Compare your moss to the photographs, drawings, and species descriptions until you find the species that best fits your sample.

   b. Use the **Key Features Path to the Keys** (pp. 16–17) to determine which illustrated key (pp. 341–379) to follow to identify your moss.

2. Compare your specimen to similar species, where confusing look-alikes are contrasted. **Bold-faced** species are so similar they are placed on the same page. You might discover that your sample is one of these instead.

3. (Optional) Collect your specimen following the suggestions on pp. 20–21. Use a microscope to study attributes that are difficult to see with a hand lens.

4. Refer to the Habitat Lists on pp. 380–383 for suggestions of species you are most likely to encounter in a given habitat.

5. Turn to these pages to learn more:

6. Finally – find another moss and repeat. Slow down and enjoy the beautiful world of mosses.

KEY FEATURE 1: GROWTH FORM

Take a look at a clump of moss, then tease it apart to examine one strand. Choose the category that best matches your specimen.

Most mosses follow one of three basic growth forms:

ACROCARP

Stems simple or sparsely forked, with the forks often running parallel to each other. Plants packed together like tufts of carpet.

Capsules arise from end or tip of stem, but later growth can disguise this trait.

Individual stems typically stand upright, but the exceptions are still rarely branched.

Mounds of moss often appear to "creep" across the ground. But tease a clump apart and you will find it composed of individual stems.

PEAT MOSS

Stems stand upright with branches in clusters of
3 or more. Some branches spread outward
and others hang down along the stem.
Many branches are crowded
at the top, forming a
mop-like head.

PLEUROCARP

Stems branch freely and at a wide angle, some irregularly,
others in a pinnate pattern, i.e., regularly divided into
opposite branches. Plants twine together to form mats.

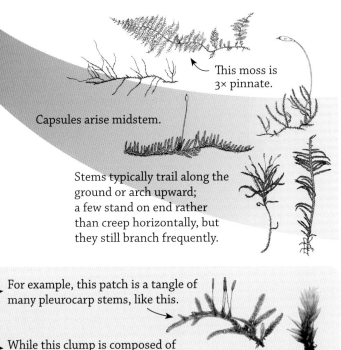

This moss is
3× pinnate.

Capsules arise midstem.

Stems typically trail along the
ground or arch upward;
a few stand on end rather
than creep horizontally, but
they still branch frequently.

For example, this patch is a tangle of
many pleurocarp stems, like this.

While this clump is composed of
many acrocarp stems, like this one.

KEY FEATURE 2: LEAF SHAPE

What is the essential shape of the leaf?

Most moss leaves fit along a continuum from very narrow and hairlike to wide egg-shaped.

Choose the category that best matches your specimen with wet leaves—dry leaves are often narrower or shriveled.

LANCE

Narrowly triangular, with generally straight rather than curved sides that gradually taper to a point.

HAIRLIKE

Very long and narrow, appearing "hairlike" to the naked eye.

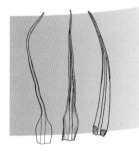    

TONGUE

Generally straight-sided coming to an abrupt tip, like a tongue or strap.

LEAFLESS

Capsules arise from mat of algal-like threads, lacking regular branches and leaves.

OVATE

Egg-shaped, arrowhead-shaped or with curved or bulging sides; relatively shorter and wider than lance-shaped leaves.

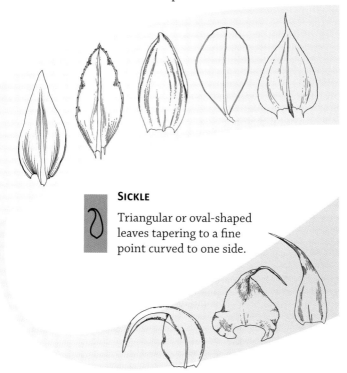

SICKLE

Triangular or oval-shaped leaves tapering to a fine point curved to one side.

PEAT MOSS

Branch and stem leaves of differing shape. Branch leaves (on left below) ovate to lance-shaped and cupped. Stem leaves (on right) triangular to tongue-shaped and flat.

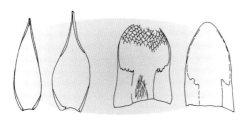

KEY FEATURE 3: MIDRIB

Hold your specimen up so the light shines through a leaf. As you tilt the sprig gently side to side, check for a fine line running down the middle of the leaf blade.

Choose the category that best matches your specimen.

LANCE WITH MIDRIB

OVATE WITH MIDRIB

SICKLE WITH MIDRIB

TRICKY CASES

FULL-BLADE MIDRIB:
When a midrib fills all or most of the leaf blade, it is difficult to recognize. Peel off a leaf and examine the clasping base where the midrib is visible.

14

All **Tongue**-shaped leaves have a midrib.

Don't bother squinting too hard to see the midrib of **Hairlike** leaves. They all have one, even if it can be hard to make out. See **Full-blade Midrib** below.

LANCE WITHOUT MIDRIB

   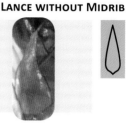

The leaves of some species, like this one, are tightly overlapping.

OVATE WITHOUT MIDRIB

SICKLE WITHOUT MIDRIB

TRICKY CASES

 Ovate leaf without a midrib.

Ovate leaf with a midrib.

PLEATED LEAVES: Vertical folds in a blade might mimic or hide a midrib.

KEY FEATURES PATH TO THE KEYS

Now put the three key features together to find which key will help you identify your moss specimen.

Or flip through the section of the book with the appropriate **GROWTH FORM** and **LEAF SHAPE/MIDRIB** tabs to browse among similar species for your specimen.

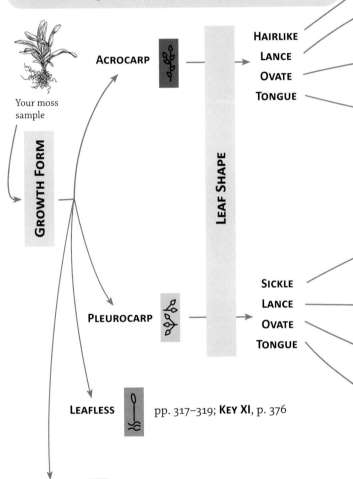

Your moss sample

GROWTH FORM

ACROCARP

LEAF SHAPE

HAIRLIKE
LANCE
OVATE
TONGUE

PLEUROCARP

SICKLE
LANCE
OVATE
TONGUE

LEAFLESS pp. 317–319; **KEY XI**, p. 376

PEAT MOSS pp. 321–339; **KEY XII**, pp. 376–379

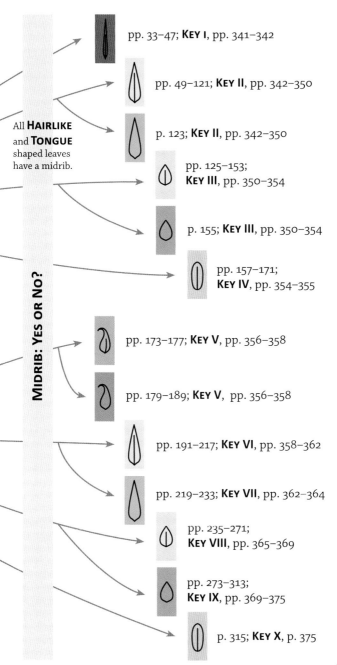

pp. 33–47; **KEY I**, pp. 341–342

pp. 49–121; **KEY II**, pp. 342–350

p. 123; **KEY II**, pp. 342–350

All **HAIRLIKE** and **TONGUE** shaped leaves have a midrib.

pp. 125–153; **KEY III**, pp. 350–354

p. 155; **KEY III**, pp. 350–354

pp. 157–171; **KEY IV**, pp. 354–355

MIDRIB: YES OR NO?

pp. 173–177; **KEY V**, pp. 356–358

pp. 179–189; **KEY V**, pp. 356–358

pp. 191–217; **KEY VI**, pp. 358–362

pp. 219–233; **KEY VII**, pp. 362–364

pp. 235–271; **KEY VIII**, pp. 365–369

pp. 273–313; **KEY IX**, pp. 369–375

p. 315; **KEY X**, p. 375

17

HOW TO LOOK AT A MOSS

FIRST, NOTE ITS SURROUNDINGS. Are you in an urban park, along a stream in a forest, in a bog? Is the moss growing on disturbed soil, the bark of a tree, a rock, a rotting log? Moss identification is often aided by knowing where the plant was growing.

Mosses grow everywhere, but that doesn't mean every sprig is an ideal specimen to study. Look for healthy, homogeneous samples and avoid bedraggled, tiny samples that lack capsules and are growing intertwined with several species.

Many mosses look very different when wet versus dry. If possible, observe it in both conditions. Dry mosses can be moistened using a spray bottle, such as those used when ironing clothes or misting houseplants. Moisten the moss clump while intentionally keeping part of the clump dry by covering it with your hand as you mist. Then you can observe wet and dry plants side by side. If the moss is already wet, pull a few shoots from the clump; they will quickly dry in the air.

Wet

Dry

Pick a small sample and begin to tease apart individual shoots. Most mosses fall into one of two groups of different growth forms. Acrocarps generally stand upright, with many stems next to each other vertically and packed together into a clump or tuft. If the stem branches, it typically divides in two with the forks running side by side. In contrast, pleurocarps generally creep with their stems running along the substrate to which they are attached (soil, bark, rock, etc.), interweaving with other stems to form mats. Their branches split off at a right angle to the main stem. **Growth form** is the **First Key Feature** that will guide your identification. Study the text and illustrations on pp. 10–11 carefully before deciding on the growth form of your sample and moving on to examine the leaves.

That's right — moss leaves are really small! You will need a hand lens of 7–20× to get a good look at them. Lower power lenses give a broader field of view, useful for initial examination, whereas higher power lenses provide the extra magnification needed to see fine detail.

To use your lens, look straight ahead and bring the lens close to your eye or glasses; then bring the moss sample up to the lens with your other hand. Play with the focus by moving the sample toward and away from the lens. Good light is essential. Tilt your head back to allow the light of the sky to shine through the leaf in order to search for a midrib and to silhouette teeth along the leaf margin.

Millimeter rulers are printed inside the front cover of the book and on the left sides of the identification key pages for convenience measuring leaves, but you might also want to carry a white plastic ruler with you.

The **Second Key Feature** to unlock the identity of your unknown moss is **leaf shape**. Most moss leaves fall along a continuum from hairlike through lance to ovate. The text and illustrations on pp. 12–13 and experience using our guide will help you become better attuned to where we drew the line between the various leaf shapes.

The **Third Key Feature** is the presence or absence of a **midrib**, a vein-like structure running lengthwise down the middle of some leaves. Most, but not all, acrocarps have leaves with midribs; leaves with and without midribs are common among pleurocarps. The text and illustrations on pp. 14–15 give tips in looking for midribs — not an easy task on leaves so small.

While you still have the leaf in front of your hand lens, check a few other characters. Examine the margin or edge of the leaf. Is it smooth or toothed? If toothed, do teeth cover the margin from apex to base, or is the margin toothed only along the upper half of the leaf? Does the edge appear to have a border distinct from the rest of the leaf blade? Typically a border is due to a rolled-down leaf margin, thus overlapping cell layers and looking dark.

Finally, search the clump or mat for sporophytes. A sporophyte consists of a spore-producing capsule elevated atop a stalk above the green, photosynthetic gametophyte of the moss. Although some species rarely, if ever, produce capsules, many mosses do so yearly. The shape and orientation of the capsule along with characters of its lid and hood are useful and sometimes essential features for identifying mosses.

COLLECTING MOSSES

A REFERENCE COLLECTION IS USEFUL FOR TEACHING others about moss diversity as well as comparing new finds to specimens that you have previously identified. Refrain from collecting where prohibited, such as in national and state parks.

Because of their diminutive size, all you need is a small sample of moss, a teaspoon to tablespoon is about right. Never collect the entire clump or mat. Avoid mixed collections in which different species grow intertwined in a tuft or mat, and if available, include some plants with capsules. A pocket knife is handy for scraping mosses from rocks and bark, and for cleaning away soil. Dripping wet plants should be squeezed gently to remove excess water.

Place your specimen in a paper sandwich bag or a packet made from a folded sheet of paper (see illustrated instructions). Label the packet with information such as: the date, geographic location, habitat (forest, bog, field, etc.), and substrate (rock, soil, bark, etc.) on which the moss was growing. Once you have identified the moss, record its name on the packet.

After returning from the field, open your packets and spread your specimens out to dry. Left moist, they will become moldy, which is why plastic bags are acceptable only for very short-term storage. The dried specimens can be kept in shoeboxes and organized as desired.

HOW TO MAKE A MOSS COLLECTION PACKET

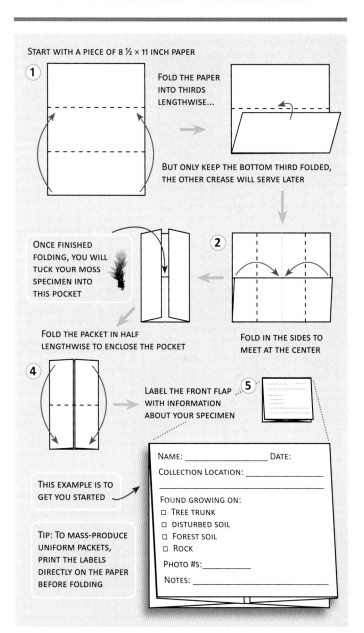

START WITH A PIECE OF 8 ½ × 11 INCH PAPER

1 FOLD THE PAPER INTO THIRDS LENGTHWISE...

BUT ONLY KEEP THE BOTTOM THIRD FOLDED, THE OTHER CREASE WILL SERVE LATER

2 FOLD IN THE SIDES TO MEET AT THE CENTER

ONCE FINISHED FOLDING, YOU WILL TUCK YOUR MOSS SPECIMEN INTO THIS POCKET

FOLD THE PACKET IN HALF LENGTHWISE TO ENCLOSE THE POCKET

4

5 LABEL THE FRONT FLAP WITH INFORMATION ABOUT YOUR SPECIMEN

THIS EXAMPLE IS TO GET YOU STARTED

TIP: TO MASS-PRODUCE UNIFORM PACKETS, PRINT THE LABELS DIRECTLY ON THE PAPER BEFORE FOLDING

NAME: _____ DATE: _____

COLLECTION LOCATION: _____
_____

FOUND GROWING ON:
☐ TREE TRUNK
☐ DISTURBED SOIL
☐ FOREST SOIL
☐ ROCK

PHOTO #S: _____

NOTES: _____

What Are Mosses?

MOST OF US AS CHILDREN LEARN ICONIC FIGURES for a tree, a bird and a flower. With maturity we learn to recognize more than one species in each of these categories. Not so with mosses, despite their ubiquity and accessibility. The book you are holding is a celebration of moss species diversity and an attempt to help you discover a larger world at your feet and fingertips. But first it is necessary to resolve some common misconceptions regarding what precisely is and is not a moss.

SPANISH MOSS is not a moss. This common name refers to both a flowering plant of the pineapple family and a lichen, which is a composite organism made of a fungus and a photosynthetic alga.

REINDEER MOSS is not a moss. It is a lichen. Scratch this lichen, and you will find a thin line of green algae beneath the outermost layer of white fungi.

OTHER LICHENS are not mosses, though often mistaken for them.

CLUBMOSSES are not mosses. They are spore-producing vascular plants with a life cycle similar to ferns.

GREEN ALGAE are not mosses even though many people use that word for the green, slimy plants in streams, ponds and swimming pools.

LIVERWORTS are not mosses. If you find a small green plant that you thought was a moss but is not found in our book, you may have found a liverwort.

There are hundreds of liverwort species growing in eastern North America. Some liverworts are not very mosslike; instead they look like flat green ribbons. They may be irregularly lobed with rounded ends, and some have stalks with umbrella-like tops (used for reproduction).

But other liverworts are easily confused with mosses. They can have creeping, flattened shoots with leaves that spread outward on opposite sides and overlap like scales. Liverworts often have a third row of tiny, hidden leaves. The leaves are either circular or deeply divided into narrow lobes and never have a midrib. In comparison, most mosses have leaves that emerge from all sides of the stem, are of similar size, are usually pointed and can have a midrib. Liverwort capsules are short-lived and thus not as commonly seen as moss capsules. They open by means of four vertical slits instead of a circular lid typical of most mosses.

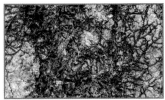

PEAT MOSSES are mosses. You will find more than a dozen species described in this book.

AND THESE ARE MOSSES:

This is not a moss

SO WHAT ARE MOSSES?

Mosses belong to a branch of the tree of life that diverged from green algae about 500 million years ago and includes all the land plants. Like other land plants, mosses have a multicellular body, contain green chlorophyll, and make their living through photosynthesis. Using the energy of sunlight, they combine carbon dioxide and water to make the sugars that are used for metabolism and to build their stems, leaves, and reproductive structures. As an evolutionary line, the mosses split early from the main branch of plants that went on to develop sophisticated conducting tissues and reproductive structures like seeds and flowers. Thus, mosses are some of the oldest and simplest plants on Planet Earth.

BASIC STRUCTURE OF MOSSES

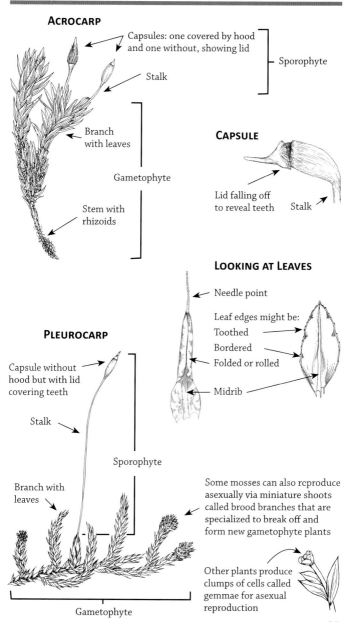

ACROCARP

Capsules: one covered by hood and one without, showing lid

Sporophyte

Stalk

Branch with leaves

Gametophyte

Stem with rhizoids

CAPSULE

Lid falling off to reveal teeth

Stalk

LOOKING AT LEAVES

Needle point

Leaf edges might be:
Toothed
Bordered
Folded or rolled

Midrib

PLEUROCARP

Capsule without hood but with lid covering teeth

Stalk

Sporophyte

Branch with leaves

Gametophyte

Some mosses can also reproduce asexually via miniature shoots called brood branches that are specialized to break off and form new gametophyte plants

Other plants produce clumps of cells called gemmae for asexual reproduction

LIFE HISTORY OF MOSSES

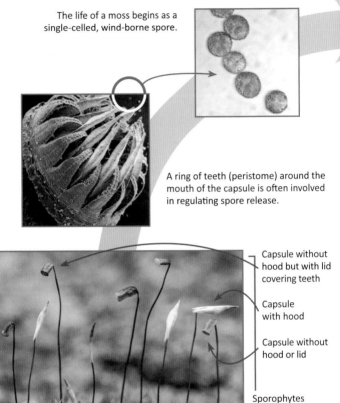

The life of a moss begins as a single-celled, wind-borne spore.

A ring of teeth (peristome) around the mouth of the capsule is often involved in regulating spore release.

Capsule without hood but with lid covering teeth

Capsule with hood

Capsule without hood or lid

Sporophytes

Gametophytes

The tip of the sporophyte enlarges under the hood to form a capsule, inside of which spores form. In a typical moss the hood falls away when the spores are ready for dispersal, and the capsule opens by means of a lid (operculum).

Under the right circumstances of moisture and temperature, a green filament emerges from the spore wall and initiates the protonema, which resembles a green algal mat.

The protonema grows and develops into the green plant that we recognize as a moss, called the gametophyte generation, so named because it produces the gametes or sex cells: sperm and egg.

At the ends of the gametophyte stems in acrocarps or on short side branches in pleurocarps, microscopic banana-shaped antheridia produce many sperm. Microscopic bottle-shaped archegonia each produce a single egg.

Archegonial shoot

Antheridial shoot

Developing sporophytes

Sperm swim and are carried by splashing or flowing water. Most travel only a short distance. Sperm that reach an archegonium swim down the neck of the bottle to fertilize the egg within. Thus begins the sporophyte generation, so named because it culminates in the production of spores.

The fertilized egg divides numerous times and the young sporophyte emerges as a spear from the top of the swollen archegonium. The stalk (seta) commonly elongates several millimeters to 10 centimeters or more, always remaining anchored below to the green gametophyte and carrying aloft the torn off upper part of the archegonium as a hood (calyptra).

WHAT GOOD ARE MOSSES?

Moss growing over an abandoned road

MANY PEOPLE WONDER IF YOU CAN EAT MOSS. Mosses produce a variety of secondary compounds that make them unpalatable and mostly indigestible to humans and most other animals. The very chemicals that make them inedible also make them attractive sources of antibacterial, antifungal, and antiviral compounds as we seek out new medicines. Some mosses have even been shown to have anticancer properties. Mosses have been used as bandages in surgical dressings and to regulate blood clotting. The fact that mosses are not eaten by most insects has led to recent assays for insect repellant compounds. Mosses are built of complex carbohydrates that require more energy to digest than most animals would gain even if they could tolerate the unpleasant taste. However, in spite of the negative caloric value, in order to obtain anti-freeze chemicals that help keep cold muscles moving, reindeer will eat certain mosses during severe winters. Mosses are also regularly eaten by woodland lemmings and barnacle geese.

Although used in earlier centuries by humans for everything from fuel, to diapering babies, to filling chinks between rocks and timbers of houses, there is much less household use of moss today. Most economic use comes from a single genus, *Sphagnum*, the peat mosses. Because of its ability to retain water and slowly release it, peat moss is widely used in the horticultural trade. Moist peat moss is used to keep plants alive during shipping. Mixed into soil, it adds water-holding capacity and organic matter. Its ability to inhibit the growth of bacteria and fungi makes it an excellent medium for germinating seeds.

Peat humus added to soil improves soil structure and water retention

This antimicrobial activity has recently been used in the production of pool and spa filters made of peat moss. Large mats of pleurocarpous mosses are rolled up and removed from forests in the Appalachians and Pacific Northwest for decorative use in planters as well as packing materials for shipping. Moss gardening with living plants is becoming increasingly popular.

Mosses serve many unsung but essential roles in the living world. Mosses are some of the first colonists of tree bark, soil, and newly exposed rock. Moss spores or leaf fragments are blown or are washed into newly exposed areas, and because mosses obtain their mineral nutrients from rain and splashed or running water, they don't need previously developed soil to live. In fact, mosses promote soil formation through physical and chemical weathering of rock and dirt. As mosses grow, bits

Underneath a mat of moss, soil is forming

of dust and humus collect among the stems, and as they die their decomposing bodies add to the developing soil. In arid areas they help stabilize soils.

Because mosses are small and can survive without being rooted in soil, they can grow where other plants cannot, such as on cliffs, boulders, steep hills, and tree trunks. Many have the ability to dry out but remain alive and dormant. When moistened by rain or even fog, they can quickly resume photosynthesis and other life processes until they dry out again. By growing where other plants cannot, mosses add to the total photosynthetic productivity of the earth on which all animals and fungi depend. The drought resistant properties of mosses are also being studied as we develop more drought-resistant crops.

Mosses absorb water from rainfall and runoff and hold it like a sponge in and around their stems and leaves. This water is then slowly released to the ground or atmosphere. Slow release of water reduces stream erosion and fluctuating lake levels. Mosses are also slow to release mineral nutrients thus permitting more gradual colonization and growth cycles in many ecosystems.

Mosses hold water like a sponge

Mosses provide homes for countless small animals that underpin entire ecosystems. What does a bobcat eat? Rodents, birds, and snakes. What do snakes eat? Among other things, frogs. What do frogs eat? Insects. Where do some of those insects live? In clumps of moss. If there is less moss, it means there will be fewer insects, fewer frogs, fewer snakes, and fewer or perhaps no bobcats.

Mosses also are important in the global carbon cycle. As mosses grow, they absorb carbon dioxide and release oxygen. In northern climates where decomposition is slow because of cold temperatures, vast amounts of carbon are sequestered in peat bogs. If global warming causes the release of this stored carbon, we may find it ever more difficult to keep carbon dioxide levels in the atmosphere within reasonable limits.

Mosses are very sensitive to the chemical and physical surface where they grow, and thus act as inexpensive indicators of air pollution and other environmental contaminants. Mosses can tell us about levels of minerals, heavy metals, moisture, and pH of roadsides, sidewalks, building walls, soils, and tree bark. Other species of indicator mosses can tell us about some of the chemicals in the air we breathe.

Beautiful mosses are all around us. Whether hiking along the Appalachian Trail, swimming at the base of a waterfall, or walking an urban sidewalk, it is hard not to be seduced by velvety carpets of moss. Most are perennial and do not die back in winter. So if not covered by snow, they are available for study in all seasons. This book is an invitation to slow down, to look closely, and to learn about and come to love some of nature's smallest plants. Enjoy!

Wet leaves flatten and straighten

Distinctive round "apple"-like capsules; without lid

Fine-toothed leaf margin

Dry leaves irregularly curled

Stem base matted with brown fuzz

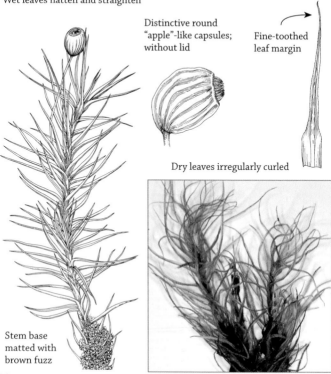

32

Bartramia pomiformis

APPLE MOSS

APPEARANCE: Dull yellow green to blue green, pillowy cushions. Stems are upright, 2–6 cm high, sparsely forked, densely clothed with hairlike curly leaves, and topped by apple-round capsules on slender stalks. When dry, leaves are loosely and irregularly curled and twisted; wet, the leaves straighten and are held at 60 degrees from stems. Stem bases are often matted with brown fuzz.

LEAVES: Hairlike, 4–6 mm long, from a widened clasping base. Edges are curled under, slimming the leaves to a hairlike tip. Midrib extends to apex. Fine teeth along edge of top half of leaf.

CAPSULES: When young, bright green globes resembling tiny apples. At maturity 1–2 mm long, inclined or perpendicular to the 1–2 cm stalk, round when moist, but elongate and deeply furrowed when dry. The convex lid falls off, revealing red teeth.

HABITAT: Soil or rocks, usually acidic though sometimes calcium-enriched. Prefers damp shaded sites such as cracks in cliffs or rock outcrops and banks of ravines or streams.

SIMILAR SPECIES

Dicranella heteromalla (p. 37) Hairlike leaves are 2–3 mm long and gently swept to one side and barely curled, wet or dry. Capsules are shaped like a white-wine glass.

Philonotis fontana (p. 125) Shares the globose capsules, but has shorter, triangular leaves, 1–2 mm long, that don't contort when dry.

Tortella tortuosa (p. 77) Leaves lack teeth that are coiled when dry and curved like an S when wet, leaves are more lance-shaped than hairlike at tips.

MICROSCOPIC FEATURES

Cells each have one low bump. Teeth on leaf edges are actually double-toothed.

Plants form patches of hairlike, silky, yellow green

Leaves are straight when wet, curled when dry

Capsules with and without lid

After lid falls off, note hairlike teeth

Capsules also have a bright yellow stalk

Midrib apparent in clasping leaf base

Ditrichum pallidum

SAFFRON MOSS

APPEARANCE: Small, upright, 3–6 mm tall, yellow-green moss with shiny, hairlike leaves which spread from stem slightly when wet and are curled up when dry.

LEAVES: Hairlike, 3–5 mm long, with a tiny widened base. Midrib fills most of blade and is difficult to distinguish except at base. Edges are smooth.

CAPSULES: Cylindrical, 1–2 mm long, upright to somewhat inclined, becoming ridged when dry, with tannish pink hairlike capsule teeth and a long-beaked lid. Stalk is 1–4 cm, bright yellow.

HABITAT: Disturbed soils, especially sandy and dry fields or partly shady woodlands.

SIMILAR SPECIES

Dicranella heteromalla (p. 37) Can best be distinguished by its curved capsules with puckered mouth and narrowly triangular teeth, compared with the erect to slightly curved capsules with unpuckered mouth and hairlike teeth of *Ditrichum pallidum*. It also has a mustard yellow capsule stalk, compared to the bright yellow capsule stalk of *D. pallidum*. In the absence of capsules, the two mosses can be indistinguishable without microscopic investigation.

Dicranum montanum (p. 41) Hairlike leaves, 2–4 mm long, taper gradually from base to apex and are tightly curled when dry.

MICROSCOPIC FEATURES

Strongly toothed leaf tips can be distinguished under microscope. Capsule teeth are divided into two forks nearly to the base and are covered in tiny bumps.

Fine, hairlike leaves all
gently swept to the side

Capsule
with hood

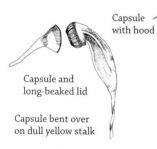

Capsule and
long-beaked lid

Capsule bent over
on dull yellow stalk

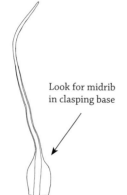

Look for midrib
in clasping base

Dicranella heteromalla

FINE HAIR MOSS

APPEARANCE: Upright stems, usually no more than 1 cm tall (occasionally to 4 cm), form patches over soil of silky, fine leaves that are often gently curved to the side. Plants range from yellow green to dark green in color. Not much changed wet or dry.

LEAVES: Hairlike, 2–3 mm long with a triangular base. The tips are usually swept to one side and are filled by the midrib, which is difficult to distinguish as such; look for it in the abruptly wider leaf base. Edges of leaf are smooth.

CAPSULES: Cylindrical to white-wine-glass shaped, 1 mm long, curved, furrowed and puckered below the mouth, with narrowly triangular teeth and a long-beaked lid. Stalks are 8–14 mm, mustard to brown.

HABITAT: Common on disturbed shaded soil, for example along edges of streams or roads, or on soil of upturned trees.

SIMILAR SPECIES

Ditrichum pallidum (p. 35) Distinguished by the capsules, which are upright on bright yellow stalks and have hairlike teeth from an unpuckered mouth.

Dicranum montanum (p. 41) Hairlike leaves, 2–4 mm long, taper gradually from wide base to narrow apex and are tightly curled when dry.

MICROSCOPIC FEATURES

Narrow egg-shaped leaf base. Tip of leaf is toothed. Capsule teeth are divided halfway into two forks, and are bumpy near the tips and vertically grooved below.

Fine, hairlike leaves of yellow or olive green

Capsule without lid

Goiter

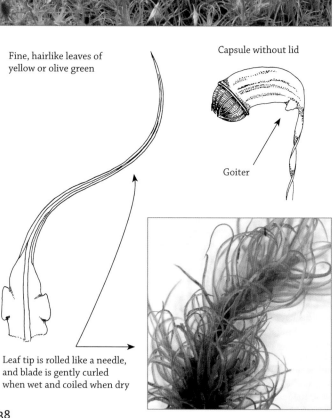

Leaf tip is rolled like a needle, and blade is gently curled when wet and coiled when dry

APPEARANCE: Upright plants are densely covered in fine hairlike leaves and form tufts 1–3 cm tall of yellowish or olive green. Leaves are spreading to gently curled when wet, tightly curled when dry. Stem bases are covered in fuzz.

LEAVES: 3–5 mm long, hairlike blade from an abruptly wider and clasping base. Tip is rolled into a needle. Leaf base is tan or clear. Midrib runs to tip. Edges are smooth.

CAPSULES: Slender curved macaroni, 1–2 mm long, with a bump at base of capsule where it joins the stalk, like an Adam's apple or goiter. Once beaked lid has fallen off, the red teeth at mouth contrast with golden capsule. Stalk is 8–15 mm tall.

HABITAT: Rotting logs, occasionally on tree trunk bases and moist forest soil, often near streams.

SIMILAR SPECIES

Dicranella heteromalla (p. 37) Prefers to grow on forest soil. The hairlike leaves are gently curled to one side wet or dry, not tightly crisped as in *Oncophorus*. Capsules lack goiter.

Dicranum montanum (p. 41) Leaves are usually 2–4 mm long and gradually tapering from base to tip. Capsules lack swelling at base.

Dicranum fuscescens (p. 45) Leaves are 4–7 mm long and gradually taper from base to tip. Capsules lack swelling at base or have only a small bump.

MICROSCOPIC FEATURES

Cells in lower outside corners of leaf are not much different from neighboring cells. Upper leaf margins are two cells thick.

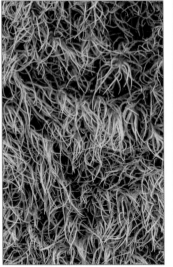

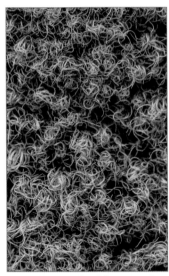

Wet leaves gently curved

Dry leaves curl and draw inward

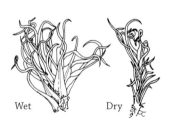

Wet

Dry

Plants form dark green, furry scabs over bark ⟶

Appearance from a distance

Capsule without lid

Dicranum montanum

CRISPY BROOM MOSS

APPEARANCE: Upright plants, 5–15 mm high (occasionally to 4 cm), form dark green, yellowish green, or brownish small patches like furry scabs over bark or rock. Stems are densely covered in leaves that are curled-contorted when dry, irregularly gently curled in all directions when wet. Base of stem is covered in white or brown fuzz. Often bearing short branchlets near top of plant with tiny, fine, ringlet-curled leaves. Some patches consist mostly of plants with reduced branchlets and tiny leaves, which can break off and asexually propagate the moss.

LEAVES: Hairlike, 2–4 mm long (less than 1 mm on the short branchlets), tapering gradually from wider base to a sharp tip. The leaves are too fine to distinguish the midrib, though it is present to tip. Edges of leaf are smooth.

CAPSULES: Short-cylindrical, 1–2 mm long, upright or gently inclined, pale yellow brown with a long-beaked lid. Stalk is 5–15 mm tall, yellow or rusty.

HABITAT: Tree bases, rotting logs, and on humus over rocks in dry open spaces.

SIMILAR SPECIES

Dicranum flagellare (p. 51) Tiny branchlets covered in scale-like leaves are produced at tops of stems. Leaves are only slightly curled when dry and have tubular tips.

Dicranum fuscescens and *D. fulvum* (p. 45) Dark green leaves are 4 mm long or more. The former has a tiny bump at base of bent-over capsule. Both have dark or rusty brown rather than tan-mustard colored capsules.

MICROSCOPIC FEATURES

Cells in lower outside corners of leaf are large and brownish, neighboring cells are thick-walled and rectangular. On backside of leaf, upper cells are mound-shaped. Leaf tip is folded to form a V in cross-section. Upper leaf edges have small teeth and are one cell thick.

Gently curled plants with gray-green sheen

Wet plants turn brighter green

Capsule with lid

Midrib apparent in wider leaf base

Paraleucobryum longifolium

SILVER BROOM MOSS

APPEARANCE: Plants form windswept patches with leaves densely packed along upright stems, 1–4 cm high. When dry, plants are whitish green to green with a characteristic gray sheen. Upon wetting the silvery cast fades and the plants become a brighter green, but the leaves maintain their gentle curl over to one side. Lower stems are covered in fuzz.

LEAVES: Hairlike, 4–8 mm long. Edges are smooth and curved upward like a canoe, nearly forming a tube. All but the leaf base is made entirely of midrib, which when viewed from the back of the leaf has faint white and green vertical stripes. Peel off a leaf and examine its base to recognize the midrib.

CAPSULES: Cylindrical, upright, 2–3 mm long, lid is long-beaked. Stalk is 1–2 cm tall. Both capsule and stalk are brownish yellow.

HABITAT: Rocks or humus over boulders, especially in moist and mountain forests; less common on tree trunks and logs.

SIMILAR SPECIES

Dicranum fulvum (p. 45) Darker green, lacking silvery color. Leaves curl in many directions.

Bartramia pomiformis (p. 33) Dull yellow green, hairlike leaves and round capsules with convex lids.

MICROSCOPIC FEATURES

As seen from back of leaf, the midrib is composed of alternating rows of green and clear cells. Cells in lower outside corners of leaf are large and brown. Tip of leaf is finely toothed.

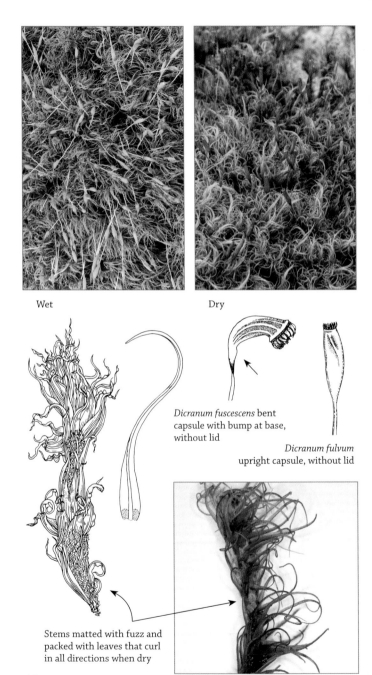

Wet

Dry

Dicranum fuscescens bent capsule with bump at base, without lid

Dicranum fulvum upright capsule, without lid

Stems matted with fuzz and packed with leaves that curl in all directions when dry

Dicranum fulvum

BOULDER BROOM MOSS

APPEARANCE: Upright plants form dull dark green or ochre-colored, woolly clumps, 2–5 cm tall. The leaves are densely packed along the stems, which are often also matted with brown fuzz. When dry, the leaves are curled in all directions; when wet, they are gently curled over to side.

LEAVES: Hairlike, 4–8 mm long, sharp-tipped leaves with a wedge-shaped base. The leaf edges are folded or rolled into a tube and faintly toothed near tip. Midrib runs to tip, though it is difficult to distinguish in the narrow blade. Pull off a leaf to see that the midrib fills ⅓ of base between slender triangles of clear cells.

CAPSULES: Cylindrical, 2–3 mm long, upright. Lid is long-beaked. Stalk is 1–1.5 cm tall, one per plant stem.

HABITAT: Dry rocks, typically acidic and in shady forests.

SIMILAR SPECIES

***Dicranum fuscescens*, CURLY BROOM MOSS**: Plants grow on bark of tree trunk bases and rotting logs, in addition to forest soil and dry rocks. Capsules are curved and horizontal, with small bump at connection to stalk.

Dicranum montanum (p. 41) Leaves are no more than 4 mm long and are very tightly curled-contored when dry.

Dicranum scoparium (p. 47) Leaves are gently swept to one side rather than curly in all directions; tips are not tubular.

MICROSCOPIC FEATURES

In *D. fulvum,* the leaf blade near tip is two cells thick, while it is one cell thick in *D. fuscescens*.

Plants have a distinctive windswept aspect
as the leaves are all gently swept to one side

Narrow leaves are folded
lengthwise, creating a
hairlike appearance

Capsule
with lid

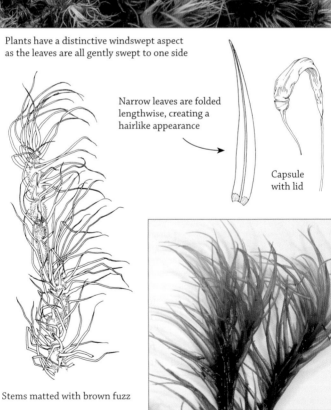

Stems matted with brown fuzz

Dicranum scoparium

WINDSWEPT BROOM MOSS

APPEARANCE: Upright plants, 2–8 cm tall, are densely covered in yellow, brown, or dark green leaves that all gently curve to one side, lending a windswept look to the mounds. Occasionally wet leaves can be straighter rather than sickle-curved; when dry they are slightly curly but not much changed. Stems are matted with brown fuzz.

LEAVES: Long-triangular, 4–8 mm long, with a transparent base and tapering blade that is folded lengthwise into a V. Midrib runs to tip but is difficult to distinguish in the narrow blade. Peel off a leaf and look for the midrib in the wider base. Very faint teeth near tip.

CAPSULES: Curved macaroni shape, 3–4 mm long with a very long-beaked lid. Stalk is 2–4 cm, mustard to rusty, solitary.

HABITAT: Very common; on forest soil, in moist and shady or open and dry areas, also on tree bases, logs and rocks.

SIMILAR SPECIES

Dicranum fulvum (p. 45) When dry, leaves curl in all directions; when wet, they are gently curled over to side. Capsules cylindrical, upright, 2–3 mm long. Grows on dry rocks.

Dicranum fuscescens (p. 45) Leaves are curled every which way, rather than all swept to one side. Capsules are curved and horizontal, with small bump at connection to stalk.

Dicranum polysetum (p. 49) Leaves are rippled or wavy. Produces multiple capsule stalks per plant.

MICROSCOPIC FEATURES

Cells of leaves are one layer thick. Upper leaf cells are usually long-rectangular (though rarely short-rectangular) with pinched-looking, perforated walls that connect cells. The cells are not bumpy. There are four ridges running along the length of the midrib on the underside of the leaf.

Leaves crinkled or rippled

D. polysetum typically produces several capsules per shoot

Capsule without lid

Stems fuzzy

Dicranum polysetum

WRINKLED BROOM MOSS

APPEARANCE: Upright plants, 2–12 cm tall, form shiny, light green or golden, loose patches over ground. Leaves are sparse and wide spreading along the stem except near top, where they are dense and held upright. Leaves are rippled, wet or dry, giving the plants a crinkly, frizzy look; tips are not contorted when dry. The stems are also often densely cocooned in white or brown fuzz from base to top.

LEAVES: Long-triangular, 7–10 mm long, with folded-over, sharp-looking tips into which the midrib disappears. Teeth run from tip halfway down leaf edges.

CAPSULES: Macaroni shape, 3–4 mm long, curved; lid has an exaggerated long beak. Stalks usually 2–5 per plant, yellow or orange, 2–4 cm.

HABITAT: Forest soil, especially in conifer forests, and on soils in dry, open rocky spaces.

SIMILAR SPECIES

Dicranum scoparium (p. 47) Leaves are not rippled, are gently curled to one side and held closer to the stem rather than spreading outward. Capsule stalks one per plant.

MICROSCOPIC FEATURES

Cells in upper leaf are long-rectangular with pinched-looking, perforated walls that connect cells. Leaf is one cell thick and cells themselves are not bumpy. On the underside of the leaf, two ridges of teeth run along the midrib.

Brood branches project stiffly from among normal leaves

Capsule without lid

Rust-colored stems show through narrow, pale green leaves

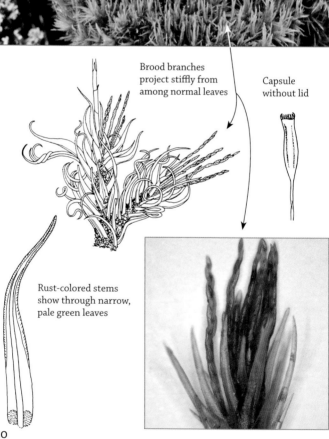

Dicranum flagellare

ASPARAGUS BROOM MOSS

APPEARANCE: Upright stems are densely covered with leaves and look like clumps of carpet, 1–4 cm high. The leaves gently curve to one side when wet, turning curly but not corkscrewy when dry. Orange stems, matted with rusty fuzz near base, and pale green leaves combine to give the plants a warm, dull tone. Stiff upright branchlets project in clusters from among upper leaves. These branchlets, called brood branches, are orange and covered with tiny, green, scale-like leaves, looking like mini asparagus stalks. Look for them by viewing a clump in profile. Brush your hand over the mound and notice how easily brood branches break off to asexually reproduce the moss.

LEAVES: Long-tapering triangle, 2–4 mm long, narrow and inrolled near top but not hairlike, base is orange-tinged. Peel off a leaf and look at the leaf base to distinguish the midrib as it can be difficult to recognize in the narrow blade. Edges of leaf are smooth.

CAPSULES: Slender-cylindrical, 2–3 mm long, upright or gently curved with a short-beaked lid. Stalk 1–2 cm and yellow brown.

HABITAT: Rotting logs and old tree stumps. Also occasionally on soil or bark at base of trees.

SIMILAR SPECIES

Dicranum montanum (p. 41) Occasional branchlets are supple rather than stiff. The "normal" leaves turn corkscrewy when dry. Prefers to live on tree trunks and bases.

Dicranum fulvum (p. 45) Leaves are 4–8 mm long. Plants lack branchlets with tiny scale-like leaves.

MICROSCOPIC FEATURES

Edges of leaf are only one cell thick. Cells are smooth throughout. Cells in lower outside corners of leaf to nearly the midrib are abruptly different, brown, large, and rounded.

Fine leaf tips are typically broken off at midblade

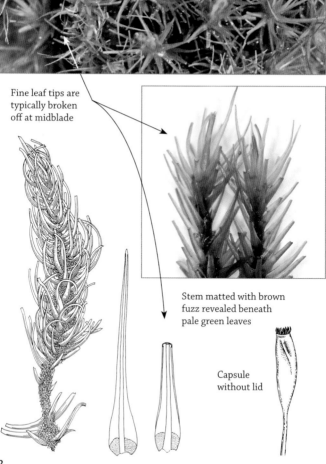

Stem matted with brown fuzz revealed beneath pale green leaves

Capsule without lid

Dicranum viride

BRITTLE BROOM MOSS

APPEARANCE: Upright stems form cushions 1–3 cm high bearing leaves that are broken off mid blade, as though plants were given a messy haircut. Wet leaves straighten and point out from reddish stems, looking spiky-starry. Dry leaves are curled and inrolled-tubular. Leaves are pale green with deep green center line. Brown fuzz on stems.

LEAVES: Long-triangular, 4–7 mm long, with a rounded and golden base, a tapering blade that is folded lengthwise into a V, and ends with fine tips which are often broken off bluntly. Midrib is wide and dark and disappears into tip. Edges smooth.

CAPSULES: Rare; cylindrical, 2–3 mm long, and upright. Stalk 10–17 mm. More frequently reproduces vegetatively via the broken leaf tips.

HABITAT: Tree trunks, tree trunk bases, and rotting logs.

SIMILAR SPECIES

Dicranum flagellare (p. 51) Tiny, asparagus-stalk-like branches are produced at tops of stems among normal wispy leaves.

Dicranum fulvum (p. 45) Plants are usually larger, 2–5 cm. Leaves lack the many broken tips.

Dicranum montanum (p. 41) Leaves no more than 4 mm long, with intact tips very tightly curled-contorted when dry.

MICROSCOPIC FEATURES

The midrib completely fills the tip of the delicate leaf tips.

When wet, narrow, wide-spreading leaves give plants a spiky appearance

Cylindrical (rather than faceted) capsules, with lid and without (drawing at left), lacking hairy hood

Midrib visible in pale, clasping leaf base rather than in opaque and rolled blade

Polytrichastrum alpinum

ALPINE HAIRCAP MOSS

APPEARANCE: Dark green, upright moss, 4–10 cm tall, superficially resembling pine seedlings, sometimes with a whitish cast, growing in patches. Leaves are evenly spaced along the stem. When wet the leaves are flat and held outward from stem, but when dry the leaves draw in slightly toward stems and their edges curl up, forming a tube.

LEAVES: Narrow lance-shaped blade with an oval, clasping base, 8–10 mm long. When dry, the leaf edges roll up to meet at the middle, forming slender, tight tubes. The leaves are thick, opaque, and come to a sharp point. Midrib reaches tip of leaf, but is visible only in pale clasping leaf base. Edges are toothed from tip to oval base.

CAPSULES: Cylindrical capsules, bent over, 3–5 mm long, lacking a disk at the base of capsule. While developing, mouth is covered by a long-beaked lid and whole capsule is protected by a hairy hood. Stalk is yellow brown and 2–5 cm tall.

HABITAT: Moist, shady, cool places, on forest soil or over rocks, often along streams and on mountains.

SIMILAR SPECIES

Polytrichum commune (p. 57) Leaves are never inrolled and tubular-looking when dry. Capsules are faceted like a box.

Polytrichum juniperinum (p. 63) and *Polytrichum piliferum* (p. 65) Have inrolled leaves that are folded or curled when wet and dry and are tipped with fine hairlike extensions.

Atrichum species (pp. 67–69, 131) Share plant shape and cylindrical capsules, but have a clearly discernable midrib running through thin leaves that crumple when dry.

MICROSCOPIC FEATURES

Cross-section of leaf shows thin strips of cells, 1-cell wide and 3–7 high, along the midrib; the uppermost cell of each stack is covered in tiny bumps.

Wet plants with wide-spreading leaves and capsules without lid or hood

Dry plants with drawn-in leaves and capsules with hairy hoods

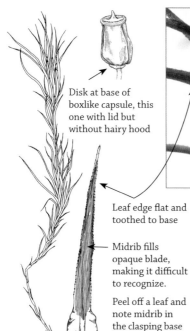

Disk at base of boxlike capsule, this one with lid but without hairy hood

Leaf edge flat and toothed to base

Midrib fills opaque blade, making it difficult to recognize.

Peel off a leaf and note midrib in the clasping base

Polytrichum commune

COMMON HAIRCAP MOSS

APPEARANCE: Large, 5–15 cm tall, upright dark green or brownish plants that superficially look like pine tree seedlings growing in thick patches. Narrow pointed leaves are held upright and pressed to stem with recurved tips when dry; when wet, they spread outward 90 degrees. Male plants are topped by splash cups, cupped rosettes of short leaves surrounding the sex organs.

LEAVES: Narrow, lance-shaped from clasping square base, 6–10 mm long. Leaves are thick, opaque, and flat, especially when wet, but never with deeply inrolled edges and although sharp-tipped, without long needle tips. Midrib is brownish, opaque, and runs to top, most visible in pale clasping leaf base; otherwise it fills leaf blade and is hard to recognize. Teeth run from tip to clasping leaf base.

CAPSULES: Four-sided, short-rectangular to cubic, like a box, with a disk at the base. Capsules are upright initially, inclined with age; covered in a very hairy hood while developing in the summer. Stalk is 5–9 cm tall.

HABITAT: Moist soil, often shaded, in fields or woodlands. Also along margins of bogs, swamps, and lakes.

SIMILAR SPECIES

Polytrichum juniperinum (p. 63) and *Polytrichum piliferum* (p. 65) Leaves end in distinct long needle points and have very inrolled, toothless leaf margins.

Polytrichastrum alpinum (p. 55) Capsules are cylindrical, not four-sided; leaves inrolled and tubular-looking when dry.

Polytrichastrum pallidisetum (p. 59) Capsules are more elongate and lack disk at base.

MICROSCOPIC FEATURES

Cross-section of leaf shows thin strips of cells, 1-cell wide and 4–9 high, along the midrib; the uppermost cell in each stack is wide and notched.

Capsules with and without lid, and covered by hairy hood

Drier plants with in-drawn leaves

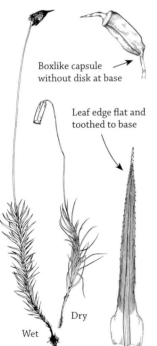

Boxlike capsule without disk at base

Leaf edge flat and toothed to base

Dry

Wet

Polytrichastrum pallidisetum

MOUNTAIN HAIRCAP MOSS

APPEARANCE: Dark green, upright plants, superficially resembling tiny pine seedlings, 3–12 cm tall. The opaque leaves are sparsely spaced along stem except for dense cluster near top and are held 90 degrees from stem when wet, closer when dry. Stem base is covered sparsely in fuzz.

LEAVES: Long, narrow sword shape, with a clasping, clear, square base, 6–10 mm long. Leaves end in a short, reddish needle point. Midrib reaches tip but is easiest to see in the clear, clasping base. Leaves are thickened; edges not rolled or folded inward and have teeth running from tip to base.

CAPSULES: Long, four-sided box-shaped, lacking a disk at the base of capsule, bent over, tan, 4–5 mm long. Lid is long-beaked and whole capsule wears a hairy hood until mature. Stalk is pale yellow and 2–8 cm long.

HABITAT: On soil or rocks in coniferous and Northern Hardwoods forests at high elevations in the Southern Appalachians and across the northern part of our range.

SIMILAR SPECIES

***Polytrichastrum ohioense*, OAK HAIRCAP MOSS**: Replacing *P. pallidisetum* in oak and other hardwood forests in the southern part of our range. Leaves sheathing its capsule stalks have golden rather than reddish needle tips of its other leaves.

Polytrichum commune (p. 57) Capsules are short, more cubic, and have a constriction and disk at base of capsule.

Polytrichastrum alpinum (p. 55) Capsules are smoothly cylindrical and leaves roll up like a tube when dry.

Atrichum species (pp. 67–69, 131) Share the general plant shape, but have thin leaves that crumple when dry.

MICROSCOPIC FEATURES

Cross-section of leaf shows thin strips of cells, 1-cell wide and 4–6 high, along the midrib; uppermost cells have irregular walls, and look oval, square-topped, or U-shaped.

Flat, waxy, blue-green leaves spread outward, forming rosettes like miniature yucca plants

Cylindrical capsules lack disk at base; without and with lid

Midrib fills opaque blade, making it difficult to recognize

Peel off a leaf and note midrib in the clasping base

Pogonatum urnigerum

YUCCA HAIRCAP MOSS

APPEARANCE: Small, upright, rosette-shaped plants, 2–5 cm tall, often branching, standing singly or in sparse tufts, looking like miniature yucca plants. Their waxy leaves have a pale blue green to dark green color, but turn brownish with age. The leaves spread outward when wet, but are held closer and upright when dry.

LEAVES: Lance-shaped above a clasping base, 3–7 mm long, opaque, flat, and often blue green in color and coated in a whitish wax. Midrib is visible in pale leaf base but becomes obscured above. Edge of leaf is toothed in the upper half.

CAPSULES: Capsules are cylindrical, upright to slightly inclined, 2–3 mm long. Stalks are 1–4 cm tall. Capsules develop in the fall, and while developing are covered in hairy hoods over long-beaked lids.

HABITAT: Disturbed soil or rocks along roads or in rocky cliff crevices. Sometimes grows on burned-over ground.

SIMILAR SPECIES

Polytrichum juniperinum (p. 63) Similar structure and blue-green color, but usually taller. The leaf margins fold inward over much of the upper leaf surface, so that edges are smooth and only the needle tip is roughened. Its capsules are angled and box-shaped rather than smoothly cylindrical.

MICROSCOPIC FEATURES

Cross-section of leaf shows thin strips of cells, 1-cell wide and 4–7 high, along the midrib; the uppermost cell in each stack being conspicuously larger, thick-walled, and bumpy.

Polytrichum juniperinum

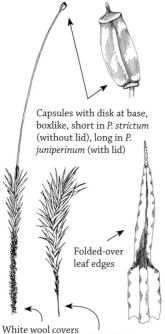

Capsules with disk at base, boxlike, short in *P. strictum* (without lid), long in *P. juniperinum* (with lid)

Folded-over leaf edges

White wool covers *P. strictum* stem

Wool lacking on *P. juniperinum*

P. strictum growing through peat moss

Polytrichum juniperinum

JUNIPER HAIRCAP MOSS

APPEARANCE: Blue green or dark green, waxy, upright, unbranched plants, typically 2–8 cm tall, superficially resembling juniper tree seedlings growing in patches over soil. When dry, the long-pointed leaves are drawn in toward stem, when wet, they spread outward. Lower stems are covered in brown hairs. Male plants are topped by orange splash cups, rosettes of short leaves around the sex organs.

LEAVES: Blue or dark green, 4–8 mm long, narrow lance-shaped from a square, pale, clasping base. The midrib extends beyond the leaf tip as a roughened rusty needle. The midrib is easiest to recognize in the pale leaf base; otherwise it is hard to distinguish because leaf margins are folded over much of the leaf. Leaf edges are smooth.

CAPSULES: Upright to horizontal, four-sided, like a box, with a disk at base, 3–5 mm long. While developing, capsules are covered in hairy hoods. Stalks are red, 2–6 cm tall.

HABITAT: Disturbed soil, often on crusts of soil over rocks, or in sandy, dry, open spaces such as along trails or in fields. Also frequent in burned-over spaces.

SIMILAR SPECIES

***Polytrichum strictum*, WOOLLY HAIRCAP MOSS**: Forms dense, deep mounds growing on peat moss hummocks or on peaty soils. Lower stems are felted with white wool; capsules are 2–3 mm long.

Polytrichum commune (p. 57) Leaves are sharply toothed along edges and lacking rough needle tips.

Polytrichum piliferum (p. 65) Smaller, with long white tips extending beyond leaves.

MICROSCOPIC FEATURES

Cross-section of leaf shows thin strips of cells, 1-cell wide and 6–7 high, along the midrib; the uppermost cell in each stack is egg- or cone-shaped.

Wet   Splash cup   Dry plants look like tiny paintbrushes

Leaves crowded near top of reddish stems

Boxlike capsule with disk at base, this one with lid but without hairy hood

Long white awn and folded leaf edges

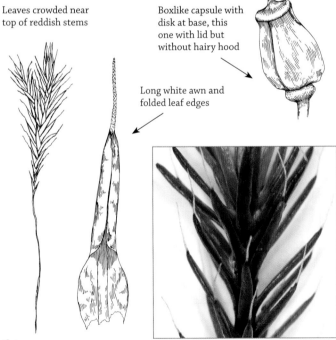

APPEARANCE: Upright plants, usually not more than 2 cm high, rarely to 4 cm, growing in loose, gray green or reddish brownish patches over ground. Leaf tips extend in long, white hairlike awns. Leaves are densely crowded near top of otherwise bare, reddish stem. When dry, leaves are drawn in toward stem, and from above the white-tipped plants look like tiny paintbrushes; when wet the leaves spread widely. Male plants are topped by red splash cups, cupped rosettes of tiny leaves.

LEAVES: Narrow lance-shaped, from an oval, sepia-colored, clasping base, 4–7 mm long, including the long, white hairs that extend from the tips. Leaf edges are folded completely over upper leaf surface, giving leaves a tubular appearance, with smooth edges and teeth only at the tips. Midrib is easiest to see in the pale clasping leaf base.

CAPSULES: Upright or inclined, brown, 2–4 mm long, 4–5 sided, like a box or prism, with a disk at the base. While developing, hairy hoods cover capsules. Stalks are 2–4 cm tall, red brown.

HABITAT: Disturbed soils, dry and sandy or amid gravel and rocks in open spaces such as road banks or pastures.

SIMILAR SPECIES

Polytrichum juniperinum (p. 63) Larger plants with leaves tipped with short brown needles instead of long white hairs.

MICROSCOPIC FEATURES

Cross-section of leaf shows thin strips of cells, 1-cell wide and 5–7 high, along the midrib; the uppermost cell in each stack is egg- or cone-shaped.

Wet plants look starlike

Dry plants look crumpled

Capsules with
and without lid

Leaf edges toothed
more than ½ of blade →

Striped midrib
fills ⅓ or more of
leaf width

Wet   Dry

SLENDER STARBURST MOSS

APPEARANCE: Plants are upright and unbranched, to 2 cm tall, with leaves densely packed along stem and either solitary or forming loose patches over ground. When wet, leaves spread out and give the plants a starlike appearance from above; when dry, leaves curl in tightly toward stem. Hydrates slowly. Plants are a dull yellow-green or whitish green color, sometimes with a hint of red.

LEAVES: Dagger-shaped and incurved like a canoe, 3–7 mm long, less than 1 mm wide. Surface of leaves is rippled when wet. Midrib is very wide, filling a third or more of upper leaf, and extending to tip. Close inspection reveals green and white stripes running along the midrib. Edges of leaf are toothed from tip to more than halfway down blade. Tiny teeth are visible along ripples on undersurface of leaf.

CAPSULES: Slenderly cylindric, 3–7 mm long, usually upright at base and curved near tip, with long beaked lid. Stalk 1–3 cm.

HABITAT: Soil mounds at base of upturned trees and similar dry, bare, disturbed soils, such as along trails or on thin soil over rocks.

SIMILAR SPECIES

Atrichum altecristatum and *A. crispulum* (p. 69) Slightly bigger overall, leaves are 1–2 mm wide. Midrib fills no more than ¼ of upper leaf width.

Polytrichastrum and *Polytrichum* (pp. 55–59, 63–65) Similar in upright, starry growth shape, but are much bigger with thick, tough leaves.

Mnium (pp. 133–137) and *Plagiomnium* (pp. 139–141) Egg-shaped leaves, often have horizontally creeping stems and upright stems, and have drooping pear-shaped capsules.

MICROSCOPIC FEATURES

Thin strips of cells, 1-cell wide and 5–10 high, run along the midrib. Leaf cells are bulging, like muffin-tops, and covered in small bumps.

Wet leaves are wavy and bright green

Dry leaves are crumpled and dark

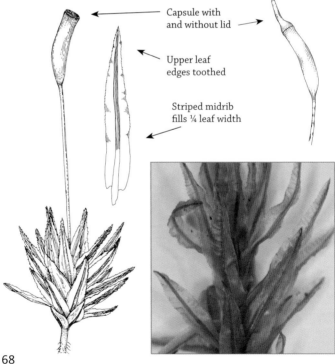

Capsule with
and without lid

Upper leaf
edges toothed

Striped midrib
fills ¼ leaf width

Atrichum altecristatum

WAVY STARBURST MOSS

APPEARANCE: Plants stand upright and unbranched, 1–3 cm tall and forming loose patches over ground. When wet, leaves spread out and give the plants a starlike appearance from above. When dry, leaves curl in tightly. Stem base is often matted with rust-colored fuzz.

LEAVES: Long, narrow swords, 2–8 mm long and 1–2 mm wide. Leaves are rippled and bright green when wet; brown and contorted when dry. Midrib reaches leaf tip and fills no more than a quarter of the width of the upper leaf. Close inspection reveals green and white stripes running along the midrib. Leaf edges are toothed above middle; near tip, margins curve up like sides of a canoe. Tiny teeth are visible along ripples on undersurface of leaf.

CAPSULES: Cylindrical and usually upright to barely curved, 2–7 mm long, capped by a long beaked lid while developing. Stalk is red, 1–3 cm.

HABITAT: Forest floor on mounds, sides of ravines or banks along roads, also in forest clearings and lawns.

SIMILAR SPECIES

***Atrichum crispulum*, CRISPY STARBURST MOSS**: Larger plants, stems are 3–7 cm tall, leaves are 5–9 mm long; lower stems sometimes covered with white fuzz. Prefers wetter, more densely shaded habitats, often along streams or swamp edges.

Atrichum angustatum (p. 67) Often smaller, stems up to 2 cm tall, with leaves less than 1 mm wide. Midrib fills a third or more of upper leaf width.

Polytrichastrum and *Polytrichum* (pp. 55–59, 63–65) Similar in upright, starry growth shape, but much bigger, with thick, tough leaves.

MICROSCOPIC FEATURES

Thin strips of cells, 1-cell wide and 4–6 high in *Atrichum altecristatum,* compared with 2–4 cells high in *A. crispulum,* run along the midrib.

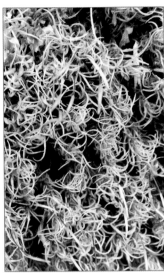

Wet leaves flatten and spread outward   Dry leaf edges roll inward, leaves curl

Capsules with lid
and hood clinging
to capsule base

Capsule without
lid or hood

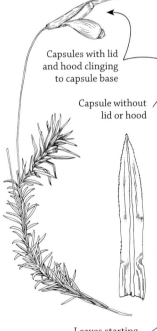

Leaves starting
to roll as they dry

Timmia megapolitana

WARRIOR MOSS

APPEARANCE: Upright, unbranched, green to yellow-green plants standing 2–8 cm tall in loose tufts. When wet, the leaves spread widely from a sheathing base. Upon drying they draw closer to the stem, the edges roll inward, and the tips curl. Superficially the plants resemble an *Atrichum* but the capsules, which are nearly always present, are very different.

LEAVES: Lance-shaped, 4–8 mm long, gradually narrowed to a sharp point. Tiny teeth project from the edge and the midrib extends all the way to the tip.

CAPSULES: Oblong-cylindric, curved, 2–3 mm long, inclined to horizontal at the end of a 1–3 cm stalk. Lid is domed with a small nib. When the lid falls, revealing the teeth, they are a wonder to examine under the hand lens: each tooth has an erect thickened base and then bends inward at a right angle over the mouth of the capsule. The hood is tardily deciduous and often remains upright behind the capsule at the tip of the stalk, reminiscent of a single-feather Indian brave headdress.

HABITAT: On soil, humus, and rock in moist, shaded, calcareous sites.

SIMILAR SPECIES

Atrichum species (pp. 67–69) Have rippled leaves with broad midribs bearing green and white stripes. Their capsules are slenderly cylindrical, mostly 3–7 mm long, upright at least at the base, and topped with a long-beaked lid; hoods are not persistent.

MICROSCOPIC FEATURES

Midleaf cells are rounded-hexagonal, green; basal cells are long-rectangular, yellow green to brown.

Wet plants with spread-out leaves

Drying leaves crumple and twist

Capsule with lid

Leaves transparent green with rolled edges

Stems matted with brown fuzz

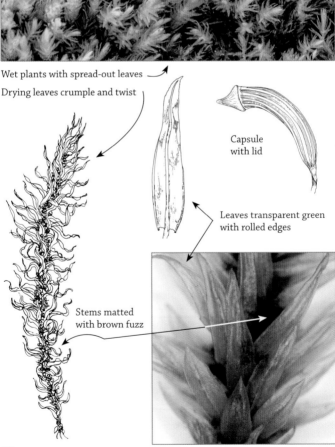

Aulacomnium palustre

RIBBED BOG MOSS

APPEARANCE: Plants are upright, pale yellow green or brownish gold, 3–10 cm tall, densely leafy, and matted with brown hairs on lower stems. Some plants produce slender, leafless stalks topped lollipop-like by a round cluster of tiny points, called gemmae, which serve in asexual reproduction. When wet, branches are bushy even though leaves spread only 50 degrees. Leaves irregularly collapse to stems when dry, looking loosely crumpled and twisted.

LEAVES: Long lance shape, 2–4 mm long, nearly parallel-sided for much of the length, narrowing to a sharp tip. Midrib is slender, extending nearly to tip and easy to see through the transparent leaves. Edges are smooth and rolled under. Leaf blade is often gently keeled lengthwise.

CAPSULES: Curved, bent over, ridged lengthwise when mature, with a short-peaked lid while developing, 2–4 mm long. Stalk is 2–4 cm tall.

HABITAT: Wetlands, such as bogs, swamps, fens and marshes with a range of pH levels.

SIMILAR SPECIES

Philonotis fontana (p. 125) Narrow, pointy, yellow-green leaves over vivid red-orange stems. Stems are often topped by a whorl of short branches with large wide leaves surrounding a cup in the center, like a flower. Other stems are irregularly short-branched.

Pohlia wahlenbergii (p. 125) White green, shiny, narrow pointed leaves over red stems.

MICROSCOPIC FEATURES

Leaves are toothed near top of leaf. Leaf cells generally roundish and bear a single small bump. Cells of lower leaf are inflated, clear or brownish.

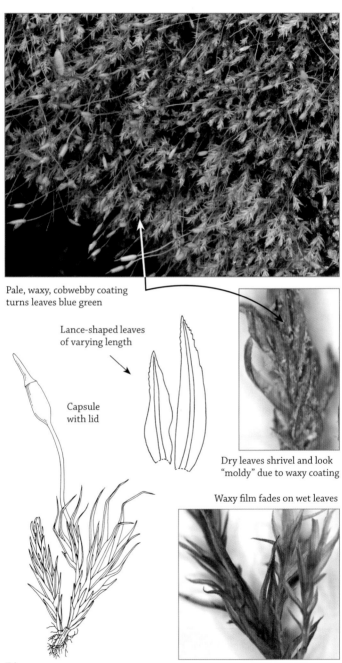

Pale, waxy, cobwebby coating
turns leaves blue green

Lance-shaped leaves
of varying length

Capsule
with lid

Dry leaves shrivel and look
"moldy" due to waxy coating

Waxy film fades on wet leaves

74

Saelania glaucescens

COBWEB MOSS

APPEARANCE: Upright plants, 4–15 mm high, with sparse, spiky leaves of a pale blue green that are covered in a white cobwebby or waxy film. Wet leaves spread 70 degrees and flatten; while dry they shrivel somewhat and look quite "moldy." Lower stems sprout golden brown fuzz.

LEAVES: Narrow lance shape, 1–3 mm long, with a sharp point. Midrib reaches apex. Edges are smooth.

CAPSULES: Cylindrical, about 2 mm long, upright, yellow brown, with a beaked lid and red teeth. Stalk 4–13 mm, yellow.

HABITAT: Soil, especially calcium-enriched, steep banks beneath overhangs, and beside roads, or on soil in cliff cracks.

SIMILAR SPECIES

Ceratodon purpureus (p. 87) Similar leaf and capsule shape, but leaves are yellow green or reddish without waxy covering and capsules are reddish purple.

MICROSCOPIC FEATURES

Cells of upper leaf are often two layers thick. The white fibers on the leaves are a diterpene produced by the plant rather than a fungus or cyanobacteria, as previously supposed.

Dry plants have corkscrew leaves

Capsule with lid; when lid falls off, long, hair-like, twisted teeth are revealed ringing mouth

Strip leaf off stem to see V-shaped transition between green blade and colorless base

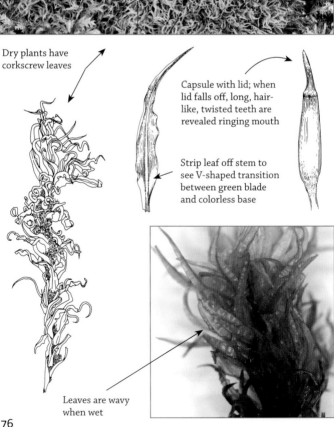

Leaves are wavy when wet

Tortella tortuosa

TALL TORNADO MOSS

APPEARANCE: Dull green to yellow green, upright plants in tufts and cushions, 1–5 cm tall; the older parts of plants turning brown and their stems densely hairy with dark reddish brown fuzz. When moist the leaves are spreading, some straight and others gently curved, which gives the plants a resemblance to propellers when viewed from above. Upon drying the leaves twist into corkscrews and curl back at the tips; the leaf bases are often shiny when dry.

LEAVES: Narrowly lance-shaped, 3–6 mm long, with the midrib extending all the way through the gradually narrowed tip. Margins lack teeth and are wavy when wet. If an entire leaf is stripped from the stem with a forceps or fingernail and examined with a hand lens, it will reveal a sharp V-shaped transition between green and colorless regions at the base.

CAPSULES: Cylindrical, upright, 2–3 mm long, with reddish, hairlike teeth twisted together in a spiral, and covered with a long, narrow lid when developing. Stalk is 1–3 cm long.

HABITAT: Usually on calcareous rock in sun or shade; also on soil, rotten wood, and sand dunes along the Great Lakes. Also found in the southern Appalachians.

SIMILAR SPECIES

Tortella humilis (p. 79) Smaller plants (rarely as tall as 1 cm) with shorter leaves (2–4 mm long) that are curled but not spirally twisted when dry.

Weissia controversa (p. 81) Smaller, standing < 1 cm tall, with leaves only 1–2 mm long. Leaf margins often inrolled.

MICROSCOPIC FEATURES

Upper leaf cells roundish, green, and covered with several small bumps; basal cells are larger, rectangular, and colorless, extending up the margins to form a V-shaped transition to the upper green cells. Elongate cells of the midrib extend beyond the round green cells at apex to form a short point.

Capsule with lid and close-up without lid showing spiral-twisted, hairlike teeth

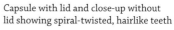

Wet leaves spread outward and are gently rippled and curved, giving plants a propeller-like appearance

Dry leaves fold and curl irregularly, and edges ripple

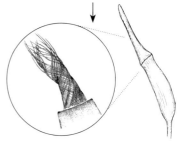

Tortella humilis

TINY TORNADO MOSS

APPEARANCE: Upright plants, 5–10 mm high, form dense clusters of dull yellow olive green. Wet leaves are flat and spread from stems, sometimes slightly rippled or curved like propellers. Dry leaves fold lengthwise and curl irregularly.

LEAVES: Lance, between 2–4 mm long; tip is pinched into an abrupt sharp point. Midrib reaches tip, blade is shallowly keeled, edges are flat, including at tip, and smooth.

CAPSULES: Upright, long-cylindrical 2–3 mm, golden, with a long-beaked lid. Teeth are hairlike and twisted, like a tornado. Stalk is yellow, 7–18 mm.

HABITAT: Bark at tree bases, logs, soil, rock, concrete, and on mortar.

SIMILAR SPECIES

Barbula convoluta (p. 161) Leaves about 1 mm long, which when dry, fold lengthwise and curve in to stem but are not much curled.

Rhabdoweisia crispata (p. 83) Plants are darker green. Capsules are shaped like tiny goblets, 1 mm tall, with a short beaked lid, and a stalk only 2–5 mm.

Tortella tortuosa (p. 77) Larger: plants are 1–5 cm high; leaves are 3–6 mm long. Grows in calcium-enriched areas.

MICROSCOPIC FEATURES

Cells of leaf are round and covered in bumps except for V-shaped region at base of leaf, which is composed of clear, rectangular cells.

Tiny, starlike plants
in clusters over soil

Capsule with hood,
with lid,
lacking both, revealing tiny
teeth ringing mouth

Edges rolled inward, giving
leaves a wormlike aspect

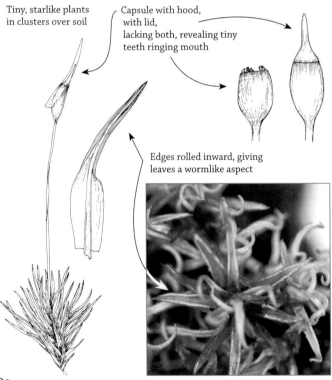

Weissia controversa

PIGTAIL MOSS

APPEARANCE: Small, upright plants, 2–5 mm tall, that grow singly or in dull, pale green or yellow lime-colored clusters. Leaves are dense along stems and when wet are flat and spread outward, starlike. Dry leaves curl into pig-tail corkscrews.

LEAVES: Lance-shaped, 1–2 mm long, with a sharp prick at the tip. The shallowly keeled blade and inrolled upper edges make the leaves look narrow and wormlike. Midrib reaches tip but is difficult to see in the tiny leaves. Edges are smooth.

CAPSULES: Upright, short or long cylindrical, about 1 mm, with tiny yellow to brown teeth at mouth. Stalks are 3–8 mm tall, dull yellow.

HABITAT: Disturbed soils in calcium-enriched open spaces such as pastures, fields, along streams, and on soil crusts over rock.

SIMILAR SPECIES

Tortella humilis (p. 79) Leaves are 2–4 mm long; edges are flat rather than inrolled. Capsules have long, twisted, and hairlike teeth.

Ptychomitrium incurvum (p. 93) Plants grow on rocks with dark olive green leaves that lack inrolled edges. Capsule hood has a deep bowl with a torn rim.

Rhabdoweisia crispata (p. 83) Plants are darker green; leaves are 2–4 mm long and though long sword-shaped, they are not tightly inrolled and tubular. Prefers to grow in moist cracks in rock.

MICROSCOPIC FEATURES

Upper leaf margins are rolled upward like a canoe. Upper cells are short, covered in many branched bumps; lower cells are rectangular, clear, and without bumps. Short clear tooth or needle at tip of leaf.

Rhabdoweisia crispata

Rhabdoweisia capsules with long-beaked lid and without, latter showing teeth ringing mouth

Urn is furrowed when dry

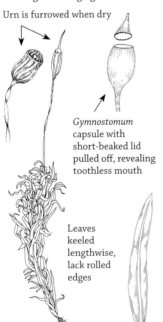

Gymnostomum capsule with short-beaked lid pulled off, revealing toothless mouth

Leaves keeled lengthwise, lack rolled edges

Gymnostomum aeruginosum

Rhabdoweisia crispata

FIREWORKS MOSS

APPEARANCE: Plants form dark green, starry clusters, 3–10 mm high, growing in seepage cracks through rock. Leaves spread wide from upright stems and are gently curled in all directions when wet, looking like small skinny starbursts. When dry, leaves are curled-contorted, though not in corkscrew ringlets. Stems can be reddish.

LEAVES: Sword-shaped, 2–4 mm long. Folded along midrib like the keel of a boat. Midrib reaches tip. Edges are smooth.

CAPSULES: Shaped like a tiny goblet, 1 mm tall, upright, with a long-beaked lid over teeth. The urn becomes strongly ribbed with age. Stalk is 2–5 mm, yellow.

HABITAT: Acidic rocks, especially moist cracks in rock.

SIMILAR SPECIES

***Gymnostomum aeruginosum*, TOOTHLESS CUP MOSS**: Plants prefer to grow on damp, calcium-enriched rock in shady spaces. Leaves are about 1 mm long. Capsules are goblet-shaped, toothless, and also usually lacking recessed, shallowly beaked lid.

Ptychomitrium incurvum (p. 93) Leaves are shorter, 1–2 mm long. Capsule hoods deeply bowl-shaped with a torn rim.

Weissia controversa (p. 81) Light green plants, with lance-shaped leaves, 1–2 mm long, sharp needle-tipped. Their inrolled edges make the leaves look tubular and wormlike. Prefers to grow on disturbed soils in open spaces and on thin soil crusts over rock.

MICROSCOPIC FEATURES

Upper leaf cells are round and smooth. Cells at leaf base and in the outside lower corners are large, clear, and thin-walled. Tiny teeth run along top of leaf. Midrib actually ends slightly below tip of leaf. Leaf cells of *G. aeruginosum* are covered in small bumps except in lower outside corners.

Wet plants with wide-spread leaves;
dry leaves curl like corkscrews

Slender cylindrical capsules,
this one with lid

Fragile teeth ring mouth and
often break off soon after
lid falls

Leaves folded lengthwise
with edges rolled under

Bryoerythrophyllum recurvirostrum

BRICK CARPET MOSS

APPEARANCE: Tiny, upright, sometimes branched plants grow in carpets 5–20 mm tall. Leaves are dull mid-green near top of stems and usually quite reddish brown near base. The densely packed leaves spread wide when wet, revealing orange-red stems; when dry, leaves curl like corkscrews.

LEAVES: Lance-shaped, 2–3 mm long, ending with a sharp point. Leaves are folded lengthwise, like the keel of a boat. Midrib reaches tip. Edges are smooth and rolled under, looking like a dark outline.

CAPSULES: Slender, cylindrical, upright, 1–3 mm long, rusty colored. After beaked lid has fallen off, the fragile teeth of capsule mouth soon break off and are absent. Stalk is 6–16 mm tall and orange.

HABITAT: Moist, calcium-enriched rock crevices and ledges in river gorges, mortar, rotten logs, tree bases, soil and humus.

SIMILAR SPECIES

Rhabdoweisia crispata (p. 83) Plants are darker green, leaves are 2–4 mm long, sword-shaped, without rolled edges. Prefers to grow in moist cracks in rock.

Tortella humilis (p. 79) Leaf margins are flat, not rolled. Capsules are golden and stalks are yellow. Capsule lid much longer. Capsule teeth are twisted into a spiral.

Weissia controversa (p. 81) Plants are 2 – 5 mm tall, never branched. Leaves are 1–2 mm long, and inrolled tubular when dry.

MICROSCOPIC FEATURES

Cells near base of leaf are large, clear, and thin-walled. Otherwise, cells are smaller, rounder, and covered densely in small bumps, which are C-shaped. Midrib is sandwiched top and bottom by small cells. Sometimes tip of leaf bears a few sharp teeth.

Purple form   Green form

Dried capsules are shriveled and brownish

Mature capsules are cylindrical and distinctively purple →

Capsule with lid

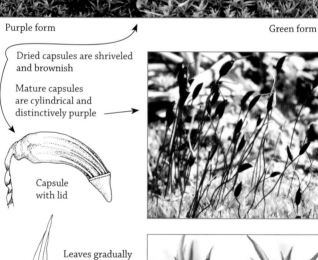

Leaves gradually taper to a point and are keeled lengthwise

86

Ceratodon purpureus

PURPLE MOSS

APPEARANCE: Small moss with upright branches up to 3 cm tall, forming dense patches of green or purple. The leaves are contorted when dry, but spread from brownish stems when wet. Easiest to identify in spring with abundant purple capsules.

LEAVES: Long, narrow-triangular, up to 2 mm long, and gradually tapering to a point. Leaves are keeled. Midrib runs to tip. Edges are smooth.

CAPSULES: Inclined to horizontal, cylindrical and rusty purple, 1–2 mm; lid is red, conical. With age, capsules become curved, brown, and grooved. Stalks 1–3 cm, reddish purple.

HABITAT: Common in disturbed, open dry spaces on acidic soil and sometimes on other surfaces including rock asphalt, and even weathered roof tops.

SIMILAR SPECIES

When fruiting in spring, the purple-red capsules and stalks make this hair-leaved moss quite unique. Otherwise, it can be confused with common mosses such as:

Pohlia nutans (p. 89) Can be distinguished by its wider leaves, red stems, and pale green leaves.

Dicranella heteromalla (p. 37) and *Ditrichum pallidum* (p. 35) Leaves are finer, wispy, and often windswept to the side. On closer inspection, their leaves have an oval clasping base that abruptly narrows to a hairlike blade.

MICROSCOPIC FEATURES

Leaf edges curl downward along length of leaf up to flat and toothed tip. Upper cells are rectangular with thin walls and without minute bumps.

Small plants are easiest to spot beneath
their abundant drooping capsules

Capsules with and without lid

Base of capsule tapers into stalk forming
a "neck" ⅓ the length of capsule

Midrib ends just
below apex

Edges are smooth
and lack border

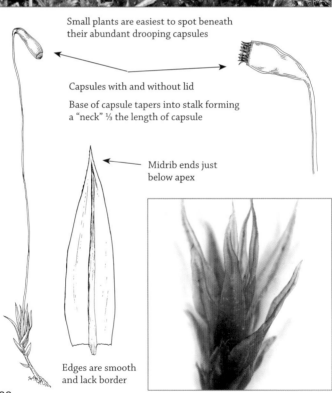

COPPER WIRE MOSS

APPEARANCE: Small, upright tufts, are usually 1–3 cm tall, yellow green, not particularly shiny. Leaves are clustered at top of red stems, held upright alongside stem, not much changed wet or dry. Lower stems are sometimes matted with rusty fuzz.

LEAVES: Dagger-shaped, 1–3 mm long, upper leaves longer than those lower on stem. Midrib reaches just below the sharp-pointed tip. Edges of leaf lack border and teeth.

CAPSULES: Cylindric-pear shaped, 3–4 mm long, drooping, the neck of capsule ⅓ the length of whole, orange when ripe. Shallow cone-shaped lid. Stalk is 1–3 cm tall, orange like a shiny penny.

HABITAT: Shady soil, on aged *Sphagnum* mounds, on rotting logs where it commonly grows with *Tetraphis pellucida* (p. 129), also in cracks of rock cliffs.

SIMILAR SPECIES

Rosulabryum capillare (p. 147) Leaves twist like corkscrews when dry; leaves are widest above middle, have a clear border along edge and a fine needle tip.

Gemmabryum caespiticium and *Ptychostomum creberrimum* (p. 91) Leaves are needle-tipped.

MICROSCOPIC FEATURES

Cells long-rectangular and thick-walled. Teeth along leaf tip are visible under microscope.

Tiny plants are easiest to spot by their abundant capsules drooping atop bright red stalks

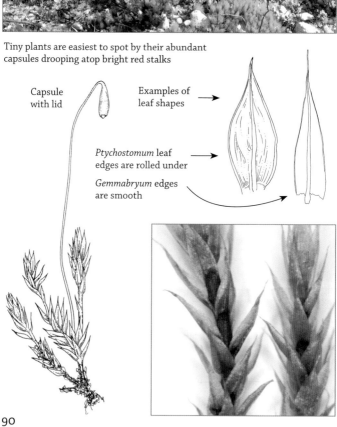

Capsule with lid

Examples of leaf shapes →

Ptychostomum leaf edges are rolled under →

Gemmabryum edges are smooth

Gemmabryum caespiticium

HANDBELL MOSS

APPEARANCE: Small, upright, 5–10 mm tall, silky, green to yellow green, compact mosses that can spread extensively over ground. Plants are most easily spotted by their capsules dangling on red stalks that project in an abundant cloud above the tiny shoots. Overlapping leaves are clustered at tops of branches and spread from stems when wet. Dry leaves are drawn in closer to the stem and are slightly crumpled. Stems are often red with rust-colored fuzz at base.

LEAVES: Lance or narrowly egg-shaped, 2–3 mm long, gradually tapering to a point beyond which the midrib can extend as a needle-prick; cupped. Midrib is red at base of leaf, fading toward point. Edges are smooth.

CAPSULES: Pear-shaped, drooping upside down, 2–3 mm long with shallow conic lid. Stalk is 2–4 cm long, red.

HABITAT: Common in disturbed sites, including lawns, on rocks or walls, or on bare soil.

SIMILAR SPECIES

Ptychostomum creberrimum, **SCARLET STALK MOSS**: Plants up to 15 mm tall, leaf edges rolled down, forming a border.

Pohlia nutans (p. 89) Leaves lack needle-like midrib extensions, live in wet places.

Rosulabryum capillare (p. 147) Leaves are broader, with only a short needle tip, and twisted in a spiral when dry.

MICROSCOPIC FEATURES

Edge of leaf has a border of long, narrow cells, which often curls down; stronger in *P. creberrimum* than in *G. caespiticium*. Upper cells of leaf diamond-shaped, 4–7× as long as wide in *G. caespiticium*, shorter in *P. creberrimum*. *G. caespiticium* has antheridia and archegonia on separate plants whereas *P. creberrimum* has both together on one plant.

Wet | Leaves flat and wide-spread when wet, folded along midrib and coiled when dry | Dry

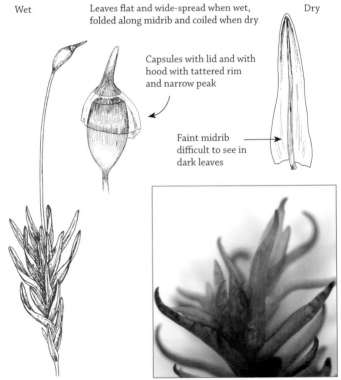

Capsules with lid and with hood with tattered rim and narrow peak

Faint midrib difficult to see in dark leaves

Ptychomitrium incurvum

GNOME'S HOOD MOSS

APPEARANCE: Small upright plants stand 2–6 mm high and are densely covered in olive to blackish green leaves that spread outward, starlike when wet and fold along midrib and curl up like pig tails when dry. Look for the unique capsules, and especially their hoods, to distinguish this species from others that form dark clusters on rock.

LEAVES: Narrow lance shape, gradually tapering to point but lacking needle-like prick, 1–2 mm long. Midrib is present, though faint in the tiny dark leaves. Edges are smooth.

CAPSULES: Egg-shaped, upright, with small teeth along mouth, up to 1 mm long. Lid is long-beaked; hoods are shaped like deep acorn caps with a narrow peak and lower half torn into shreds. Stalk is 2–3 mm tall.

HABITAT: On rock, especially in cracks of boulders in hardwood forests in all but the northernmost part of this guide's range.

SIMILAR SPECIES

Weissia controtroversa (p. 81) Plants grow on disturbed, calcium-enriched soils and are typically pale or lime green colored, with wormlike leaves. Capsule hoods are one-sided, rather than bowl-shaped.

Rhabdoweisia crispata (p. 83) Leaves are like long, slender swords, 2–4 mm; capsule hoods are not bowl-shaped.

MICROSCOPIC FEATURES

Leaf near point is two cells thick, with cells on the upper surface rounded and bulging. Cells near leaf base are clear, yellow, and rectangular.

Wet leaves spread outward

Dry leaves are stiff and pressed to stems

Capsules with lid, hairy hood, and lacking both lid and hood

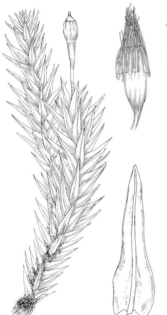

Capsule mouth open and ringed with reflexed teeth

Leaves gradually taper to point but lack needle tip extension

Ulota hutchinsiae

ROCK TUFT MOSS

APPEARANCE: Plants form dry, pincushion-like tufts 1–2 cm high on rock that are dull green or brown above and dark green or black at the base. The stiff, upright plants are densely covered in leaves that are held close to stem, and barely curved, but not contorted and curly when dry. When wet, they spread slightly outward, looking prickly.

LEAVES: Long triangular, coming to a point, but not particularly sharp and without a needle tip, 2 mm long. Midrib reaches tip. Edges are smooth.

CAPSULES: Cylindrical, or tall urn-shaped, 2 mm long, upright, with 8 vertical ribs and 8 teeth that fold down to outside of capsule when mature. Lid is beaked and hood is densely hairy. Stalks 3–4 mm tall lift capsules above leaves.

HABITAT: Very common on dry rocks, rarely on trees.

SIMILAR SPECIES

Schistidium apocarpum (p. 111) Leaves are tipped with a fine, white, hairlike needle. Capsules are hidden among leaves.

Bucklandiella microcarpa (p. 117) Plants are 2–4 cm tall; clumps are more open and yarnlike. Wet leaves flare out nearly 90 degrees when wet. Leaves are keeled. Capsules lack hairy hood while developing.

Orthotrichum anomalum (p. 107) Capsule teeth do not fold down from mouth when dry and mature. Capsule hood is only sparsely hairy. Grows on calcium-enriched rocks.

Ulota coarctata (p. 97) Capsules are inclined, and pear-shaped with puckered mouths.

MICROSCOPIC FEATURES

Cells at base and top of leaf are very, very thick-walled. Cells have one bump.

Wet leaves spread wide

Dry leaves neatly pressed to stem or barely twisted

Hairy capsule hoods

Capsules with and without lid showing puckered mouth

Stalk lifts capsule well above leaves

Base of capsule tapers into stalk

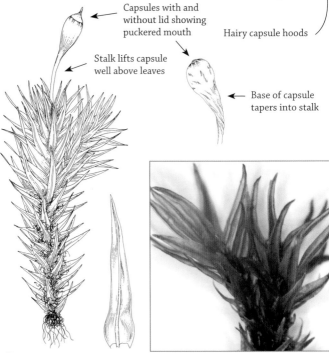

Ulota coarctata

PUCKERED TUFT MOSS

APPEARANCE: Upright plants, 3–10 mm high, form small, dull, olive green clusters on tree trunks. When dry, leaves are straight or slightly twisted, not curly nor neatly pressed to stem. When wet, leaves straighten and flare out slightly. Lower shoots are brown, while new growth at branch tips is light green.

LEAVES: Narrow lance shape, 2–3 mm long, gradually tapering to a point. Midrib to tip. Leaf edges are smooth and not strongly bordered by inrolled edges.

CAPSULES: Pear-shaped, about 2 mm long, pale, with a puckered mouth and capsule base that gradually tapers into stalk. Teeth draw in tight to mouth when dry. Lid is beaked and hood is hairy. Stalks 3–4 mm tall lifting capsules well above leaves.

HABITAT: Tree trunks in moist woods, such as along streams. Occasionally also on calcium-enriched dry boulders.

SIMILAR SPECIES

Drummondia prorepens (p. 101) Plants trail in dark lines along bark rather than crowded into clusters. Leaves are 1–2 mm long. Capsules are tubby goblet-shaped, not tapered into stalk.

Ulota crispa (p. 99) Leaves are tightly curled-contorted when dry. Capsules are not rounded or puckered at top.

Ulota hutchinsiae (p. 95) Grows on rocks; capsules are cylindrical or vase-shaped, mouth is not puckered.

Orthotrichum sordidum (p. 105) Leaves are straight and neatly pressed to stem when dry. Capsules abruptly join stalk and are partially hidden among leaves.

MICROSCOPIC FEATURES

Midrib ends below leaf tip. Cells of upper leaf are round and usually smooth or occasionally have a bump. Lower leaf cells rectangular and angled outward from midrib toward leaf edges.

Wet leaves straight and spread out   Dry leaves curl tightly

Capsules with lid, with hairy hood and lacking both, latter showing reflexed teeth at mouth

Narrow leaves gradually taper to a point but lack needle extension

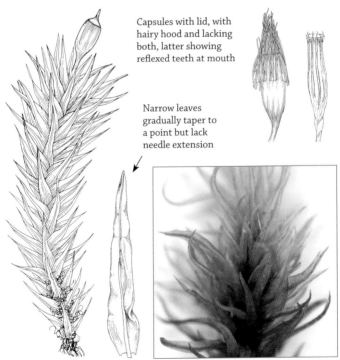

Ulota crispa

CRISPY TUFT MOSS

APPEARANCE: Upright plants form dense, rounded mounds 5–10 mm high of dull, dark olive green on tree trunks. When dry, leaves are tightly curled-contorted. Wet leaves straighten and spread outward, revealing reddish brown stems matted with fuzz.

LEAVES: Narrowly lance-shaped, coming to a sharp point but without needle or hair extensions, 2–3 mm long. Midrib is strong to tip. Edges are smooth and usually lack a dark border from curled leaf edges. Pale and translucent except for dark green midrib and red leaf base.

CAPSULES: Cylindrical or when older, constricted below the mouth into a vase shape, 2 mm long, the base gradually tapers to stalk, pale yellow. Dry capsules expose the 8 tan, reflexed teeth around mouth. Lid is beaked and hood is long-haired. Stalks 2–4 mm tall lift capsules well above leaves.

HABITAT: Tree trunks.

SIMILAR SPECIES

Ulota coarctata (p. 97) Also on trees but leaves are not much contorted when dry, and capsules are rounded and puckered at top, like a toothless mouth.

Ulota hutchinsiae (p. 95) Grows on rocks; leaves are pressed to stem when dry, rumpled but not curled-contorted.

Orthotrichum sordidum (p. 105) Generally similar except its leaves are held straight and pressed to stem when dry. Capsules lack long tapering base.

MICROSCOPIC FEATURES

Midrib ends just below leaf tip. Upper leaf cells are round and each has one small bump.

Short, upright clusters are connected in trailing lines over bark

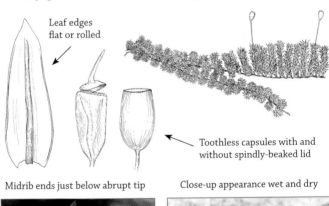

Leaf edges flat or rolled

Toothless capsules with and without spindly-beaked lid

Midrib ends just below abrupt tip

Close-up appearance wet and dry

Drummondia prorepens

TRAILBLAZER MOSS

APPEARANCE: Recognizable as distinctive lines of starlike (wet) to budlike (dry) plants on tree bark; clusters of numerous, short, blackish to olive green branches stand upright from trailing primary stems. Leaves are dense and overlapping like pointed, folded shingles when dry but spreading outward up to 75 degrees when wet.

LEAVES: Lance-shaped, coming to an abrupt point, 1–2 mm long, keeled along midrib like a boat. Midrib ends just below tip. Edges are smooth.

CAPSULES: Tubby goblet shape, about 1 mm long, upright with a wide, toothless mouth. Lid is a spindly beak and hood flares out from a peaked top, hairless. Stalk is 2–4 mm tall and holds capsule well above shoots.

HABITAT: Bark of trees, especially hardwoods such as oaks.

SIMILAR SPECIES

Orthotrichum sordidum (p. 105) Plants form clusters, rather than trailing in dark lines along bark. Leaves are 2–3 mm long. Capsules are toothed, long cylindrical, and with a hairy hood.

Orthotrichum stellatum (p. 103) Plants form clusters, rather than trailing in dark lines along bark. Leaves are about 2 mm long. Capsules are toothed, long cylindrical, and just peeking out from amid leaves.

Ulota coarctata (p. 97) Plants form clusters, rather than trailing in dark lines along bark. Leaves are 2–3 mm long. Capsule are toothed, pear-shaped, and gradually tapering into stalk.

MICROSCOPIC FEATURES

Leaf cells are smooth, round, and thick-walled. (Compare with bumpy *Ulota* and *Orthotrichum* cells.) Capsules have 16 very short, square teeth.

Wet leaves spread wide, giving plants a starry appearance

Dry leaves stiff and tightly pressed to stems

Capsules with and without lid

Capsules just peek out from shoot tips

Rolled-down leaf edges

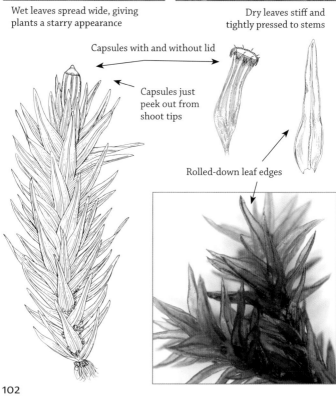

Orthotrichum stellatum

BALD BRISTLE MOSS

APPEARANCE: Upright plants, 3–5 mm tall, in small clusters. Leaves are densely crowded and are drawn together tightly and erect when dry, like forest green dry paintbrushes. Wet plants turn bright lime green and look starry as leaves spread outward 60 degrees near top of stems, 45 degrees farther down.

LEAVES: Lance shape, about 2 mm long, coming to a short-angled point. Midrib is strong to tip. Leaf edges are smooth and curled down, making the borders look dark.

CAPSULES: About 2 mm long, cylindrical, becoming vase-shaped with 8 vertical ribs upon drying, strongly constricted below wide-flaring mouth bearing 8 reflexed teeth. Hoods are hairless. Capsules are on 1 mm stalks barely emerging above the leaf tips.

HABITAT: Tree trunk bark, occasional on logs or stumps.

SIMILAR SPECIES

Orthotrichum anomalum (p. 101) Grows on rock, plants are 1–2 cm tall. Capsule and a bit of stalk are raised above leaves. Capsule hoods are hairy.

Orthotrichum sordidum (p. 105) Larger, tufts grow 6–10 mm tall. Capsule hoods are hairy. Capsule teeth are reflexed.

Orthotrichum strangulatum (p. 109) Plants grow on rocks in tufts 5–10 mm high; leaf tips are sharp. Capsule hoods are hairy. Capsule teeth are often upright.

MICROSCOPIC FEATURES

Midrib ends well below leaf tip, about 10–15 cells. Upper leaf cells are round and each has two small bumps on both top and bottom surfaces. Capsule teeth covered in tiny bumps.

Wet

Dry

Capsules half-hidden among leaves

Plants grow on tree trunks

Capsules with lid and
without showing reflexed teeth

Rolled-down,
dark leaf edges

Orthotrichum sordidum

UMBRELLA BRISTLE MOSS

APPEARANCE: Upright plants form dull cushions 6–10 mm deep on tree trunks. When dry, stems are densely covered in dark green, upright-appressed leaves, like neatly folded umbrellas. When wet, leaves are lighter green and yellower, and spread 45 degrees from stems.

LEAVES: Lance shape, 2–3 mm long, coming to a sharp tip but lacking a needle or hair extension. Midrib strong to tip. Leaf edges are smooth and curled down, looking dark.

CAPSULES: 1–2 mm long, cylindrical or vase-shaped, i.e., drawn-in below the mouth, with 8 ribs and 8 orange reflexed teeth, at least when older and dry. Developing capsules have a beaked lid over the mouth and wear a hairy hood. Stalk is short, about 2 mm, and lifts capsule halfway above leaf tips.

HABITAT: Tree trunks, especially of hardwoods.

SIMILAR SPECIES

Drummondia prorepens (p. 101) Plants trail in dark lines along bark rather than crowded into a cluster. Leaves are 1–2 mm long. Capsules lifted well above shoots.

Orthotrichum stellatum (p. 103) Smaller, plants are only 3–5 mm high. Capsule hoods are smooth, hairless.

Orthotrichum strangulatum (p. 109) Dry leaves curve in toward branches when dry. Capsules are more hidden among leaves so only the tip peaks out above. Prefers to grow on calcium-enriched rocks.

Ulota coarctata (p. 97) Dry leaves are slightly untidy. Capsules are lifted well above leaves and are rounded and puckered right at top, like a toothless mouth.

MICROSCOPIC FEATURES

Midrib ends 8–10 cells below leaf tip. Upper leaf cells are round and have 2–3 small bumps on top and bottom surfaces. Lower leaf cells are long-rectangular with thick, irregular walls. Capsule teeth are covered in bumps and lattice-like at tips.

Dry above; wet below

Plants grow on dry, calcium-enriched rocks

Capsules with lid, with and without hairy hood

Capsule stalks extend capsules beyond branches

Rolled-down, dark leaf edges

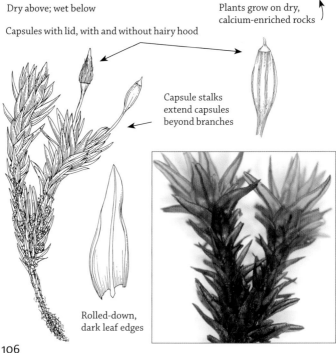

Orthotrichum anomalum

RIBBED BRISTLE MOSS

APPEARANCE: Stiff, upright plants form dull, dark green or blackish mounds 1–2 cm high on rock. Leaves stand upright, drawn together and barely crumpled when dry; spreading outward slightly when wet, revealing starlike, brighter green tips.

LEAVES: Broadly lance-shaped, 2–3 mm long, coming to a short, blunt point. Midrib is strong to just before tip. Leaf edges are smooth and curled down, making the borders look dark.

CAPSULES: Cylindrical, about 2 mm long, with 8 full-length vertical ribs alternating with 8 short ribs, especially evident when dry. Capsule teeth split into 16 and are held upright rather than reflexed when dry; hood is sparsely hairy. Stalks about 3 mm long lift capsules and a bit of stalk above leaves.

HABITAT: Rocks, dry and calcium-enriched.

SIMILAR SPECIES

Orthotrichum strangulatum (p. 109) and *O. sordidum* (p. 105) Capsules partially hidden among leaves: just the tip or half the capsule peaks out above leaves, respectively. The latter prefers to grow on tree bark, as does *Orthotrichum stellatum*, (p. 99) which is also much smaller, plants only 3–5 mm high.

Ulota hutchinsiae (p. 95) Plants form loose mats over acidic rocks. Capsules have only 8 ribs, have 8 teeth, and their hoods are very hairy.

Ulota coarctata (p. 97) Grows on trees; capsules are rounded and puckered at top, like a toothless mouth.

MICROSCOPIC FEATURES

Midrib ends just a cell or two below tip. Upper leaf cells are round and thick-walled, and each has two small bumps on both top and bottom surfaces. Lower leaf cells are rectangular without particularly thickened walls. Bases of capsule teeth are marked with wavy lines.

Wet leaves straighten and spread slightly

Dry leaves arch inward tightly

Capsules with and without lid, just peeking from among leaf tips (see photos above)

Rolled-down, dark leaf edges

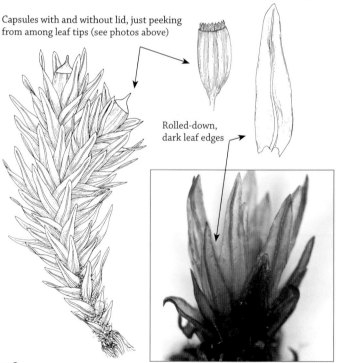

108

Orthotrichum strangulatum

SHY BRISTLE MOSS

APPEARANCE: Small upright plants form stiff, dull brown, dark green, or blackish tufts, 5–10 mm tall on rock. The bright green tips of branches are visible only when plants are wet and leaves straighten and spread slightly. Dry leaves draw in and curve toward branches, thus resembling desiccated artichokes.

LEAVES: Long, narrow triangles, 2–3 mm, with a short-angled, sharp tip. Midrib is present to tip. Leaf edges are smooth and rolled downward, appearing dark.

CAPSULES: Upright-cylindrical, 1–2 mm long, the mouth being slightly smaller than the girth of the barrel, with 8 strong vertical ribs, dark brown. Teeth are usually upright, sometimes reflexed; hoods are hairy. Stalks are so short that capsules barely peek out from among tips of leaves.

HABITAT: Dry, calcium-enriched rocks in open spaces.

SIMILAR SPECIES

Orthotrichum anomalum (p. 107) Plants form mounds 1–2 cm tall. Capsules are barely, but completely, raised above the leaves.

Orthotrichum sordidum (p. 105) Plants grow on tree bark. Leaves are stiffly erect and pressed to stems when dry. Capsules are constricted at mouth.

Orthotrichum stellatum (p. 103) Smaller, plants are only 3–5 mm high. Capsule hoods are smooth, hairless. Capsules are constricted at mouth. Grows on trees.

MICROSCOPIC FEATURES

Midrib ends quite a few cells below leaf apex. Leaf edges are several layers thick and rolled down. Capsule teeth are covered in tiny bumps.

Wet

Note bright orange teeth fringing capsules

Dry

Needle tip

Stubby capsules, revealing orange teeth
ringing mouth after lid has fallen off

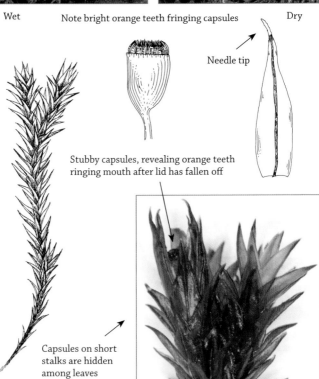

Capsules on short
stalks are hidden
among leaves

Schistidium apocarpum

PRICKLY CANNIKIN MOSS

APPEARANCE: Upright plants, 1–4 cm tall, grow in patches over rock. When dry, the white needle tips of leaves stand out against the dark green or rusty brown of this stiff hard-scrabble moss. Wet leaves are lime green with translucent tips. Dry plants hold their leaves upright or barely curved and pressed to stem; moistened leaves flare out slightly.

LEAVES: Narrow triangular, 1–3 mm long, with white or translucent hairlike needle tips, often curved to side. Midrib is present but difficult to see in the narrow leaves. Edges of leaves are smooth.

CAPSULES: Upright, shaped like tiny acorns or cups, 1 mm long, and hidden among leaves. When the short-beaked lid has fallen off, the wide mouth reveals a fringe of erect bright orange teeth. Stalk is less than 1 mm tall.

HABITAT: Dry rocks, either acidic or calcium-enriched in somewhat less-exposed habitats.

SIMILAR SPECIES

Bucklandiella microcarpa (p. 117) Capsules are raised on stalks usually more than 4 mm tall.

Grimmia pilifera (p. 119) Plants are less densely packed. Midrib is prominent; plants are not red-tinged. Capsule lids are long-beaked over recurved teeth.

Orthotrichum anomalum (p. 107) and *Ulota hutchinsiae* (p. 95) Leaves without needle tips. Capsules emerge above the height of the leaves.

MICROSCOPIC FEATURES

On the underside of the leaf, near the tip, the midrib is covered with bumps. Edges of leaf curl downward and are often two cells thick. Cells near base of leaf are wavy and thick-walled.

Wet   Dry

Cuplike capsules hidden
among shoot tips

Capsules without
lid showing bright
orange teeth
along wide mouth

Typical appearance at a distance when dry

Schistidium rivulare

BROOK CANNIKIN MOSS

APPEARANCE: Dark green, brown, or sometimes light green plants, 1–5 cm tall, form scruffy patches over rocks. Older growth is dark green or brown and predominates; the new green growth at branch tips is usually visible only when plants are moistened. Leaves are stiff, spiky, and drawn tightly to stems when dry, but don't flex open much when wet.

LEAVES: Narrowly triangular or lance-shaped, 1–3 mm long, strongly folded along midrib like the keel of a boat, often slightly curved to side. Midrib is strong to tip. Edges are smooth and rolled under, creating a dark border. Some leaves have a tiny, pale tip, but none have a needle-like projection.

CAPSULES: Upright, wide-mouthed cups, 1 mm long, orange with a red rim and red teeth that spread wide, like eyelashes when mature; mouth is covered with a beaked lid while developing. Stalk is negligible and therefore capsules are hidden among leaves.

HABITAT: Wet rocks in streams and dry rocks in seasonally wet habitats.

SIMILAR SPECIES

Codriophorus acicularis (p. 115) Leaves are more pear-shaped, and are not folded along midline. Capsules are raised clearly above leaves on stalks.

Schistidium apocarpum (p. 111) White hairlike points project beyond the ends of leaves.

MICROSCOPIC FEATURES

Edges of leaf near tip of leaf are multiple layers thick in patches and bear shallow teeth. Basal leaf cells are rectangular, weakly wavy, and thick-walled. Midrib is smooth.

Wet leaves spread out, revealing yellow-green shoot tips

Dry leaves are drawn in tightly and shoots look black and scraggly

Capsules arise from branch tips; these are with and without beaked lid

Blunt-tipped leaves

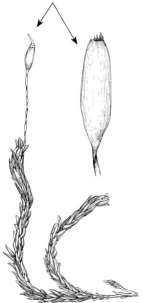

Codriophorus acicularis

BLUNT BOULDER MOSS

APPEARANCE: Creeping, blackened old stems irregularly fork into upward-arching, yellow-green branches and form shaggy patches on wet rocks. The shoots, 2–11 cm long, are densely covered in leaves which, when wet, spread outward, and when dry, are drawn in tightly, scale-like and often slightly curved to the side near the ends of branches. The narrow, upright capsules that are raised above the branches are a useful field character as well.

LEAVES: Elliptical to broadly lance-shaped, 2–3 mm long, coming to a blunt tip. Midrib ends just below leaf tip. Edges are smooth, or barely roughened at the apex.

CAPSULES: Upright cylindrical, 2–3 mm long; lid is long-beaked. Stalk is red to dark red and 3–15 mm tall, raising capsules above leaves.

HABITAT: Wet rocks, usually acidic, in stream beds or the spray-zone of waterfalls, often submerged or soaked.

SIMILAR SPECIES

Schistidium rivulare (p. 113) Has longer-pointed, sharper leaf tips that are folded along midrib. Capsules are short, wide-mouthed cups hidden among leaves.

Platylomella lescurii (p. 253) Smaller plants in similar habitats with broadly ovate leaves about 1 mm long; capsules are curved and on stalks 1–3 cm tall.

MICROSCOPIC FEATURES

Leaf edges are rolled downward. Upper cells are covered, on both surfaces, with small bumps. Cells of lower leaf have wavy walls.

Dark, dull, short-branched shoots are densely covered in sharp leaves that are drawn in tightly when dry and spread widely when wet

Capsules arise from branch tips and are held well above leaves; these are without lid

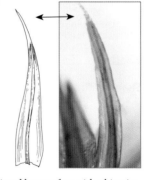

Long-pointed leaves often with white tips

Bucklandiella microcarpa

ROCK CANNIKIN MOSS

APPEARANCE: Plants form dark yellow green, dull clumps of moss over rock, 2–4 cm high. Creeping older stems covered in brown to blackish leaves turn upright with greener leaves and numerous short, stubby side branches, densely covered in sharp leaves. When wet, leaves arch outward up to 90 degrees. When dry, leaves are upright, or gently curved, and pressed tight to branches.

LEAVES: Lance-shaped, 2–3 mm long, gradually tapering to a short, sharp, white prick. The white tips are more pronounced on some leaves than on others. Blade is slightly keeled. Midrib runs to tip. Edges of leaf are smooth and curled down at least on one side from base to about midleaf, but not to tip.

CAPSULES: Oblong-cylindrical, about 2 mm long, with a long beaked lid. Stalk 5–8 mm.

HABITAT: Acidic, dry rocks, also occasionally on rocky soils.

SIMILAR SPECIES

Grimmia pilifera (p. 119) Leaves are 3–4 mm long, and capsules on 1-mm-tall stalks and thus hidden among leaves.

MICROSCOPIC FEATURES

Leaf cells are elongate with thick wavy walls except in lower outside leaf edges, where cells are square, straight-walled, and clear.

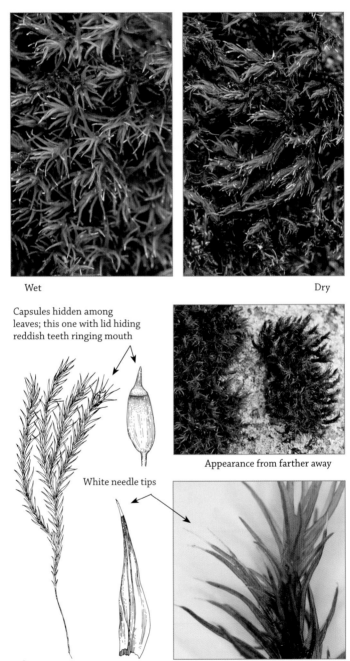

Wet

Dry

Capsules hidden among leaves; this one with lid hiding reddish teeth ringing mouth

Appearance from farther away

White needle tips

Grimmia pilifera

HOARY CANNIKIN MOSS

APPEARANCE: Upright plants form mounds, up to 1–4 cm high, of dark brown or olive green over rock. Stems divide irregularly into clusters of short branches. Wet leaves spread outward 45 degrees. Dry leaves are blackish with white needle tips and tightly drawn in, shoots thus resembling dry pine cones.

LEAVES: Lance shape, 3–4 mm long, slightly keeled and typically coming to a rough, white awn. Midrib is prominent to apex. Leaf edges are smooth and curled down on at least one side near base.

CAPSULES: Egg-shaped, about 1 mm long, with a long-beaked lid and recurved red teeth. Stalk is only 1 mm tall; thus capsules are hidden among leaves.

HABITAT: Rock: dry, usually acidic or granitic boulders.

SIMILAR SPECIES

Bucklandiella microcarpa (p. 117) Wet leaves flare and arch away nearly 90 degrees. Capsules are raised above leaves.

Schistidium apocarpum (p. 111) Leaves 2–3 mm, midrib is difficult to see. Plants are clumped more densely, often tinged with red. Capsule lids short-beaked over erect teeth.

MICROSCOPIC FEATURES

Outer basal leaf cells are clear, square, and have thickened cross-walls; neighboring basal cells are wavy-walled and longer. Most leaf cells are small, round, two layers thick, at least along leaf edges.

Plants form brittle, blackish, and crusty patches over rock, revealing hints of red and green when wet

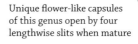

Unique flower-like capsules of this genus open by four lengthwise slits when mature

Midrib runs to tip of narrow leaf blade

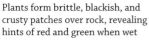

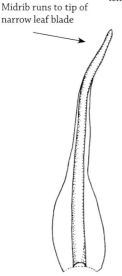

Andreaea rothii

NEEDLE-LEAVED LANTERN MOSS

APPEARANCE: Small, blackish plants form crusty patches over rock. Plants break and crumble when dry, and change little when wet, but reveal subtle hints of red and green color. Stems are erect to reclining, simple or sparsely forked, 5–20 mm tall. The spiky leaves are sparse along stems and often curved outward like a sickle. Look carefully for the unique capsules to distinguish this genus from other dark rock mosses.

LEAVES: Lance-shaped, 1–2 mm long, narrowed to long needle tips. The midrib is visible in the leaf base; otherwise it is hard to distinguish as leaves are dark and most of the narrow leaf blade is filled by the midrib. Strip off a leaf and hold it up to the light to inspect its base. Leaf edges smooth.

CAPSULES: Football-shaped capsules split lengthwise when mature into four ribbons folded like tiny flowers or Chinese lanterns. Capsules top a stubby stalk, not much taller than the tops of leaves.

HABITAT: Acidic rocks, shaded or out in the open, dry or wet, but often where water seeps over rock periodically.

SIMILAR SPECIES

Andreaea rupestris (p. 155) Similar except its leaves are wider and they lack a midrib and needle-like tips.

Schistidium apocarpum (p. 111) When dry, the white needle tips of leaves stand out against dark plants. Acorn-shaped capsules bear a fringe of red teeth along mouth when mature.

Schistidium rivulare (p. 113) Narrow, but not needle-like lance-shaped leaves are slightly folded lengthwise. Capsules are short, wide-mouthed cups hidden among the leaves.

MICROSCOPIC FEATURES

Cells are rounded, like muffin tops, but not covered in bumps or pits on back side of leaf.

Dense, round, sea urchin appearance
typical of *L. glaucum*; capsules infrequent

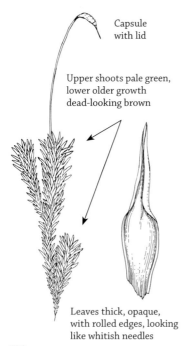

Capsule
with lid

Upper shoots pale green,
lower older growth
dead-looking brown

Leaves thick, opaque,
with rolled edges, looking
like whitish needles

Capsules frequent on *L. albidum*;
plants form looser clusters

Leucobryum glaucum

PINCUSHION MOSS

APPEARANCE: Upright plants form dense, usually round cushions on the ground, like white-green sea urchins, brighter green when wet. Densely packed stems are 1–9 cm high, covered in leaves that are held stiffly straight or very slightly curved away from stem. When teased apart, upper stems are opaque pale green and previous growth below is dead-looking brown.

LEAVES: Lance shape, 4–8 mm long, with a flat, clear, egg-shaped base (with air bubbles inside visible with a hand lens) from which extends an opaque blade with inrolled edges, forming a trough or tubular stocky needle shape. Midrib is lacking, edges are smooth.

CAPSULES: Cylindrical, 2 mm long, curved over, with a small bump at base and a long-beaked lid. Stalk is rust-colored, 9–17 mm tall. Capsules are infrequently produced; the plants reproduce vegetatively from bits of branches or leaves that break off.

HABITAT: Forest soil, often over mounds in the ground that are the remains of nearly decomposed logs, or growing on more recently fallen logs.

SIMILAR SPECIES

***Leucobryum albidum*, WHITE MOSS**: A smaller species more common in the southern part of our range; less than 1 cm tall, with leaves only 2–4 mm long. Clumps are sometimes not as dense and mounded.

Paraleucobryum longifolium (p. 43) Leaves appear silvery covering a dark green instead of uniformly whitish. Leaves are hairlike rather than thickened/tubular.

MICROSCOPIC FEATURES

Thick fleshy leaves are composed mainly of midrib, which consists of green, cholorphyll-containing cells sandwiched between layers of large, colorless cells. Actual leaf blade is reduced to a narrow band of clear cells on either side of midrib.

Philonotis fontana shoots often end in a whorl of short branches

Round *Philonotis* capsule with lid

Drooping *Pohlia* capsule without lid

Male plants topped by crownlike reproductive structure

Philonotis leaves

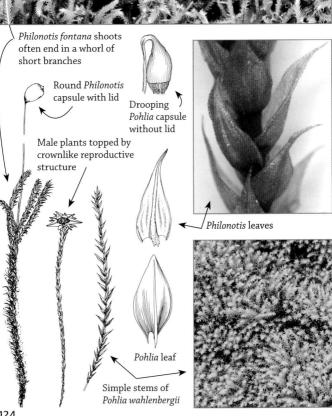

Pohlia leaf

Simple stems of *Pohlia wahlenbergii*

Philonotis fontana

FOUNTAIN MOSS

APPEARANCE: Upright, irregularly short-branched plants of soggy places, with vivid red stems, usually 3–10 cm tall (up to 16 cm), bearing whitish to bluish green leaves. By late summer many stems are topped by a whorl of short branches surrounding a circle of petal-like leaves around a cup. Brown fuzz mats the base of stems. Wet leaves flare out 35 degrees from stems. When dry, the leaf bases remain angled outward, while the tips curl irregularly back inward or to one side.

LEAVES: Triangular with a long, narrow, tapering tip, 1–2 mm long. Often pleated. Midrib runs to tip. Leaf edges are rolled downward and are usually smooth, or sometimes tiny teeth are apparent near leaf tip.

CAPSULES: Globose when wet but egg-shaped and furrowed when dry, horizontal, 2–3 mm long, with a conic lid. Stalk is 2–5 cm tall and reddish.

HABITAT: Wet rocks and soil next to streams, or in a seepy ditch or spring.

SIMILAR SPECIES

***Pohlia wahlenbergii*, BLEACHED SEEP MOSS**: Leaves lack pleats, spread up to 80 degrees from stems when wet, and their edges are not rolled.

Ptychostomum pseudotriquetrum (p. 127) Red stems with wider, dark green, unpleated leaves. Plants are usually only 2–4 cm tall.

MICROSCOPIC FEATURES

Leaf edges are toothed; some teeth are single, others are double. On the lower surface of leaf, each cell has one bump on the end nearest the leaf base.

Plants are sparsely covered in leaves that flare out widely when wet revealing red stems

Capsule with lid

Midrib often red brown

Rolled edges form border

Basal corners of leaf run onto stem as slender fins

Red stems covered by brown fuzz, especially near base

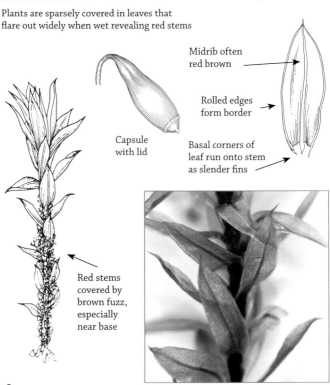

Ptychostomum pseudotriquetrum

MARSH CARDINAL MOSS

Appearance: Plants form dark green or reddish tufts of upright stems, 2–4 cm tall. Reddish stems are not much forked, are matted with brown fuzz and sparsely covered in leaves, which become denser toward top of shoots. Wet leaves are flat and spread 80 degrees from stems, dry leaves shrivel and curl slightly with the edges rolling in more, making leaves appear narrower.

Leaves: Long egg shape, usually 2–3 mm, with a fine, sharp tip. Midrib runs to apex, sometimes just beyond, and is often red brown. Edges of leaf are smooth and curl downward, forming a dark border. Outside lower corners of leaf run down onto stem in slender fins.

Capsules: Long pear- or club-shaped, 3–5 mm long, gradually tapering to stalk, bent over or hanging upside down. Lid is conical. Stalk is usually 1–3 cm tall.

Habitat: Wet, mineral-enriched soil or rocks in swamps or sedgy fens, beside ponds, or in seepy cracks in cliff ledges.

Similar Species

Philonotis fontana (p. 125) By late summer, many stems are topped by a whorl of short branches with large wide leaves surrounding a cup in the center, like a flower. Leaves are often pleated and more triangular in shape.

Microscopic Features

Cells of upper leaf are 2–3× as long as wide. Darker, long cells running along edge form a border. Cells along edges of lower outside corners rectangular. Leaf tip can be slightly toothed.

Plants characteristically grow atop tree stumps

Intermixed shoots topped with either pencil-like capsules or flower-like gemmae cups

Capsule without lid showing unique 4 teeth

Gemmae cups

Leaves denser and larger farther up stem

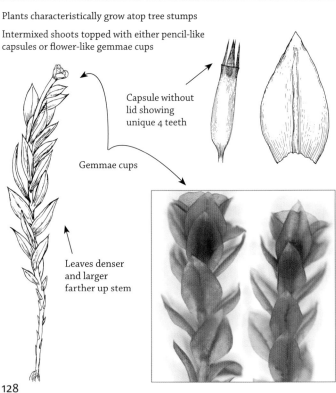

Tetraphis pellucida

FOUR-TOOTH MOSS

APPEARANCE: This quintessential stump-top moss forms turfs of upright, unbranched stems, 8–15 mm tall, sparsely covered in leaves, which are dark green but turn pale reddish brown with age. Leaves are slightly denser and longer toward top of stems. Stems are often topped by capsules that resemble sharp pencils or by rosettes of small leaves that look like nests of eggs. The nestlike gemmae cups serve in asexual reproduction. When old, they shrivel into round "buds." When dry, leaves are drawn in and look slightly messy on gently curling stems. Wet leaves spread out about 45 degrees.

LEAVES: Egg-shaped, 1–2 mm long, coming to a sharp point. Midrib is strong and ends just below tip. Edges are smooth, flat, and lack a pale border.

CAPSULES: Slender-cylindrical, 2–3 mm high, erect, brown to yellow brown with a pointed lid over four orange-brown, upright teeth, making capsules look like a bird beak or the tip of a sharpened pencil. Stalk is 6–14 mm tall and often twisted when dry.

HABITAT: Rotting logs and especially atop old tree stumps.

SIMILAR SPECIES

Plagiomnium cuspidatum (p. 139) Sparse oval leaves that are strongly toothed. Also, its sterile branches tend to trail vinelike over the ground. Capsules are not upright or 4-toothed.

Pohlia nutans (p. 89) Leaves are 2–3 mm long and lance-shaped. Capsules are pear-shaped and drooping, mouth with 16 teeth.

MICROSCOPIC FEATURES

Rounded cells throughout. No long narrow cells running along leaf margins.

Wet, wide-spreading leaves give plants a rose-like appearance from above

Dry plants are shriveled and twisted

Capsules with and without lid

Leaf blade smooth, rather than rippled

Base tapers into stem

Atrichum crispum

OVAL STARBURST MOSS

APPEARANCE: Plants are erect, unbranched, to 5 cm tall, pale green to olive green in mounds or patches. When wet, leaves spread away from the stem, giving a rose-like appearance from above, but upon drying the leaves fold upward along the stem and become shriveled and twisted. They are slow to rehydrate after wetting.

LEAVES: Long oval, typically 4–7 mm long and about 2 mm wide, tapering to an acute tip and also distinctly tapering to the point of attachment to the stem. Strong midrib runs to the apex. Small marginal teeth project outward, spinelike, from tip nearly to the base. When wet, the leaf surface is flat to slightly V-folded along the midrib, but without the ripples or ruffles of other *Atrichum* species.

CAPSULES: Upright to inclined, cylindrical, 2–3 mm long, with long-beaked lids. Stalk is 1–3 cm tall.

HABITAT: Wet, usually sandy soil along streams and in roadside ditches of shaded sites; also on moist sandstone.

SIMILAR SPECIES

Other *Atrichum* species (pp. 67–69) Have rippled or ruffled leaf surfaces when wet, and leaf bases are parallel-sided rather than distinctly tapering.

Plagiomnium species (pp. 139–141) Often have some creeping stems as well as erect ones.

Mnium species (pp. 133–137) Have teeth in pairs along the leaf margin.

MICROSCOPIC FEATURES

Midrib bears a few obscure ridges of tissue 1 cell wide and 1–4 cells high. Leaf teeth and cells on the leaf margin have low wrinkled wall thickenings.

Plants starlike from above with wet, wide-spread leaves over red stems

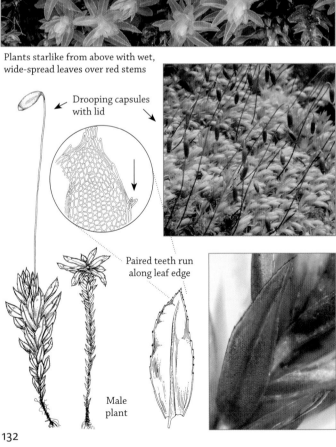

Drooping capsules with lid

Paired teeth run along leaf edge

Male plant

Mnium hornum

LIPSTICK THYME MOSS

APPEARANCE: Upright plants stand 2–5 cm high, with pale yellow green to dark green leaves evenly and sparsely spaced over a red, unbranched stem that is densely matted with brown fuzz near base. Male stems are topped by longer leaves that are clustered around a budlike center. The leaves are flat and upright or spread away from stem when wet; when dry they curl and shrivel.

LEAVES: Long oval, 3–5 mm long, about 4× as long as broad, with a short triangular tip. Midrib ends at apex. Edge is bordered and toothed from tip past midpoint. Each toothy point is in fact forked into a double tooth. To see this, hold a leaf edge up to the light and perpendicular to your eye and tilt it side to side. If it is a *Mnium*, then with practice you should make out two tiny pinpricks of light, rather than just one as in *Plagiomnium*.

CAPSULES: Football shape, 3–5 mm long, with a short neck, bent over to upside down, tan. Lid is conic. Stalk 2–5 cm, single, orange.

HABITAT: Wetlands, in swamps, along streams or in damp woods on soil or rock; prefers acidic habitats.

SIMILAR SPECIES

Arrhenopterum heterostichum (p. 171) Shoots somewhat flattened, lacking reddish tint, typically growing in dry oak woods. Leaves rounded at apex rather than short-peaked.

Mnium marginatum (p. 135) Similar species found in calcium-enriched habitats; leaves are broader, 2–3× as long as wide.

Plagiomnium species (pp. 139–141) Leaves have single teeth rather than double, and creeping stems are usually mixed in a colony with the upright stems.

MICROSCOPIC FEATURES

Midrib actually ends 2–3 cells shy of leaf tip and has a few teeth near tip on underside of leaf. Cells of leaf blade are round or hexagonal.

Stems upright and starlike

M. spinulosum has dark reddish brown capsule teeth, compared with yellow-tan teeth of *M. marginatum*

M. spinulosum capsules lack neck; this one without lid

M. marginatum capsules have a short neck; this one with lid

Double teeth

Mnium marginatum

BORDERED THYME MOSS

APPEARANCE: Upright plants, 1–3 cm tall, with unbranched, reddish stems growing in loose clusters. Leaves are larger and closer together near top of stems, and are usually pale green, though sometimes brownish. Dry leaves curl and shrivel into ruffles. Wet leaves straighten not quite all the way, remaining somewhat curvy.

LEAVES: Oval, 2–5 mm, about 2–3× as long as broad, tapering to a sharp point. Translucent or reddish border encircles leaf. Midrib reaches tip and is sometimes reddish. Leaf is toothed at least near the tip, sometimes down to middle. Each toothy point is forked into a double tooth. Hold a leaf edge up to the light and tilt it side to side. If it is a *Mnium*, then with practice you should make out two tiny pinpricks of light, rather than just one as in *Plagiomnium*.

CAPSULES: Cylindrical, 2–4 mm long, with a short neck, bent over at least to the horizontal. Lid is beaked and covers yellow to light brown teeth during development. Stalk is orange or reddish, single, and 13–25 mm tall.

HABITAT: Calcium-enriched places on rocks, soil, and even tree trunk bases.

SIMILAR SPECIES

***Mnium spinulosum*, SPINY THYME MOSS**: Has broader dark green leaves. Capsules are accented by showy dark reddish brown teeth. Capsule stalks are often double or triple. Grows in acidic locations.

Mnium hornum (p. 133) Leaves are about 4× as long as broad; prefers acidic habitats.

Plagiomnium species (p. 139–141) Leaves have single teeth rather than double, and creeping stems are usually mixed in a colony with the upright stems.

MICROSCOPIC FEATURES

Upper leaf cells round with walls thickened at the corners. Midrib toothless, or with small teeth on backside of leaf tip.

135

Dead leaf cells turn blue, see arrow above

Drooping capsule
without lid

Oval or elliptic leaves
with midrib that ends
below blunt point

Shallow double teeth
line leaf edges near tip

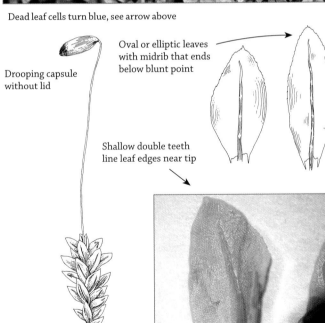

BLUE THYME MOSS

APPEARANCE: Upright, unbranched plants, usually 1–3 cm tall, form dark green or rust-colored loose clusters. Leaves are sparse, but slightly more crowded and larger near top of reddish stems. Dry leaves are gently crumpled; wet leaves spread out and flatten. Lower stems are often fuzzy. Dead leaf cells turn a distinctive blue.

LEAVES: Oval or elliptic, 2–3 mm, with a blunt point. Midrib ends well below tip. Leaf toothed at least near the tip, sometimes down to middle with very short, often double teeth that are so small they look single with a hand lens. Border lacking, lower leaf corners run down onto stem.

CAPSULES: Cylindrical, 2–4 mm long, with a short neck, bent over to upside down, lid is convex. Stalk is red, single, and 1–2 cm.

HABITAT: Bark at tree bases and stumps. Occasional on other substrates in damp forests.

SIMILAR SPECIES

Atrichum crispum (p. 131) Leaves are larger, 4–7 mm long, and more strongly toothed. Midrib runs to apex of leaf.

Mnium marginatum (p. 135) Leaves are pale green, 2–5 mm long, sharply pointed and with a border of clear or reddish cells along edge.

Rhizomnium punctatum (p. 143) Leaves are round-tipped, 3–6 mm long, sometimes with a single tooth at top. Edges are smooth with a very pronounced border.

MICROSCOPIC FEATURES

Upper leaf cells are round with walls thickened at the corners. Cells along leaf edge are longer and sometimes form a weak, pale, one-cell wide border. Teeth are unicellular and stubby. Lower leaf corners run down onto stem.

Starry, upright fertile and prostrate ladder-like vegetative plants intertwine in loose clump

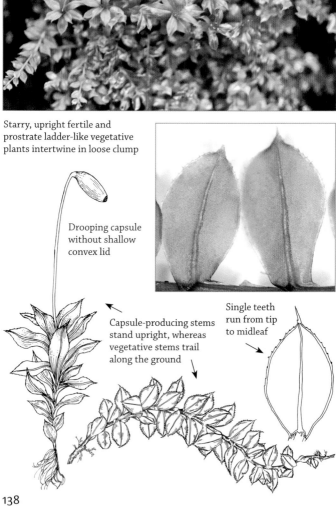

Drooping capsule without shallow convex lid

Capsule-producing stems stand upright, whereas vegetative stems trail along the ground

Single teeth run from tip to midleaf

Plagiomnium cuspidatum

BABY TOOTH MOSS

APPEARANCE: Vegetative stems trail along the ground like a vine, with leaves neatly in two rows; stems with capsules stand upright. Both growth habits intertwine to form loose, dark green tufts 2–3 cm tall. Leaves are sparse along green stems except at tops of upright stems, where they are clustered and crowded. Leaves range from deep green to yellow green and are flat and flare outward when wet and are crumpled and twisted when dry.

LEAVES: Oval, or elongate-oval, 3–4 mm long, sometimes widest above middle, coming to a short, sharp tip. (Leaves in clusters at top of upright stems are slightly larger.) Midrib reaches apex. Faint border runs along edge of leaf as well as single teeth from tip to mid-leaf. Lower outside corners of leaf run down onto stem.

CAPSULES: Cylindrical, 2–3 mm long, hanging upside down, yellow or brown, with a convex lid. Stalks are yellow, single, 1–3 cm tall.

HABITAT: Moist shady habitats including forest soil, bark at tree bases, poor lawns, among rocks or in wet, grassy fields.

SIMILAR SPECIES

Mnium species (pp. 133–137) Plants are upright only, without trailing vegetative shoots. Teeth along leaf edges are double.

Plagiomnium ciliare (p. 141) Teeth run all the way from tip to base of 5–8 mm long leaf. Also leaf is more straight-sided tongue-shaped.

MICROSCOPIC FEATURES

Midleaf cells are rounded, not sharply angled hexagons. Teeth on leaf edge are composed of a single cell.

Fertile stems upright while vegetative stems trail along ground

Vegetative stems of *P. medium* few and short

Capsules with lid

P. ciliare fertile stems each produce one capsule stalk, whereas those of *P. medium* produce multiple capsules

Midrib runs beyond leaf tip

Pale border and teeth run from tip to base of leaf

Plagiomnium ciliare

SABER TOOTH MOSS

APPEARANCE: Vegetative stems trail along the ground like a vine, with leaves neatly in two rows; stems with capsules stand upright. Both growth habits intertwine to form loose, dark green tufts 3–6 cm tall. Leaves are sparsely spaced except at tops of upright stems, where they are clustered in a rosette. Leaves are shiny green to yellow green, flat, and flare outward when wet, and are crumpled and twisted when dry. Lower stems are covered in brown fuzz.

LEAVES: Tongue-shaped, 5–8 mm long, with a rounded apex. Midrib extends beyond tip of leaf as short point. Faint border of pale cells runs along edge of leaf, as well as regular, single, long and sharp teeth from tip to base. Lower outside corners of leaf run down onto stem.

CAPSULES: Cylindrical, brown, hanging upside down, 3–5 mm long, lid is conical. Capsule stalk is single (one per fertile shoot), brown, 2–5 cm tall.

HABITAT: Forest soil, on rotting logs, tree bases, on rocks in shady swampy areas or along streams.

SIMILAR SPECIES

***Plagiomnium medium*, GREATER TOOTH MOSS**: A larger plant with leaves up to 12 mm long at tips of upright stems. Creeping vegetative shoots are typically few and short; fertile shoots often with 2–5 capsules.

Mnium species (pp. 133–137) Plants are upright only, without trailing vegetative shoots. Teeth along leaf edges in pairs.

Plagiomnium cuspidatum (p. 139) Leaves are smaller, egg-shaped, 3–4 mm long, and have teeth that run no more than ⅔ the length of the leaf.

MICROSCOPIC FEATURES

Teeth along leaf edge are often composed of 1–4 cells. Cells in middle of leaf rounded and neatly lined up in diagonal rows.

Loose clusters of shoots with round egg-shaped leaves

Stems of *R. appalachianum* are fuzzy throughout

Leaves sometimes end in a single tooth at tip

Drooping capsule with lid

Brown fuzz sprouts at base of leaves along lower stems of *R. punctatum*

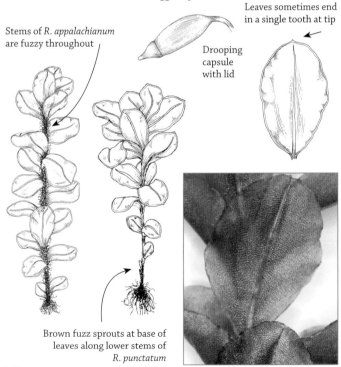

Rhizomnium punctatum

RED PENNY MOSS

APPEARANCE: Plants form loose clusters of upright stems, 1–5 cm tall, with round or egg-shaped leaves. The stem, midrib, leaf border and even leaf interior are usually tinged with red. Coarse brown fuzz sprouts from junction of leaves with lower stem. The sparse leaves spiral around the stem. When wet they are flat, angled outward 45 degrees at base, and from midleaf to tip are further arching, giving the plants an open aspect. Dry leaves curl and shrivel. Some plants are topped by a whorl of small leaves around a cup, like a flower.

LEAVES: Round egg shape, widest above middle, 3–6 mm long, often with a single tooth at top. Midrib ends just below the leaf tip. Edges are smooth with a pronounced, often red border, like a hem running around the leaf.

CAPSULES: Swollen-cylindrical, 2–4 mm long, drooping upside down; lid is beaked. Stalk is orange, 2–3 cm.

HABITAT: Wet rocks, rotting wood and soil along stream banks or in soggy woods.

SIMILAR SPECIES

***Rhizomnium appalachianum*, APPALACHIAN PENNY MOSS**: Stems are 4–12 cm tall and densely matted with brown fuzz throughout, at least by late summer. Leaves 7–13 mm long.

Mnium stellare (p. 137) Leaves are 2–3 mm long, oval or elliptic with a blunt point; midrib ends well below tip. Has toothed edges at least near apex. Dead cells turn blue.

MICROSCOPIC FEATURES

Border of leaf is two layers thick, at least near tip of leaf. Upper stems lack either coarse or fine hairlike rootlets.

Wet leaves spread outward into flat-topped, circular rosettes

Shield-shaped leaves are widest above midleaf and end in needle point →

Drooping capsule with lid

Dry leaves draw inward

Leaves clustered at tip of stem

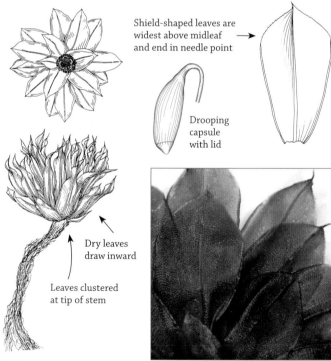

Rhodobryum ontariense

ROSE MOSS

APPEARANCE : Dark green, upright plants, 1–4 cm tall, with leaves all clustered at top of stem in a circular flowerlike rosette 1–2 cm in diameter. Upon drying the leaves fold upward, like flower petals at night, and become gently rippled and contorted. Plants are connected underground by runners.

LEAVES: Shield-shaped, widest above the middle, 5–10 mm long. Midrib extends beyond peak of leaf tip as a sharp needle point. Margins are toothed in the upper third of leaf. Lower leaf edges roll under.

CAPSULES: Pear-shaped, 4–7 mm long, drooping upside down, with a cone-shaped lid. Stalks are 2–4 cm tall, often in clusters of 1–6 per plant. Colonies expand vegetatively by runners.

HABITAT: Forest soil, humus, rotten logs, and tree bases in shady moist areas; also on rocks, especially limestone.

SIMILAR SPECIES

Plagiomnium species (pp. 139–141) Leaves cluster at top of stems in a rosette that is not as flattened as in *Rhodobryum,* and some leaves are scattered along stem below. Leafy stems usually trail along ground like a vine. Leaves are more egg- or tongue-shaped.

Rhizomnium appalachianum (p. 143) Leaves are round egg-shaped, with a rounded top and at most one tiny prick at apex. Leaves bases run down stems.

MICROSCOPIC FEATURES

Cells at leaf border are long and narrow; otherwise, cells are long-hexagonal with rounded corners.

Ovate leaves of varying width end in a tiny pricklike extension of the midrib

Drooping capsule with lid

Leaf edges clear and often rolled

Leaves clustered near top of stems, sparse below amid brown fuzz

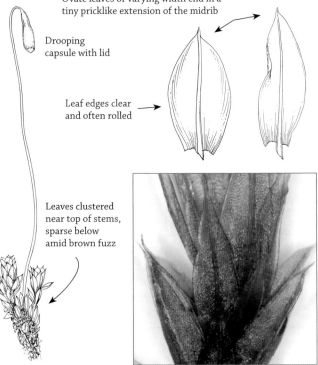

Rosulabryum capillare

CLUSTER MOSS

APPEARANCE: Upright, dark green to brown plants, usually less than 1 cm tall, are crowded together into very dense patches. Leaves are tightly clustered at top of stem and sparse below, often interspersed with brown hairs. When wet, leaves are erect or slightly flared. When dry, the leaves are twisted into a spiral cluster except for the wispy tips. Brown threadlike appendages can often be found at junction of stem and leaves and serve as a means of asexual reproduction.

LEAVES: Oblong-elliptic, 2–3 mm long, widest at the middle, with a short needle point at tip that is an extension of the midrib. The midrib is often reddish brown near base of leaf. Edges of leaves are smooth, bordered by long, clear cells and often the very edge of leaf is also curled under.

CAPSULES: Long pear-shaped and drooping upside down, 3–5 mm long, lid is a shallow cone. Stalk is red, 1–4 cm tall.

HABITAT: Moist soil, humus, or rocks, especially along roads; also on bark of trees and tree bases and on decaying wood.

SIMILAR SPECIES

Bryum argenteum (p. 149) Typically silvery, and even when green its leaves are scale-like and tightly packed on stem, giving its shoots a wormlike appearance.

Gemmabryum caespiticium (p. 91) Usually 1 cm tall or less; its narrowly egg-shaped leaves do not spiral twist when dry. Leaf ends are drawn out to longer tip.

Pohlia nutans (p. 89) Leaves lack a border; leaf ends are drawn out to longer tip. Capsules on copper-colored stalks.

MICROSCOPIC FEATURES

Leaf cells are thin-walled and not more than 3× as long as wide, except 1–3 rows of long, narrow, thick-walled cells forming a border at edge of leaf.

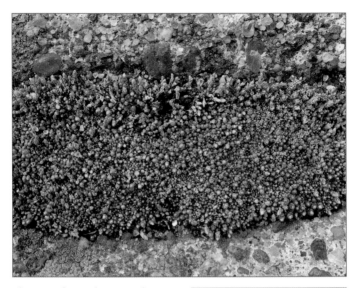

Plants are silvery pale green and growing in a typical habitat: a dry sidewalk seam

Drooping capsule with lid

Short stems are densely covered in overlapping, scale-like leaves, giving shoots a cylindrical appearance

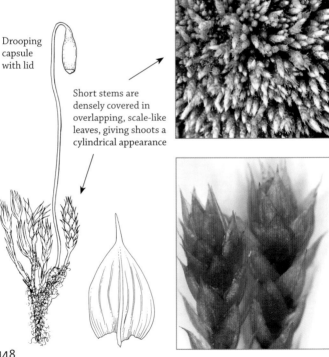

APPEARANCE: Silvery to pale green plants stand upright, often forked, usually no more than 1 cm tall, forming compact turfs that are velvety to the touch. Leaves are so tightly packed and overlapping along stems that they give branches a wormlike aspect and hide red stems. Not much changed wet or dry.

LEAVES: Tiny, around 1 mm long, and scale- or cup-shaped, with a sharp point at tip, sometimes extending as a short needle. Leaves are whitish-colorless near the tip, turning green near the base. Too small to see with a hand lens, the midrib ends below the tip. Edges are smooth.

CAPSULES: Elongated cylindrical or pear-shaped, 1–2 mm long and pink or reddish to brown, hanging upside down from 1 cm tall stalks. Lid is a shallow cone.

HABITAT: Common in urban areas on a wide variety of substrates, including hard dry soils, gravel, sand, concrete, stone and brick walls, and roofs. Characteristic of cracks and seams in sidewalks and brick patios, along paths and railways, in gardens and fields.

SIMILAR SPECIES

Rosulabryum capillare (p. 147) Green brown and its stems are not wormlike, but rather twist in a spiral when dry; leaves are 2–3 mm long.

Gemmabryum caespiticium and *Ptychostomum creberrimum* (p. 91) Leaves lance-shaped, 2–3 mm long, with a midrib that continues as a needle tip beyond the leaf. Plants do not have a whitish cast.

Myurella species (p. 273) Shoots are wormlike and pale green but creeping to erect in loose mats rather than densely packed turfs. Typically on moist calcium-rich rock or soil.

MICROSCOPIC FEATURES

Midrib ends below tip of leaf. Leaves lack a border of long narrow cells.

149

Small rosette-shaped plants
colonize disturbed soil such
as in bare garden beds

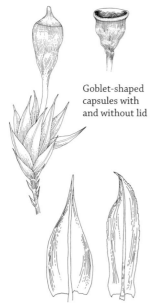

Goblet-shaped
capsules with
and without lid

Examples of leaf shape variety

Physcomitrium pyriforme

GOBLET MOSS

APPEARANCE: Small, pale green, upright plants, 3–10 mm high. Leaves are contorted when dry; when moist, they spread out to form rosettes in clumps or scattered on bare ground. Easiest to spot and identify in the spring when it forms its tiny goblet-like capsules.

LEAVES: Egg-shaped or dagger-shaped leaves, usually 3–4 mm long, narrowing to a sharp point. Midrib ends at tip or sometimes just beyond as a short, sharp needle. Thin, translucent leaves have large cells that are visible with hand lens, lending a pebbly appearance to surface. Edge of leaf is very faintly toothed.

CAPSULES: Spherical to pear-shaped when green and immature, becoming goblet- or top-shaped as they mature and dry, upright, 1–2 mm long. When beaked lid has fallen off, capsule is open at top and lacks teeth. Stalks are 5–15 mm tall, lifting capsules well above leaves.

HABITAT: Disturbed bare soil in open sunny spaces, such as lawns, garden beds, fields, roadsides, and moist stream banks.

SIMILAR SPECIES

Funaria hygrometrica (p. 153), *Gemmabryum caespiticium* (p. 91), and *Ptychostomum creberrimum* (p. 91) Similar leafy plants but with drooping, pear-shaped capsules on stalks 2–5 cm tall; however, lacking capsules, can be indistinguishable from *Physcomitrium* in the field.

MICROSCOPIC FEATURES

Cells along leaf margins are long and narrow, forming a faint border. Cells at base are inflated.

Plants with distinctive asymmetric, drooping capsules atop long stalks that twist as they change moisture level

Short rosette or bulb-shaped clusters of leaves

Capsule mouth beneath "chin;" this one old, with lid

Egg-shaped leaves taper to a tiny prick at tip

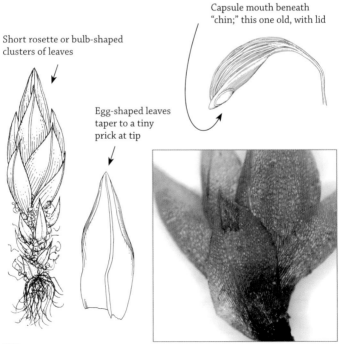

Funaria hygrometrica

BONFIRE MOSS

APPEARANCE: Small, upright, pale green plants, 3–10 mm tall, their red stems topped by a rosette or bulb-shaped cluster of leaves. The uniquely asymmetric drooping capsules are the surest means of identifying this species.

LEAVES: Egg-shaped, 2–4 mm long, cupped, translucent, and composed of very large cells, easily seen with a hand lens, giving the leaf surface a pebbly appearance. Midrib runs beyond apex, forming a tiny white needle tip. Edges of leaf are smooth.

CAPSULES: Asymmetric, swollen pear-shaped, 2–4 mm long, drooping. Immature capsules are bright green with a red ring around the convex lid. Dried capsules are reddish brown, furrowed, and bent just behind the mouth. Stalks are 2–5 cm tall and curl and twist with changes in moisture.

HABITAT: Disturbed soil, especially burned-over areas, such as campfire sites; also along roads, in lawns, gardens, fields, potted plants, or beside building foundations.

SIMILAR SPECIES

Physcomitrium pyriforme (p. 151) Has very similar looking leaves and can be reliably distinguished in the field only when its upright, tiny, goblet-shaped capsules are present.

Gemmabryum caespiticium and *Ptychostomum creberrimum* (p. 91) Have similar-shaped leaves, but lack the large clear cells that lend the pebbly aspect to *Funaria* leaves, and their drooping capsules are narrower and with a symmetrically placed mouth.

MICROSCOPIC FEATURES

Cells are hexagonal, large and thin-walled near tip of leaf, slightly longer below. Edges of leaf are not lined with a border of long, narrow cells.

Wet plants open to reveal
hints of green and red

Dry plants look like crusty
brown-black scabs over rock

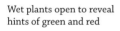

Capsule before
and after opening
lengthwise along 4 slits

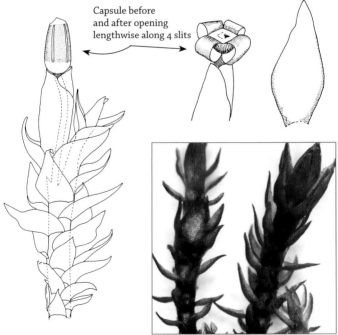

Andreaea rupestris

BROAD-LEAVED LANTERN MOSS

APPEARANCE: Small, brown-black, crusty plants forming large mats over rock, 5–30 mm tall. When dry, plants break and crumble easily, and their leaves are overlapping and held close to stems. When wet, leaves spread outward from stem and reveal hints of red and green color, especially at stem tips. Look carefully for the unique capsules to distinguish this genus from other dark rock mosses.

LEAVES: Triangular to fiddle-shaped with a blunt tip, gently cupped, up to 1 mm long. Midrib lacking. Edges are smooth.

CAPSULES: Football-shaped capsules split lengthwise when mature into four ribbons folded like tiny flowers or Chinese lanterns. Capsules top a stubby stalk, not much taller than the tops of leaves.

HABITAT: Rocks: acidic boulders or ledges, generally dry and out in the open but subject to seasonal seepage, such as snow melt or waterfall spray.

SIMILAR SPECIES

Andreaea rothii (p. 121) Similar except its leaves have a midrib and are narrower with more needle-like tips.

Schistidium apocarpum (p. 111) When dry, the white needle tips of leaves stand out against dark plants. Produce upright, acorn-shaped capsules with a fringe of red teeth along mouth when mature.

Schistidium rivulare (p. 113) Narrow, but not needle-like lance-shaped leaves are slightly folded lengthwise. Capsules are short, wide-mouthed cups hidden among the leaves.

MICROSCOPIC FEATURES

Cells are rounded, like muffin tops, and covered in bumps or pits on back side of leaf.

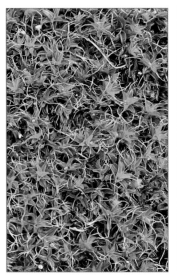
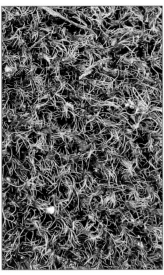

Plants look like pineapple tops as wet leaves spread outward from stems

Dry leaves arch and twist inward like clusters of long-nailed talons

Capsule with long-beaked lid over hairlike teeth

Long hair-tips

Leaves are folded lengthwise

Syntrichia ruralis

TALON MOSS

APPEARANCE: Upright plants look like long pineapple tops when the plants are wet and the leaves arch and spread far away from stems. When dry, leaves with their long, white, hairlike tips twist inward toward the stems, resembling dark braided cords of talons. Shoots have reddish stems and the leaves are blackish or reddish below, fading to yellow orange and green at tips of branches.

LEAVES: Tongue shape, 2–4 mm long, clasping at base with a blunt top from which extends an incredibly long, rough white hair. Leaves are folded lengthwise along the midrib like a keel. Dark midrib reaches apex. Edges are smooth and curled downward, forming a dark border.

CAPSULES: Cylindrical, 2–4 mm, upright, rust-colored, with a long-conic lid over long, twisted, hairlike teeth at mouth. Stalk is reddish and 5–20 mm tall.

HABITAT: Soil and rock in calcium-enriched, often dry habitats.

SIMILAR SPECIES

Grimmia pilifera (p. 119) Leaves lance-shaped with a sharp tip. Capsules have short teeth and are hidden among leaves.

MICROSCOPIC FEATURES

Cells at base of leaf are very large, clear, and inflated and in a large group that forms an upside-down U shape on either side of midrib. Otherwise, leaf cells are small, round, and densely covered in C-shaped bumps.

Wet plants open into rosettes
of tongue-shaped leaves

Dry leaves shrivel
and fold lengthwise,
resembling noodles

E. ciliata leaf with
tiny needle tip

E. procera leaf tip obtuse
and lacking needle

Brown threads grow
from stems of *E. procera*,
lacking on *E. ciliata*

Capsules with and
without long-beaked
lid and socklike hood

Encalypta ciliata

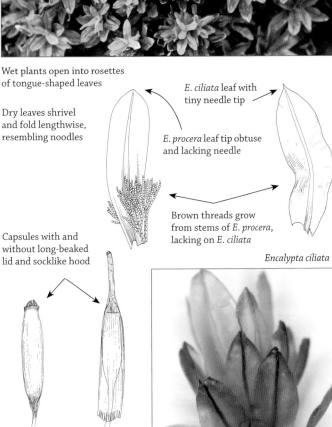

158

Encalypta procera

BLUNT EXTINGUISHER MOSS

APPEARANCE: Upright plants are 4–8 cm tall, typically form sparse patches or grow singly. Leaves are densely crowded in a rosette and are dull, yellow green near top and brown at base of stem. Wet leaves spread out 45–75 degrees from stem, flat, while dry leaves shrivel and fold along midrib, looking like skinny noodles. Threadlike brown projections grow from stems and serve as asexual propagules.

LEAVES: Tongue-shaped, 2–5 mm long, with a clasping base and a rounded or obtuse tip that is cupped like a hood and ends in a tiny prick. Midrib is strong and runs to tip. Edges are smooth and rolled under at base, forming a fine border.

CAPSULES: Rare; cylindrical, 3 mm long, upright, spirally ribbed, tan with a long-beaked lid. Hood covers entire capsule, has a pointy tip and fringe at base, looking like tiny rockets or fire extinguishers. Stalk is 12–20 mm tall, rusty. More often reproduces vegetatively via threadlike projections on stems.

HABITAT: Soil crusts over calcium-enriched rocky ledges or in cracks of those cliffs.

SIMILAR SPECIES

Encalypta ciliata, **SHARP EXTINGUISHER MOSS**: Plants are 5–20 mm tall; capsule stalks are 4–14 mm and yellow or tan. Leaves end in a tiny yellow needle. Produces capsules more often, lacks brown fuzzy projections on stem.

MICROSCOPIC FEATURES

Cells of leaf are roundish and covered in C-shaped bumps, except cells at base of leaf, which are smooth and rectangular.

Plants form dense clusters of short rosettes of tongue-shaped leaves

Capsules with lid covering long hairlike teeth; this one also with hood

Leaves abruptly taper and end in a tiny prick

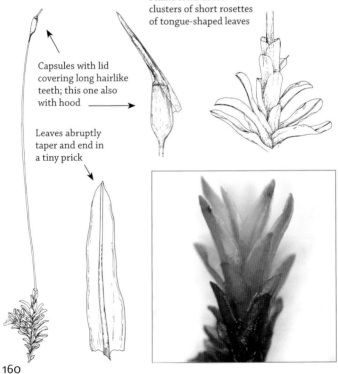

Barbula convoluta

BEAR-CLAW MOSS

APPEARANCE: Upright plants, usually less than 5 mm tall, though sometimes up to 15 mm, which form dense carpets of dull olive green tinged with yellow. Leaves are densely clustered, starlike, on short stems. Wet leaves spread wide and flat; dry leaves fold lengthwise and curve in toward stem.

LEAVES: Tongue-shaped, about 1 mm long; tips are rounded or short-beaked. Midrib extends beyond tip as a short, sharp needle. Leaf edges are smooth; blade is flat, like a narrow tongue.

CAPSULES: Capsules are upright, cylindrical, like a tapering cigar, 1–2 mm long. Lid is long-beaked; when beak is gone, mouth is ringed by long, twisted hairlike teeth. Stalk is yellow, 1–2 cm tall.

HABITAT: Disturbed soils enriched with calcium, in open spaces such as along roadsides, fields, and old walls.

SIMILAR SPECIES

Pohlia nutans (p. 89) Leaves are longer and more lance-shaped, 2–3 mm long, lack short needle tips, and have reddish stems.

Gemmabryum caespiticium and *Ptychostomum creberrimum* (p. 91) Leaves are cupped, lance-shaped to narrowly ovate with long needle tips, 2–3 mm long, and barely change between wet and dry. Stems are matted with brown fuzz.

Tortella humilis (p. 79) Leaves are 2–4 mm long and curl irregularly when dry.

MICROSCOPIC FEATURES

Cells are covered in C-shaped bumps. Lower edges of leaf are rolled downward.

Short dark plants recognizable by their unique, squat, nutlike capsules

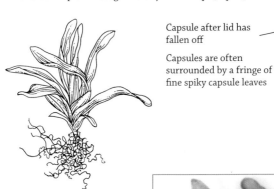

Capsule after lid has fallen off

Capsules are often surrounded by a fringe of fine spiky capsule leaves

Narrow strap-shaped leaves spread wide when wet and turn crumpled and dark when dry

APPEARANCE: Upright plants, 1–2 mm tall, form dull dark green to brownish, dense patches on soil. The leaves spread wide from the short stems when wet and are curled and crumpled when dry. Easily overlooked or ignored unless the distinctive, nutlike capsules are present.

LEAVES: Narrow tongue- or strap-shaped, 1–4 mm long, with blunt, rounded tips. Fine midrib runs nearly to apex, visible only with high-powered hand lens. Edges are smooth.

CAPSULES: Asymmetric, shaped like tiny nuts squatting on the ground, 3–4 mm long, brown, with a beaked lid. Ringed by a fringe of fine, spiky, brown, awned leaves. Lacking a stalk. The broad upper surface of the capsule is angled to face maximum sunlight.

HABITAT: Shaded soil, often along roads and paths, or on thin soil crusts over rocks.

SIMILAR SPECIES

No other moss has stalkless capsules reminiscent of plump penguins or grains of wheat like those of *Diphyscium*.

In the absence of capsules, the dry crispy leaves superficially resemble those of other small mosses with narrow, contorted dried leaves, such as *Tortella humilis* (p. 79) or *Weissia controversa* (p. 81). Rehydrated, the rounded leaf tips will separate *Diphyscium* from the sharp-tipped, sword-shaped leaves of *Tortella* or *Weissia*.

MICROSCOPIC FEATURES

The leaves owe their dark and dull appearance to the multilayered leaf tips and leaf blades covered top and bottom with bulging and bumpy cells.

Tiny plants growing on a cobble beside a stream

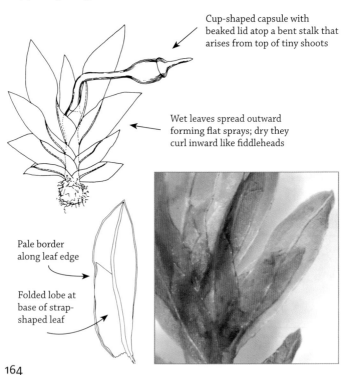

Cup-shaped capsule with beaked lid atop a bent stalk that arises from top of tiny shoots

Wet leaves spread outward forming flat sprays; dry they curl inward like fiddleheads

Pale border along leaf edge

Folded lobe at base of strap-shaped leaf

Fissidens bryoides

PIXIE POCKET MOSS

APPEARANCE: Upright stems are 3–11 mm tall and densely packed with feather-shaped leaves in two columns, thereby causing the plants to resemble flat sprays of miniature ferns. When dry, the leaf tips curl under like a fiddlehead or violin scroll.

LEAVES: Feather or tongue shape, 1–2 mm long, with folded lower lobe, blade coming to a short, sharp point. Midrib ends at apex. Smooth leaf edge has a border, hard to see, but hold a leaf up to the light—it is there!

CAPSULES: Tiny, cylindrical cups, up to 1 mm long, upright, with a conical lid. Stalk is 3–10 mm, yellow, usually bent over, and arises from tip of leafy shoot.

HABITAT: Wet rocks and soil in the shade, often in or near streambeds. If you see a minute *Fissidens* on a rock beside a river, call it *bryoides*.

SIMILAR SPECIES

Fissidens adianthoides and *F. dubius* (p. 169) Share habitat, but larger; stems are over 1 cm tall, leaves are at least 2 mm long. Capsules arise from middle of leaf shoot.

Fissidens osmundioides (p. 167) Plants are typically a little larger, leaves lack clearly defined border.

MICROSCOPIC FEATURES

Cells along leaf edge are long, narrow and clear (as opposed to not differentiated or round and clear). Cells in interior of leaf blade hexagonal and slightly bulging like muffin tops.

Shoots resemble flattened sprays of feathers

Capsule with long-beaked lid arises from stem tip

Leaf tip ends in a short prick but lacks teeth at apex

Leaves have a folded lobe and pale midrib but lack definite pale border

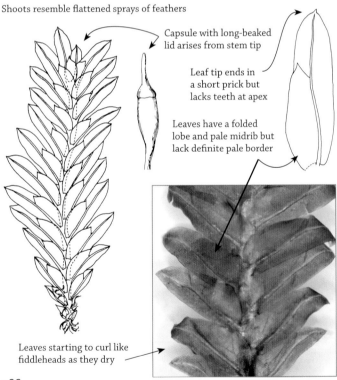

Leaves starting to curl like fiddleheads as they dry

Fissidens osmundioides

FERN POCKET MOSS

APPEARANCE: Upright plants are usually 5–20 mm tall, bearing feather-shaped leaves angled outward 80 degrees to both sides of stem, thereby causing the plants to resemble flat sprays of miniature ferns. When dry, the leaf tips curl under like a fiddlehead or violin scroll.

LEAVES: Asymmetric tongue shape, 1–2 mm long, with folded lower lobe, blade coming to an obtuse or acute point with a short prick. Translucent midrib ends at tip. Edge is smooth and without a clearly defined border.

CAPSULES: Cylindrical, about 1 mm long, slightly inclined, with a beaked lid. Stalk 2–7 mm, arising from tip of leafy shoot, red and upright or curved.

HABITAT: Soil, humus, or rocks in moist, shady swamps, acidic or basic.

SIMILAR SPECIES

Fissidens adianthoides and *F. dubius* (p. 169) Leaves have tiny jagged teeth at tip and a pale border along blade. Capsule stalk arises from middle of leafy shoot.

Fissidens bryoides (p. 165) Plants are typically less than 10 mm tall; leaves have a border, although difficult to see.

MICROSCOPIC FEATURES

Long cells of midrib are exposed to end, with midrib ending 3–4 cells shy of leaf apex. Edge at leaf tip is shallowly toothed, lacking clearly defined border cells.

Plants resemble flattened sprays of miniature ferns

Capsules with and without beaked lid atop stalk that arises midstem

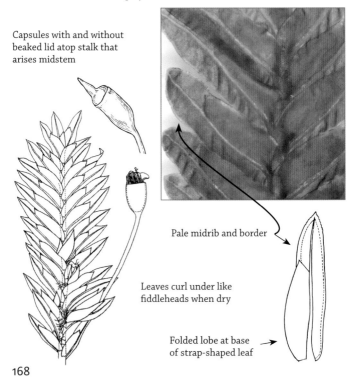

Pale midrib and border

Leaves curl under like fiddleheads when dry

Folded lobe at base of strap-shaped leaf

Fissidens adianthoides

MAIDENHAIR POCKET MOSS

APPEARANCE: Upright stems are usually 2–5 cm tall and densely packed with feather-shaped leaves in two columns, thereby causing the plants to resemble flat sprays of miniature ferns. When dry, the leaf tips curl under like a fiddlehead or violin scroll. Brown fuzz common along lower stem.

LEAVES: Feather or tongue shape, 2–4 mm long, with folded lower lobe, blade coming to a short, sharp point. Pale midrib ends just below the tip. Leaf edge has a pale or whitish border, hard to see, but hold a leaf up to the light—it is there! Tip of leaf is faintly rough or toothed.

CAPSULES: Tiny, red, cylindrical cups, 1–2 mm long, slightly bent, with a long-beaked lid. Stalks are usually 1–2 cm tall, red, and arising from the middle of leafy shoot.

HABITAT: Shady, wet areas, often near waterfalls, streams, and seeps; on rocks, soil, rotting wood, and tree trunk bases.

SIMILAR SPECIES

Fissidens dubius, **FAN POCKET MOSS**: Tends to be smaller, usually less than 2 cm tall, and in moist rather than wet areas. Leaves are similar with pale border and toothed apex.

Fissidens bryoides (p. 165) Plants are much smaller, 3–11 mm tall; capsule stalks arise from the end of the leaf branch.

Fissidens osmundioides (p. 167) Plants are smaller, 5–20 mm tall. Leaves lack clearly defined border and teeth at tip. Capsule stalk arises from tip of leafy shoot.

MICROSCOPIC FEATURES

Cells are generally flat in *F. adianthoides*; bulging like muffin tops in *F. dubius*. Midrib ends a few cells shy of leaf tip, which is jaggedly toothed. Leaf edge is bordered by 3–5 rows of pale cells; blade is 1 cell thick in *F. adianthoides,* commonly 2 cells thick here and there in *F. dubius*.

Plants are covered in tissue-paper-thin leaves of pale apple or yellow green that are only slightly crumpled when dry

Capsule without lid

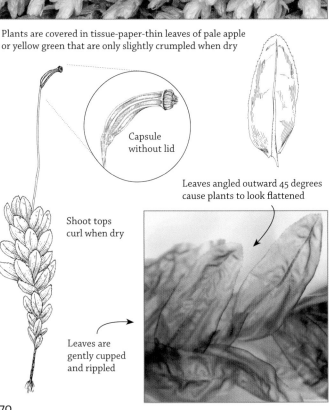

Leaves angled outward 45 degrees cause plants to look flattened

Shoot tops curl when dry

Leaves are gently cupped and rippled

Arrhenopterum heterostichum

GOOSE EGG MOSS

APPEARANCE: Plants form patches of upright yellow or fuzzy brown stems, 2–4 cm high, unbranched or densely forked, and covered with tissue-paper thin, pale apple- or yellow-green leaves. Wet leaves angle outward 45 degrees from either side of stem, giving shoots a flattened appearance; not changed when dry except leaves become shiny and slightly crumpled, and shoot tips curl under like fiddleheads on stems with crowded leaves.

LEAVES: Oblong-ovate, longer and tongue-shaped at stem apex; 1–4 mm long; round-tipped, gently cupped and wavy. Midrib ends just below leaf point. Top ½ of leaf is bordered by jagged teeth.

CAPSULES: Curved slender macaroni-shape, 3 mm long, with a beaked lid. Stalk is 6–17 mm tall and reddish orange.

HABITAT: Soil especially on slopes of ravines in dry, airy woods, such as oak forests; also at base of trees.

SIMILAR SPECIES

Atrichum crispum (p. 131) Grows on wet sandy soil, along streams or ditches. Leaves are long oval-shaped, 4–7 mm with a short sharp peak, bordered by teeth to base; shrivel and twist when dry.

Fissidens adianthoides (p. 169) Grows in wet areas such as seeps and along streams. Shoots are very flattened and leaves come to a short-triangular point and have a folded-over lobe near base.

Mnium hornum (p. 133) Grows in damp woods or wetlands. Leaves come to a short-triangular point, are bordered by paired teeth over half the length, and twist and curl when dry. Some stems and leaves are tinged with red.

MICROSCOPIC FEATURES

Cells are roundish and smooth: at most bulging but not covered in bumps; thick-walled.

Irregularly branching plants in a variety of colors, upright or trailing in wetlands

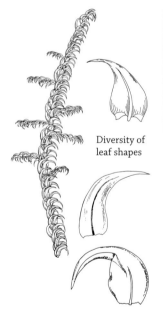

Diversity of leaf shapes

Drepanocladus aduncus

Shoots "braided" with dense, sickle-shaped leaves; shoot tips curved like a hook

Scorpidium revolvens

SCORPION MOSS

APPEARANCE: Irregularly to pinnately branching, upward arching or trailing shoots of shiny red, purple red, or black brown growing in water. Branches look loosely braided due to their densely crowded leaves with long curled tips from erect bases. Dry leaves fold down along midrib, still curled, but looking scraggly rather than juicy.

LEAVES: Sickle shape, 3–4 mm long, narrow tips curling into complete loops, concave. Midrib reaches to above midleaf. Surface is unpleated; edges are smooth.

CAPSULES: Curved-cylindrical, 2–3 mm long with a conical lid. Stalk 3–5 cm, red.

HABITAT: Wetlands, moderately calcium-enriched such as fens, often submerged.

SIMILAR SPECIES

Drepanocladus aduncus, **CROCHET HOOK MOSS**: Leaves are 1–5 mm long, usually sickle-shaped, but sometimes narrow tips are straight rather than curled when growing in especially wet circumstances. Tops of pinnate shoots curl over in a hook.

Sanionia uncinata (p. 177) Leaves are pleated, wet or dry, and bases spread away from stems. Not typically dark red colored. Leaves with more drawn-out tips and more coiled. Plants are found typically in drier habitats.

Scorpidium scorpioides (p. 283) Leaves are egg-shaped, lack midrib, and are wrinkly when dry.

MICROSCOPIC FEATURES

Cells in lower outside corners of leaf are clear and slightly larger than neighboring basal cells, which are thick-walled, darker, and pitted. Inflated and clear stem cells often strip off with leaves in dissection. Outer corner leaf cells of *D. aduncus* are inflated and yellow or brown. Outer capsule teeth bases are striped rather than dotted.

Plump, stout shoots arch upright or creep along the ground
in regular or irregular feather-like sprays of olive green or golden brown

Populations typically
lack capsules

Midrib is hidden
among pleats

Densely crowded,
wrinkled leaves

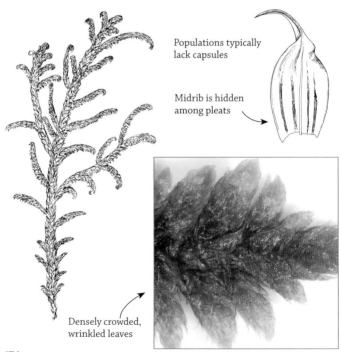

Rhytidium rugosum

WRINKLED CLIFFTOP MOSS

APPEARANCE: Robust olive green to golden brown plants forming loose mats, 3–9 cm high; creeping or sometimes ascending to nearly standing upright, especially the ends of the stems, which are often hooked. Branching varies from irregular and sparse to regularly feather-like. Stems and branches seem unusually plump, especially when wet, due to densely crowded leaves. Otherwise similar wet or dry.

LEAVES: Sickle-shaped at end of shoots, tips curved toward the lower side of stem or branch; lance-shaped lower down on shoots, straight tips. Leaves are 3–4 mm long on stems, smaller on branches, narrowed to a long tapering point; surface is strongly wrinkled. Midrib extends at least to midleaf; edges are smooth.

CAPSULES: Rarely seen; slightly inclined to horizontal, curved, cylindrical, 2 mm long. Stalks are 2–3 cm long.

HABITAT: Either on rock or thin soil overlying rock enriched with calcium and magnesium such as limestone, dolomite, basalt, or gabbro; commonly on dry, exposed rock ledges or bluffs.

SIMILAR SPECIES

Scorpidium scorpioides (p. 283) Grows in wet habitats and has leaves without a midrib.

Abietinella abietina (p. 269) Might resemble *Rhytidium* when wet, but upon drying its stems and branches become thin and wiry. Largest leaves are less than 2 mm.

Pleurozium schreberi (p. 287) Has blunt-tipped leaves that are neither curved nor wrinkled and lack a midrib.

MICROSCOPIC FEATURES

Corners of the leaf base have numerous small, square cells sharply contrasting with the much longer cells elsewhere. The ends of those longer leaf cells often project outward from the leaf surface.

Wet plants are full but lack sheen   Dry plants are sparser but shiny

Capsule with lid

Plants form soft mats of pale green or gold, arching, regularly branching stems

Narrow leaves are densely packed but curled into complete loops, giving shoots a loose, "bubbly" appearance

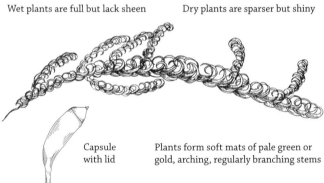

Sanionia uncinata

CANDY CURL MOSS

APPEARANCE: Plants form soft, loose mats of creeping or upright-arching, fairly regularly branching stems 4–10 cm long of yellow or pale olive. Leaves are densely crowded, spreading at a 70-degree angle to shoot with tips curled around to form a loop. Similar wet or dry, though leaves look fuller when moist and are shiny when dry. Shoot tips are hook-shaped.

LEAVES: Narrow sickle-shaped, 3–4 mm long, curved into a loop, pleated wet or dry, often with a cupped or rolled blade. Midrib is present at least to middle but faint and difficult to distinguish among the vertical pleats. Edges are smooth.

CAPSULES: Cylindrical, 2–3 mm long, curved and bent over to horizontal; lid is conical, teeth are mustard-colored. Stalk 1–3 cm, red.

HABITAT: On thin crusts of soil, usually over rock, also on rotting wood, and bark at tree bases. Typically in dry coniferous forests but also in moist areas.

SIMILAR SPECIES

Ptilium crista-castrensis (p. 179) Leaves are similarly curved and pleated, but plants are much more regularly branched, neater, and resemble plumes.

Hypnum lindbergii (p. 187) Leaves are 1–3 mm long, curved but not forming complete circles, lacking a midrib and only slightly pleated when dry.

MICROSCOPIC FEATURES

Edge of leaf near apex is toothed. Cells in outside lower leaf corners are clear and thin-walled. Stem cells strip off with leaf in dissection and are also clear and thin-walled, but larger.

Upright, diamond-shaped, pinnate-branched plumes of shiny golden green

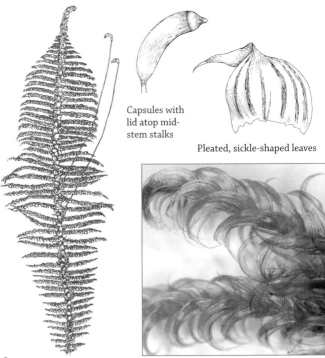

Capsules with lid atop mid-stem stalks

Pleated, sickle-shaped leaves

Ptilium crista-castrensis

KNIGHT'S PLUME MOSS

APPEARANCE: Forms distinctive, 4–10-cm-tall, diamond-shaped pinnate plumes of shiny green or gold, with branches becoming progressively shorter toward the stem tip. Stems arch upright and are densely covered by pleated, sickle-shaped leaves. The very tips of the stems are narrow and hooked. Not much changed wet or dry.

LEAVES: 2–3 mm long, triangular with a long-tapering tip that curls completely over to one side, like a sickle. Stem leaves are considerably wider than branch leaves and are less pleated, making it easier to check for a midrib, which is lacking, but the vertical pleats are deceptive. Edges are smooth.

CAPSULES: Macaroni-shaped, 2–3 mm long, dark brown, lid is short-conical. Stalk 3–4 cm, rust-colored.

HABITAT: Forest soil and rotten logs in areas ranging from dry to swampy.

SIMILAR SPECIES

Sanionia uncinata (p. 177) Longer, narrower leaves are similarly curved and pleated but plants are less regularly branched, creating a messier, less plumelike appearance.

Hypnum imponens (p. 181) Shares sickle-shaped leaves, regular pinnate branching, and a golden green sheen, but lacks the upright plume growth pattern and pleated leaves.

Ctenidium molluscum (p. 189) Prefers to grow in calcium-enriched woods and wetlands and is silvery green with unpleated leaves with rounded earlobe-like bases.

Thuidium delicatulum (p. 271) Branches are irregularly 2–3× divided, giving its "fronds" a more fine, lacy, snowflake-like aspect. Also the very small leaves (1 mm) are not long-tipped and curved to the side and they have a midrib.

MICROSCOPIC FEATURES

Leaf cells are long and narrow and lack any bumps.

Regularly branching plants look like golden green silk embroidery

H. curvifolium

H. imponens capsule nearly upright, with lid

H. curvifolium capsule curved, with lid

Leaves parted to either side of stem

Hypnum imponens

BROCADE MOSS

APPEARANCE: Plants form loose mats that look like glossy green brocade embroidery tinged with yellow and orange. The regularly pinnate, rust-colored stems and branches are densely packed with overlapping leaves that appear neatly braided or parted with a comb to either side of the stem. Not much changed wet or dry.

LEAVES: Stem leaves are 2 mm long; branch leaves are slightly smaller, long-triangular, cupped, with a gently rounded base. The leaves all curve to the side, like a sickle. Midrib is lacking; edges are smooth.

CAPSULES: Cylindrical, 2–3 mm long, barely bent, brown; lid is conical to beaked. Stalks 1–3 cm, orange brown.

HABITAT: Common on soil, rotting logs, and rocks in moist forests.

SIMILAR SPECIES

***Hypnum curvifolium*, GREATER PLAIT MOSS**: Very similar to *H. imponens* but with curved and bent over capsules. Leaves are 2–3 mm long and neatly parted and curled along branches. Tends to be more common in the southern half of the region covered by this guide.

Brotherella recurvans (p. 185) Lacks any orange tint, is even more shiny, and has very bent-over capsules. Only the very tips of the leaves curl off, like a fringe of tiny sharp hairs, just escaping from tight flat stems, compared to the whole leaf being curled in *Hypnum imponens*.

Hypnum pallescens (p. 183) Smaller plants; leaves are about 1 mm long; capsules are 1–2 mm long, stalks 6–15 mm.

MICROSCOPIC FEATURES

When a leaf is pulled off the branch, sometimes a few uninflated branch cells remain attached to the lower corners of the leaf. Lower leaf corner cells are small, brown, and square. There are tiny, flat, toothed scales in the junction of the branch to the stem, visible once the leaves are removed.

Wet plants full and feather-like

Dry plants look like silk threads

H. pallescens upright capsules with lid

Capsules abundant

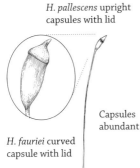

H. fauriei curved capsule with lid

Regularly branching shoots look like fine, dark ochre green embroidery, especially when dry

Hypnum pallescens

LESSER PLAIT MOSS

APPEARANCE: Carpets of shiny, dark ochre-green moss, with light green tips, creep like satin threads over bark and rock. Branches are regularly pinnate and densely covered with leaves. The leaves overlap, with their tiny sharp tips curled way under, giving the branches the tight and tidy look of embroidery floss. Not much changed wet or dry. Often produces a cloud of capsules.

LEAVES: Tiny egg-shaped triangular, up to 1 mm long, cupped, with a long, curved tip, like a sickle. All tips curve in the same direction. Midrib is lacking and edges are smooth.

CAPSULES: Abundant, cylindrical, 1–2 mm long, slightly curved and tilted, lid is peaked. Stalk 6–15 mm.

HABITAT: Tree trunk bases most often, but also on rotting logs and rocks.

SIMILAR SPECIES

Hypnum fauriei, **FAIRY PLAIT MOSS**: Very similar to *H. pallescens* but with leaves up to 2 mm long and capsules well curved and bent over.

Hypnum imponens (p. 181) Tends to have an orange cast, is a bit bigger with leaves about 2 mm long, and branches very regularly. Capsules are barely curved atop 1–3-cm stalks.

Schwetschkeopsis fabronia (p. 227) Plants branch irregularly and resemble fine combed strands of hair. Leaf tips are not curved to one side and capsules are very uncommon.

MICROSCOPIC FEATURES

Edge of leaf is finely toothed from base of leaf to tip; lower edges can curl under. Cells are long and narrow except at base of leaf, where the cells are yellow rectangles, and in the lower outside "lobes" at least three rows of cells are dull, thick-walled squares.

Plants form compact, slightly flattened mats with a striking golden green sheen

Inclined capsule with lid

Leaves are densely packed together with fine, curved tips

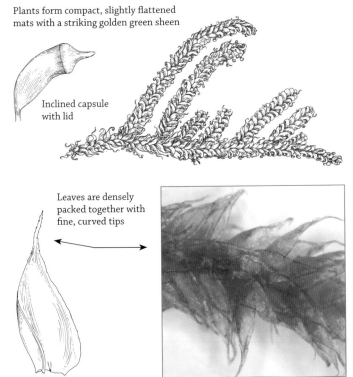

184

Brotherella recurvans

APPEARANCE: Green, yellow green, or golden creeping moss that shines like a scrap of satin on the forest floor. The leaves are densely packed together, overlapping, and appear braided or parted with a comb to either side of rust-colored and regularly branched stems. The sprays are somewhat flattened and the moss forms compact, low mats that change little wet or dry, always strikingly shiny.

LEAVES: Egg-shaped, abruptly narrowing to a sharp, narrow tip which is gently curled to the side of branch. Leaves are 1 mm long and slightly cupped and overlapping. Lacking midrib and teeth along edges.

CAPSULES: Chubby, short-cylindrical, curved, brown, 1–2 mm long, mouth lidded with a long beak while developing. Stalk is 7–17 mm tall, orange brown.

HABITAT: Rotting logs, bases of trees, soil and humus in moist shady places, especially forests with hemlock.

SIMILAR SPECIES

Hypnum imponens (p. 181) Similarly glossy, horizontally spreading moss with long leaf tips curved to the side. Tends to be orange-tinged, and larger; its leaves are 2 mm long and gradually taper to narrow tips.

Entodon cladorrhizans (p. 293) Also shiny with similar shaped but larger leaves, about 2 mm long. Leaf tips not curled to sides of branch but strongly flattened into one plane.

MICROSCOPIC FEATURES

Tips of leaves are toothed. Cells in most of leaf are long and narrow, except in outer corners of leaf base, where they are yellow, thin-walled, and swollen like balloons. Neighboring basal cells are enlarged and clear.

Plants often arch upright, forming thick, soft, pale mounds

Curved capsule with lid

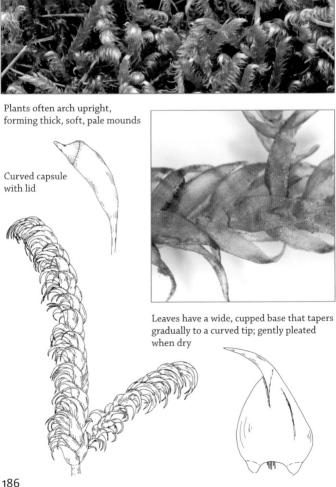

Leaves have a wide, cupped base that tapers gradually to a curved tip; gently pleated when dry

Hypnum lindbergii

PALE PLAIT MOSS

APPEARANCE: Irregularly and infrequently branched stems, sometimes creeping but tend to stand upright, giving the tufts of moss a soft cushiony height, rather than lying flat and low across the ground. Stems are green or brownish and moderately densely covered by semi-glossy, pale green or yellowish leaves. Similar wet or dry, though leaves pleat somewhat when dry.

LEAVES: Long-triangular, 1–3 mm long, with a gently rounded base and a tapering tip, cupped. Somewhat pleated when dry. Midrib is lacking and edges of leaves are smooth.

CAPSULES: Bent over and curved-cylindrical, 2–3 mm long, pleated or wrinkled when dry, lid is beaked. Stalk 2–5 cm.

HABITAT: Moist forests, swamps, stream banks, meadows, and poor lawns; on soil or logs. Tends to prefer calcium- and nutrient-enriched habitats, nestled among grasses.

SIMILAR SPECIES

Hypnum imponens (p. 181) Generally more dense, flat, and orderly. Its leaves are more curled and tend to be neatly curved to one side, appearing to be braided.

Hygrohypnum ochraceum (p. 281) Leaves are less densely packed and their tips twist. Midrib varies, but at least occasionally leaves have a strong midrib, unlike *Hypnum* leaves, which never have a midrib. Plants are darker green.

MICROSCOPIC FEATURES

When a leaf is pulled off the branch for inspection, often a few enlarged and transparent branch cells remain attached to the lower corners of the leaf. Lower leaf corner cells are inflated and clear like bubbles, clearly different from nearby small and thick-walled cells. At the junction of the branch to the stem, once the leaves are pulled off, there is a characteristic lack of the tiny, flat scales that are generally typical of this group of mosses.

Regularly branching plants
are densely covered in leaves
that spread widely wet or dry

Capsules
with lid

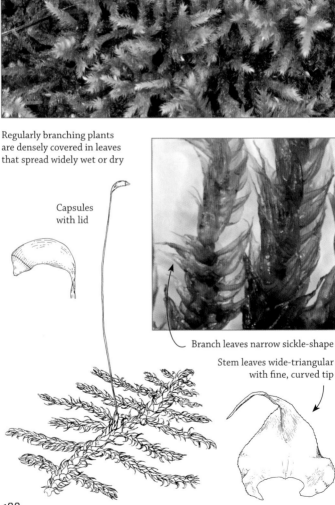

Branch leaves narrow sickle-shape

Stem leaves wide-triangular
with fine, curved tip

Ctenidium molluscum

FEATHER COMB MOSS

APPEARANCE: Creeping moss forms soft, shiny mats ranging from silver-tinged pale green to golden green. Stems are pinnately branched, and end in a tiny balled-up fist of developing leaves. Leaves spread outward nearly 90 degrees or curl when wet. Not much changed when dry, but appearing more fuzzy due to erratic, wispy leaf tips.

LEAVES: Stem leaves are 1–2 mm long, wide-triangular with a slender tip that wisps off to the side; surface is rippled or smooth. Branch leaves are narrower and about 1 mm long, smooth. Midrib is lacking. Edges are smooth.

CAPSULES: Cylindrical, bent over to horizontal, 2 mm, lid is short-beaked. Stalk is 13–20 mm and smooth, orange or red.

HABITAT: Forest soil, rotting wood, and tree trunk bases in moist, calcium-enriched places.

SIMILAR SPECIES

Eurhynchiastrum pulchellum (p. 241) Leaves have midrib and tips are straight, not curved to side; capsule lid is long-beaked.

Hypnum imponens (p. 181) Branch and stem leaves all same size, 2 mm long, shaped like gradually tapering, triangular sickles. Branch leaves appear braided.

Brotherella recurvans (p. 185) Leaves are cupped and overlapping; only the very tips curl off, like a fringe of tiny sharp hairs, just escaping from the very shiny and tightly flat stems.

MICROSCOPIC FEATURES

Leaf edge is minutely but sharply toothed from tip to base. Stem leaf bases have wide, clasping lobes. Branch leaves are different; unclasping and narrower. Long skinny upper cells of branch leaves have a bump or bulge at end nearest leaf tip. Cells in lower outside corners of leaf are small and square.

Long, stringy, sparsely dividing branches look bushy when wet and threadlike and curled upward like hooks when dry

Wet branch tips look like blunt paintbrushes

Base wide but unruffled, blade narrowed but lacking prick at tip

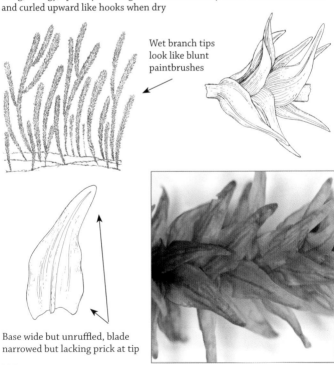

Anomodon viticulosus

GREATER TONGUE MOSS

APPEARANCE: Forms dense, thick mats of dull lime or mustard green, often 5 cm deep. Main stems are creeping and nearly bare, irregularly producing leafy branches that arch upward and curl when dry like a hook. Branch tips look like blunt paint brushes, not stringy tails. Wet branches look bushy as leaves spread outward; dry, they look more threadlike as the leaves are drawn inward and are gently swept to the side and crumpled.

LEAVES: Triangular with oval base tapering to an obtuse point, 2–4 mm long. Base is wide, but not ruffled and clasping, and blade tapers to tip, rather than rounding out to a tongue shape. Leaf tips appear more pointy and narrow when dry, but lack an actual needle tip. Midrib nearly reaches tip. Edges of leaf are smooth.

CAPSULES: Very rarely produced in North America.

HABITAT: Calcium-enriched dry rocks and walls in cool forests, occasionally on trees near base.

SIMILAR SPECIES

Anomodon attenuatus (p. 239) Ends of branches are of two types, blunt and curled under or narrowed and stringy.

Anomodon minor (p. 315) Leaves are only 2 mm long, very blunt and round at tip, not as crumpled when dry, held straight rather than curved.

Anomodon rugelii (p. 315) Leaves are quite curled and crumpled when dry, leaves have a small point at end of rounded leaf tip.

MICROSCOPIC FEATURES

Cells of leaves are round and covered in several small, craggy bumps, except those along bottom edge of leaf, which are long and clear. Leaves carefully removed from branches lack small earlobe-shaped extensions in the lower outside corners that are found with other *Anomodon* species.

Plants look like shiny yellow or green bristly pipe cleaners or stars from above

Capsule with lid

Heart-shaped base tapers to narrow, channeled tip

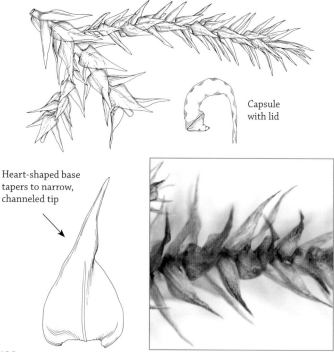

Campyliadelphus chrysophyllus

BRISTLE STAR MOSS

APPEARANCE: Creeping, irregularly branching plants, like bristly pipe cleaners, form loose patches of slightly shiny green or yellow. The leaves spread widely from the stems and are densely or remotely spaced on stem.

LEAVES: Triangular, 1–3 mm long, tapered from a heart-shaped base to a very narrow tip, the sides of which are curved upward, like walls of a canoe. Midrib is very fine and usually extends to about midleaf. Edges of leaf are smooth.

CAPSULES: Cylindrical, curved, 2–3 mm long, inclined to drooping, contracted below mouth when dry; lid is conical to short-beaked. Stalk 1–3 cm.

HABITAT: Soil or rocks that are frequently moist and usually calcium or nutrient enriched, also on logs and tree bases.

SIMILAR SPECIES

Campylium stellatum (p. 195) Leaves are of similar size, but lack a midrib and taper to a very long, narrow, channeled tip bent outward from erect base.

Campylophyllum hispidulum (p. 307) Leaves are less than 1 mm long, lack a midrib, and are squat egg-shaped abruptly narrowed to a fine tip.

Drepanocladus polygamus (p. 195) Leaves are 2–4 mm long, with even longer leaf tips, straight or slightly arching-spreading from shoots.

MICROSCOPIC FEATURES

Cells in lower corners of leaves are square to short-rectangular and fairly thick-walled with dense contents.

Leaf tips very narrow and channeled

Midrib present in *D. polygamus*;
lacking in *C. stellatum*

Capsule without lid

C. stellatum shoots look like
clusters of tiny stars from above

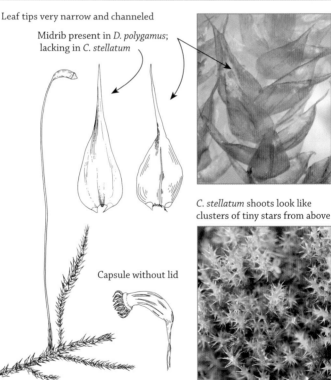

194

Drepanocladus polygamus

STIFF STAR MOSS

APPEARANCE: Yellow green or golden brown stems lay prostrate or arch upward, branch irregularly and form shiny carpets. Leaves are crowded and held stiffly upright or flare outward 30 degrees when wet, some are slightly curved. Plants are not much changed when dry; branches and leaves are just slightly more curled with lightly twisted tips.

LEAVES: Stem and branch leaves are lance-shaped, 2–4 mm long, tapering to a slender tip which is either straight or curving down and is often rolled lengthwise, forming a U-shaped channel. Midrib reaches midleaf or into narrow tip. Edges are smooth.

CAPSULES: Cylindrical, curved, 2–3 mm long, nodding, with a conical lid. Stalk is 2–4 cm, reddish brown.

HABITAT: Mineral-enriched wetlands such as fens or wet fields, on soil.

SIMILAR SPECIES

Campylium stellatum, **YELLOW STAR MOSS**: Leaves lack a midrib and leaf base is erect with tip, flaring out nearly at a right angle to the stem, giving the plants the appearance of spiky pipe cleaners, or from above, clusters of tiny stars.

Drepanocladus aduncus (p. 173) Leaves arching, sickle-like from base to slender tip. Branches quite regularly.

MICROSCOPIC FEATURES

Lower outside leaf corners feature clusters of enlarged and clear or golden to orange cells. Otherwise, cells long and narrow.

Upright, regularly branching plants form soft mounds in moist habitats

Capsules with lid atop stalks that arise midstem

H. paludosum leaves

H. blandowii leaf

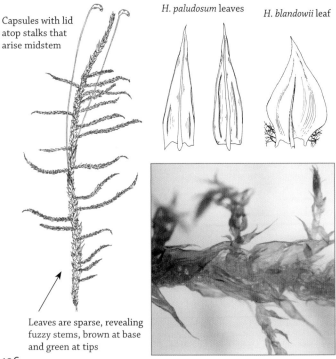

Leaves are sparse, revealing fuzzy stems, brown at base and green at tips

Helodium paludosum

NARROW-LEAVED BEARD MOSS

APPEARANCE: Plants form soft tufts of yellow green, upright, pinnately branching stems that stand up to 6 cm tall. Stem is covered in hairs, easily perceptible between well-spaced leaves: brown near base of stem and green near tip. Leaves spread out from stem slightly when wet. When dry, they are slightly crumpled and held close to stem.

LEAVES: Lance-shaped, 1–2 mm long, pleated. Prominent midrib runs nearly to tip. Edges are smooth and rolled under, especially when dry.

CAPSULES: Cylindrical, 2–4 mm long, curved and bent over to horizontal, reddish brown with a conic lid. Stalk 2–3 cm, reddish brown.

HABITAT: On soil or rotting logs or bark of tree bases in swampy woods, fields or brush.

SIMILAR SPECIES

Helodium blandowii, **WIDE-LEAVED BEARD MOSS**: Leaves are egg-shaped. Plants are 5–10 cm tall with pinnate branches of equal length. Capsules are 3–4 mm long; stalk is 4–6 cm tall. Grows in calcium-enriched brushy wetlands.

Calliergon giganteum (p. 261) Stems are not matted with hairlike projections. Ovate leaves are sparsely spaced, with an earlike ruffle at basal corners, in which can be seen bubble-like cells that stand out obviously from surrounding cells.

Cratoneuron filicinum (p. 257) Stems have narrow, finger-like tips. Leaf edges are not rolled under.

MICROSCOPIC FEATURES

Stems are covered with hairs called paraphyllia. Leaves stripped off in dissection have hairlike projections from outside lower corners. Leaf cells are long, narrow, and smooth or with one bump at the end nearest the tip of leaf.

Upright, regularly branching plants look like golden green foxtails

Populations typically lacking macaroni-shaped capsules

Deeply pleated leaves are held stiffly straight

Rust-colored fuzz on stems

Tomentypnum nitens

GOLDEN FEN MOSS

Appearance: Golden green to yellow brown plants stand upright, usually 5–10 cm high, and divide regularly into opposite branches, forming mounded tufts. Stiff straight leaves are crowded and spread little, even when wet, and are shiny when dry. The stems, which look like furry foxtails, are matted with rust-colored fuzz.

Leaves: Long, lance-shaped, very pleated, 3–4 mm long. Midrib nearly reaches tip, though hard to distinguish amid all the pleats. Edge of leaf is smooth.

Capsules: Uncommon; bent-over macaroni shape, lid is conical. Stalk is 3–5 cm tall and rusty brown.

Habitat: Wetlands such as calcium-enriched fens.

Similar Species

Calliergonella cuspidata (p. 285) Plants similar in size and form, but stems are not matted with rusty fuzz. Leaves are egg-shaped with rounded tip, not pleated, 2 mm long.

Cratoneuron filicinum (p. 257) Plants are a similar color with reddish fuzz along stems, but leaves are unpleated, egg-shaped triangular coming to a slender tip that curves gently to side, 1–2 mm long.

Microscopic Features

Cells of leaf blade are long, narrow squiggles, except for a few thick-walled, rectangular cells at leaf base. Cells in outside lower corners of leaf are not enlarged or much different.

Tease apart a dense, feathery clump to see individual olive green, treelike shoots

Plants can sprawl along ground rather than stand treelike in very wet, shady sites

Leaves are unpleated, wet or dry, with jagged teeth at tip

Branches are typically flattened and arch downward

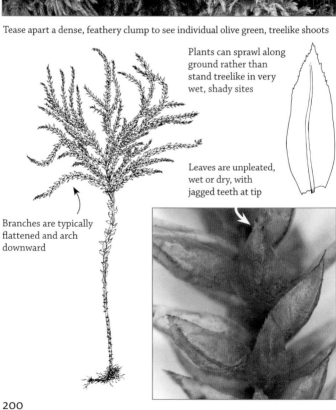

Thamnobryum alleghaniense

SHRUB MOSS

APPEARANCE: Plants look like miniature trees, 3–7 cm high with flattened branches arching down from top of upright secondary stems. (The actual primary stems are wiry rootlike strands running along the ground.) Secondary stems are stiff and sheathed in sparse leaves; branch leaves are denser and dull olive green. Wet leaves spread away from branches; dried, their tips curve inward while the bases spread outward. Plants can sprawl along the ground and lose their treelike upright posture when growing in particularly wet, shady sites.

LEAVES: Long egg-shaped, 1–3 mm long, coming to a narrow or broad point; cupped but unpleated wet or dry. Conspicuous midrib ends below tip, which is bordered by large, jagged teeth.

CAPSULES: Cylindrical, 2 mm long, bent over to horizontal atop a ruddy brown 9–16-mm-tall stalk.

HABITAT: On rock or logs in damp shady places, such as vertical rock faces in a waterfall ravine.

SIMILAR SPECIES

Climacium americanum (p. 203) Typically grows on soil in frequently flooded sites. Leaves pleated and have small lobes at base. "Tree branches" arch upward rather than downward.

Climacium dendroides (p. 203) Typically grows on soil in wetland habitats, such as swamps and along streams. Leaves are long-triangular, pleated, and shiny yellow green when dry.

Brachythecium rivulare (p. 247) Although plants can be upright with treelike branches, they lack the "trunk" bearing sparse leaves. Lower corners of triangular leaves run down stem and have large clear cells visible with hand lens when leaves are stripped from stem.

MICROSCOPIC FEATURES

Cells of branch leaf tips are diamond-shaped.

Typical shoots resemble a mini tree with "trunk and crown"
In flooded areas *C. americanum* can sprawl sideways rather than standing erect

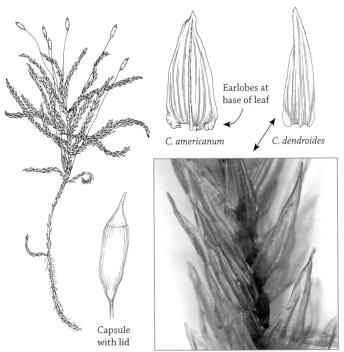

Earlobes at
base of leaf

C. americanum   *C. dendroides*

Capsule
with lid

Climacium dendroides

PALM TREE MOSS

APPEARANCE: Plants look like mini palm trees, 3–9 cm high, with their short horizontal or arching branches sprouting in a cluster from the top of upright secondary stems. (The actual primary stems are wiry strands running below ground.) Stems and branches are red; leaves are shiny yellow to yellow green. When wet, stem leaves cling to stems and branch leaves spread out only 40 degrees; when dry, branch leaves draw in tight and upright.

LEAVES: Branch leaves are long-triangular, 2–3 mm long, pleated. Stem leaves are egg-shaped, cupped, and clasp the stem. Midrib reaches leaf tip. Leaf edges are toothed, especially near apex.

CAPSULES: Rarely produced; cylindrical, upright, 2–3 mm, brown, lid is beaked. Stalks 2–5 cm and often more than one per plant when present.

HABITAT: Soil in wetlands, such as in swamps or along streams.

SIMILAR SPECIES

***Climacium americanum*, LOBE-LEAVED TREE MOSS**: Grows either upright as mini palm trees or sprawls sideways along the ground in frequently flooded sites. It tends to be dull, and its leaves have small lobes at the base.

Philonotis fontana (p. 125) Sometimes has a tuft of short branches spreading from the top of the stem. Leaves are 1–2 mm long; capsules are globose when wet, egg-shaped and furrowed when dry, bent over horizontal.

Thamnobryum alleghaniense (p. 201) Grows on rock or logs in damp shady limestone ravines. Leaves are unpleated.

MICROSCOPIC FEATURES

Cells of upper branch leaves are 5–9× longer than wide, compared to those of *Climacium americanum*, which are only 2–5× as long as wide.

Wet *B. salebrosum* plants are bushy, like foxtails

Dry *B. oxycladon* shoots with drawn-in leaves look yarnlike

Shaggy, irregularly branching, shiny shoots are densely covered in leaves

Smooth stalk, lacking bumps; this capsule with lid

B. salebrosum leaves are cupped and pleated when dry

B. oxycladon leaves are strongly pleated, wet or dry

Brachythecium salebrosum

GOLDEN FOXTAIL MOSS

APPEARANCE: Shaggy, mostly yellow green, occasionally darker green, shiny mats of foxtails. Stems creeping and branching irregularly, branches both horizontal and upright. Leaves are dense along branches, held in close when dry and slightly spreading when wet, overlapping like long-pointed scales with their fine tips feathering out.

LEAVES: Lance-shaped, 2–3 mm long, gradually narrowing to a point. Pleated, especially when dry and gently cupped. Midrib ends just below tip. Edges are smooth.

CAPSULES: Stubby macaroni-shape, about 2 mm long, inclined to horizontal, curved, reddish brown; a short-pointed lid covers mouth while developing. Stalk is smooth, 1–2 cm high.

HABITAT: A common weedy moss on soil, humus, rock, rotten logs, and bases of trees; found in urban, disturbed, and woodland habitats.

SIMILAR SPECIES

***Brachythecium oxycladon*, PLEATED FOXTAIL MOSS**: Leaves are strongly pleated and slightly more ovate, wet or dry. Capsules are 2–3 mm long, slightly to somewhat inclined, slightly curved; stalk is smooth.

Brachythecium rutabulum (p. 245) Leaves are usually smooth or barely pleated, darker green. Capsule stalk is minutely bumpy.

Callicladium haldanianum (p. 289) Similar size and shagginess, but leaves lack a midrib and do not overlap as much.

MICROSCOPIC FEATURES

Enlarged, rectangular, clear cells with thin walls in outside corners of leaf base compared with small, square, and darkened cells in look-alike *B. oxycladon*. *B. salebrosum* produces both antheridia and archegonia on one plant, whereas *B. oxycladon* has separate sexed gametophytes.

Sciuro-hypnum plumosum

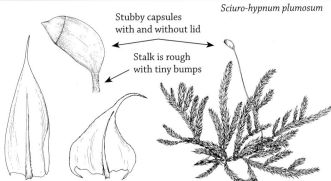

Stubby capsules
with and without lid

Stalk is rough
with tiny bumps

S-h. plumosum branch leaf, *S-h. reflexum* stem leaf;
note length of midrib

Sciuro-hypnum reflexum

Sciuro-hypnum plumosum

SATIN FOXTAIL MOSS

APPEARANCE: Shiny green to yellow or brownish green, loose to dense mats. Stems are creeping, to 5 cm long, irregularly to somewhat pinnately branched, the branches often curved. Leaves are fairly crowded, when wet spreading from the stems, but lying next to the stem or weakly diverging when dry, giving the stems a thread- or yarnlike appearance.

LEAVES: Ovate-triangular to broadly lance-shaped, coming to a narrow sharp point; edges are smooth. Stem leaves are 1–2 mm long, branch leaves closer to 1 mm. The midrib ends about midleaf, and the leaves are often curved toward one side especially near the stem tips; not or barely pleated.

CAPSULES: Inclined to horizontal, short cylindrical, curved, 1–2 mm long; stalks are reddish brown, 7–20 mm tall; surface is roughened with fine bumps near top, smooth below.

HABITAT: On wet to moist rocks, commonly near streams.

SIMILAR SPECIES

Sciuro-hypnum reflexum, **WOODLAND FOXTAIL MOSS**: Prefers to grow on bark at base of trees or on logs or stumps. Smaller with branches are curved in various directions. Leaves are about 1 mm long, usually not curved, and with midribs extending to leaf point. Entire capsule stalk is rough.

Brachythecium rivulare (p. 247) Plants are whitish or yellow green with branches that often stand upright from horizontal stems. Leaves, 2–3 mm, are egg-shaped coming to a short point, not curved off to one side.

Brachythecium salebrosum (p. 205) Plants grow on any surface in open disturbed areas; dark or yellow green. Leaves are 2–3 mm long, pleated and shiny when dry. Capsule stalks smooth.

MICROSCOPIC FEATURES

Edges have tiny teeth near apex and sometimes nearly to base. Upper leaf cells are elongate, smooth. Antheridia and archegonia are on separate branches on the same plant.

Slender, straight shoots, sprawling or erect, are crowded into grass-colored mats

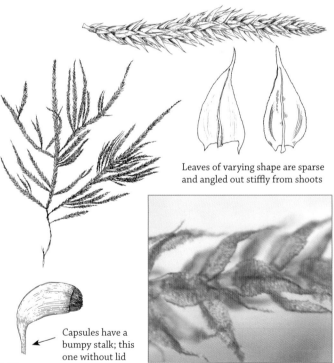

Leaves of varying shape are sparse and angled out stiffly from shoots

Capsules have a bumpy stalk; this one without lid

Bryhnia graminicolor

GRASS-COLORED MOSS

APPEARANCE: Plants form pale green, yellow green, or brownish mats composed of crowded, delicate, straight shoots up to 2 cm long. Stems can be trailing or erect and are moderately covered by leaves that spread outward when wet. Dry leaves shrink but their bases stay arched outward stiffly from stems, giving shoots a dull and sparse appearance.

LEAVES: Lance-shaped, with a slightly rounded base and gradually tapering to a slender point; stem leaves are 1 mm long, branch leaves about half that. Midrib reaches into narrow tip; held up to strong light, the spines projecting from the back of the midrib may be seen with a hand lens. Edges are smooth.

CAPSULES: Cylindrical, bent over, about 2 mm long. Stalk is bumpy and about 7–15 mm tall.

HABITAT: On rock or soil in moist shady places such as stream banks, crevices in cliffs, and under ledges to more open habitats such as steep road banks; usually in calcium-enriched areas.

SIMILAR SPECIES

Anomodon rostratus (p. 217) Plants of similar color but form dense carpetlike mats; leaves are held tight to stem when dry and flare out only slightly when wet; capsules are upright.

Hygroamblystegium varium (p. 211) Shoots are up to 15 cm long, but often shorter. Leaves lack rough midrib backside, and capsule stalks are smooth.

Platydictya confervoides (p. 229) All leaves less than 0.5 mm long; midrib is lacking, though hard to see in tiny leaves. Stringy shoots are dark and rigid. Capsule stalk is smooth.

MICROSCOPIC FEATURES

Shallow teeth are visible along leaf edge nearly to base. Cells near leaf tip have a small bump projecting from end nearest leaf tip on underside of leaf. Small spines also project from midrib on the undersurface of leaf.

Hygroamblystegium varium midrib ends beyond midleaf, sometimes extends beyond tip, sometimes curvy

Leptodictyum riparium midrib ends well below tip and is not curvy

Leaves are sparse and have a bold midrib

Leaves spread out widely or are held close to shoots

Capsules with and without lid

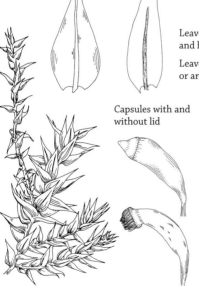

Hygroamblystegium varium

TANGLED THREAD MOSS

APPEARANCE: Scraggly, creeping moss forming patches composed of a jumble of green, irregularly branched, fuzzy-looking threads. Plants in streams and on dripping rocks often with upright branches. It bears the epithet *varium* for good reason: leaves even on the same plant can vary depending on water or nutrient availability. Plants range from blackened and bristly to pale yellow green and soft. Stems are up to 15 cm long, but are often shorter, and the sparse leaves are held close to or spreading outward from branches.

LEAVES: Leaves are very variable. Lance to egg-shaped, 1–2 mm long, coming to a short or long point, blunt or sharp. Midrib runs at least to midleaf, sometimes extending beyond the leaf as a short point, sometimes curving gently above midleaf. Edges of leaf are smooth.

CAPSULES: Cylindrical, slender, curved, 1–3 mm long, contracted below mouth when dry; lid is conical with a nib. Stalks 1–3 cm.

HABITAT: Wide range of habitats from fairly dry forest soil, rocks, logs, and tree trunks to wet rocks or wood near or submerged in streams or swampy habitats.

SIMILAR SPECIES

***Leptodictyum riparium*, WET THREAD MOSS**: Leaves are 2–5 mm long, midrib ends well below tip and is not curvy.

Bryhnia graminicolor (p. 209) Shoots are only up to 2 cm long. Midrib has tiny spines, as visible when back of leaf is held up to strong light. Capsule stalks are bumpy.

Campylophyllum hispidulum (p. 307) Leaves are up to 1 mm long, egg-shaped from a wide base, lacking a midrib. Strongly reflexed leaves give plant a spiky appearance.

MICROSCOPIC FEATURES

Cells of midleaf are irregular oval or diamond-shaped 2–7× as long as wide.

These aquatic plants are limp, flat, and irregularly branching and they turn brittle upon drying

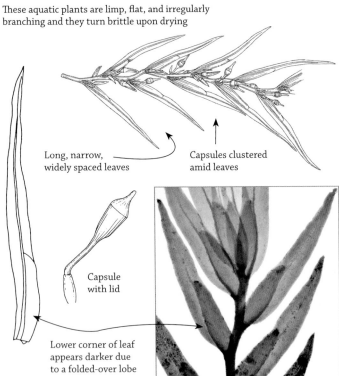

Long, narrow, widely spaced leaves

Capsules clustered amid leaves

Capsule with lid

Lower corner of leaf appears darker due to a folded-over lobe

Fissidens fontanus

LIMP POCKET MOSS

APPEARANCE: Aquatic moss with flexible, freely branched stems up to 12 cm long but usually less than half that. The narrow leaves are well spaced and attached alternately on either side of the stem so they do not overlap. Plants are flattened with leaves in one plane, giving the look of a fern frond or feather. Upon drying the plants become very brittle.

LEAVES: Narrowly lance-shaped, 2–7 mm long, gradually tapering to an acute tip. Lower corner of leaf is folded over into a small pocket, looking darker than surrounding tissue. Margin lacks a border and teeth. Midrib ends a bit short of the apex.

CAPSULES: Erect, short-cylindrical, up to 1 mm long on equally short stalks, often clustered with up to five attached at a single leaf base. Lids are conical with a short beak.

HABITAT: Attached to rocks, sticks, logs, and tree bases; submerged in flowing or still water.

SIMILAR SPECIES

Other *Fissidens* species (pp. 165–169) Have leaves more closely spaced, with the base of one clasping the leaf above it. Some have leaf borders and/or small teeth at the leaf tip.

Fontinalis species (pp. 231–233) Also grow submerged but are generally larger plants with stems over 10 cm long and are not flattened with leaves in two rows.

MICROSCOPIC FEATURES

Midrib ends 15–35 cells short of the leaf apex. The folded basal lobe is smaller than in other *Fissidens* and extends less than half the leaf length.

Stiff, thin, dark olive green threads with bushy ends

Wet plants look more feathery

Typical cluster
of branchlets
at branch tip

Slender, gradually
tapering, tiny leaves
have a midrib, but it
is difficult to see

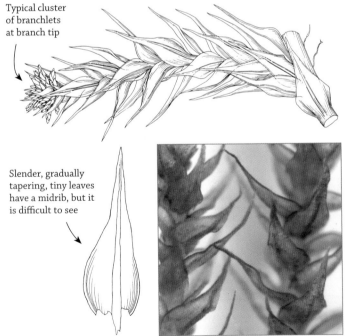

Leskeella nervosa

FRAYED STRING MOSS

APPEARANCE: Slender, irregularly branched, creeping shoots form delicate, stiff mats of dull, dark green or brown. Branches sometimes end in fuzzy clusters of tiny branchlets, which break off and reproduce the moss asexually. Wet leaves spread about 30 degrees, causing shoots to look feathery. Dry branches look like tiny strands of yarn, with fine leaf tips escaping from the rounded, chainlike leaf bases.

LEAVES: Lance-shaped; stem leaves about 1 mm long, branch leaves 0.5 mm, with an ovate base that narrows to a slender, sharp, straight tip. Midrib ends at apex, but is too fine to see. Edges are smooth.

CAPSULES: Cylindrical, 2–3 mm long, erect or slightly curved, brown, with a conical lid and yellow teeth. Stalk 9–15 mm.

HABITAT: Bark of tree trunks and bases, on logs, and on calcium-enriched rocks.

SIMILAR SPECIES

Hygroamblystegium varium (p. 211) Stem and branch leaves are both 1–2 mm long. Lacks clusters of branchlets.

Platygyrium repens (p. 223) Dry plants look like silky disks of oily golden brown and green with branches that curl upward, like hooks. Branches often end in fuzzy clusters of tiny branchlets.

Platydictya subtilis and *P. confervoides* (p. 229) Stem and branch leaves up to 0.5 mm long. Leaves without midrib, but so small that it would be hard to see even if it were there.

MICROSCOPIC FEATURES

Leaf tip edges lack teeth. Cells are smooth, bumpless.

Plants form a carpet of densely packed, cylindrical branches

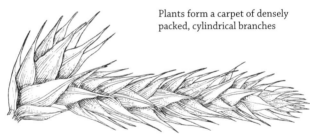

Capsules uncommon; this one showing beaked lid

Sharp, fine, pale leaf tip

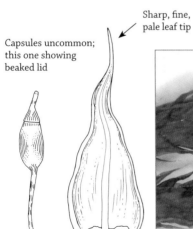

216

Anomodon rostratus

YELLOW YARN MOSS

APPEARANCE: Forms dense mats that look like yellow green, short pile carpet, not at all shiny. The upright and irregularly dividing branches are cylindrical as their densely packed, sharply pointed leaves are drawn in tightly and scale-like when dry, and, when wet, flare out only slightly. Branch tips are blunt, rather than long and stringy.

LEAVES: Triangular about 1 mm long with a long, drawn-out tip that tapers to a delicate point with a pale needle-like prick at the tip. Midrib disappears into the pointy tip. Edges are smooth and rolled under, and leaves usually look not-quite-fully hydrated, always a little puckered.

CAPSULES: Elliptical urn-shape, upright, 1–2 mm long, atop dark brown 7–13-mm-tall stalk.

HABITAT: Tree trunk bases and calcium-enriched rock.

SIMILAR SPECIES

Anomodon attenuatus (p. 239) Ends of branches are of two types, blunt and curled under or narrowed and stringy. Leaves lack a pale needle tip.

Anomodon rugelii (p. 315) Leaves are wide and ruffled at base, narrowing to a tongue-shaped blade, minutely toothed but not delicately needle-tipped.

Anomodon minor (p. 315) Leaves are blunt and rounded at apex, lack even tiny teeth at tip.

Anomodon viticulosus (p. 191) Leaves are 2–4 mm long and gradually tapered from wide, unruffled base to narrow tip, but lack a pale, delicate needle tip.

MICROSCOPIC FEATURES

Cells of leaves are round and covered in several small, craggy bumps, except those along bottom edge of leaf, which are long and clear.

Shiny plants with crowded leaves form scruffy mats on rock

Sematophyllum demissum shoot tips are curled like cat paws (see photo above); those of *S. marylandicum* are flat and straight

Sematophyllum marylandicum

S. *demissum* leaf

Capsules with and without lid

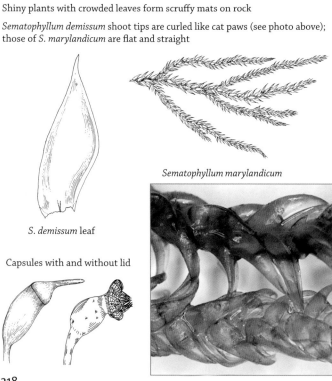

Sematophyllum demissum

CURLED SCRAP MOSS

APPEARANCE: Small, scruffy-looking moss forms shiny golden olive green mats over wet rocks. Shoots divide irregularly, are densely packed with leaves, and curl slightly at ends, like cat paws. Wet leaves spread up to 70 degrees from branches and weakly curve in one direction.

LEAVES: About 1 mm long, ovate at base tapering to a slender point, shallowly cupped. Midrib is lacking. Edges are smooth.

CAPSULES: Swollen and short cylindrical, 1 mm long, curved, bent over or horizontal, with a bent-beaked lid, often strongly constricted below mouth when dry. Stalk is reddish and 6–12 mm tall.

HABITAT: Acidic wet rocks near streams.

SIMILAR SPECIES

***Sematophyllum marylandicum*, FLAT SCRAP MOSS**: A larger plant with straight branches; leaves are 1–2 mm long. Capsule stalks 1–2 cm. Grows on wet rocks in and beside streams.

Hygrohypnum eugyrium and *H. luridum* (p. 281) Leaves are 1–2 mm long, sometimes strongly curved to one side of stem, widest above the middle rather than at base, short-tipped, and deeply cupped. Some leaves have a midrib, others do not.

MICROSCOPIC FEATURES

Cells at tip are short, but midleaf cells are 12× as long as wide. Lower cells are pitted, but two rows of cells in lower outside corners of leaf are dramatically larger and different from neighboring cells. Cell walls of capsule are thickened in the corners.

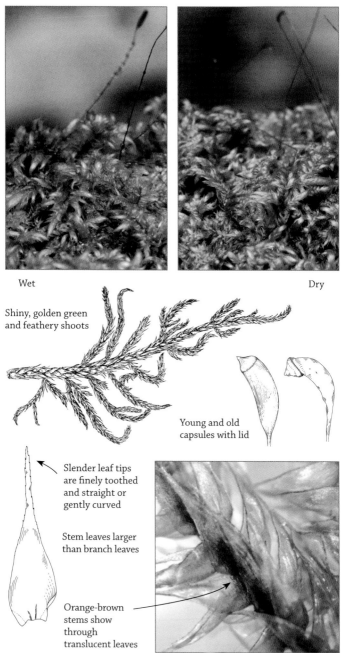

Wet   Dry

Shiny, golden green
and feathery shoots

Young and old
capsules with lid

Slender leaf tips
are finely toothed
and straight or
gently curved

Stem leaves larger
than branch leaves

Orange-brown
stems show
through
translucent leaves

220

Heterophyllium affine

SOUTHERN GLOSS MOSS

APPEARANCE: Plants form golden green, shaggy mats with shoots that divide freely and fairly regularly, resembling sprays of feathers. Dry plants are shiny, with the branch tips curling gently down. Densely crowded leaves are drawn in tightly together over branches when dry, only their fine tips escaping. Wet leaves angle 45 degrees out to the side and become quite translucent, revealing reddish brown or orange stems and branches beneath.

LEAVES: Lance-shaped, gradually tapering to a slender point, either straight or sometimes curled to one side and weakly sickle-like, gently cupped. Stem and branch leaves are of differing size: stem leaves are 2–3 mm long, branch leaves are smaller and narrower. Midrib is lacking. Teeth are visible along tip when the leaf is held up to strong light.

CAPSULES: Cylindrical, nearly upright to inclined, 2–3 mm long, curved with a conical lid. Stalk is reddish orange, 2–4 cm tall.

HABITAT: Rotten logs, soil, humus, rock, and tree bases in moist forests of the Southern Appalachians.

SIMILAR SPECIES

Callicladium haldanianum (p. 289) Leaves 1–2 mm long, egg-shaped, with smooth edges; range extends north to Canada.

Brotherella recurvans (p. 185) Leaves are 1 mm long, more oval-shaped at base with all tips curled neatly to one side, giving shoots a very tidy, smooth appearance. Capsules are barely bent.

MICROSCOPIC FEATURES

Several short rows of cells in the lower outside leaf corners are inflated large squares, clear or yellow, and differentiated from linear neighboring cells.

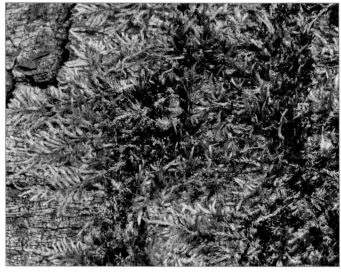

P. repens forms silky, "oily" patches of golden brown and green on tree bark

Midrib is lacking, but this is difficult to see in the tiny, overlapping leaves

Capsule with lid

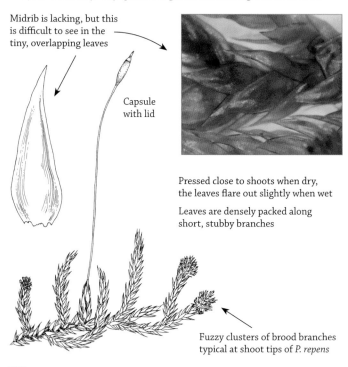

Pressed close to shoots when dry, the leaves flare out slightly when wet

Leaves are densely packed along short, stubby branches

Fuzzy clusters of brood branches typical at shoot tips of *P. repens*

Platygyrium repens

OIL SPILL MOSS

APPEARANCE: When dry, this small moss forms distinctive disks of glossy or oily-looking dark green to golden brown green on tree bark. Short branches stand upright from horizontal stems and are densely covered in leaves. Dry branches barely curl irregularly upward with appressed leaves. When wet, leaves are dull and dark green and flare out 45 degrees. Often produces tiny branchlets, called brood branches, in fuzzy clusters amid leaves at branch tips and which function in asexual reproduction.

LEAVES: Lance- to egg-shaped, about 1 mm long, with a straight, narrow tip. Leaves are so small it is hard to see that the midrib is lacking and edges of leaves are smooth.

CAPSULES: Upright, cylindrical, about 2 mm long on 1–2-cm-tall stalks. Mouth is capped by a beaked lid while developing.

HABITAT: A very common moss of tree trunks, tree trunk bases, and rotting logs; less common on acidic rocks.

SIMILAR SPECIES

Anacamptodon splachnoides (p. 263) Produces leaves sparsely along branches, and when wet, they spread up to 90 degrees, giving branches a spiky, starry appearance. Lacks brood branches.

Leskea gracilescens (p. 265) Forms long, fine, stringy branches sparsely covered with leaves that are cupped even when dry, looking like tiny necklace chains. Lacks brood branches.

Pylaisia selwynii (p. 225) Is smaller and tends to be a uniform shiny dark green when dry. Its leaf tips are wispy fine and swept to the side on curled branches. Lacks brood branches.

MICROSCOPIC FEATURES

Lower leaf edges can be rolled. Most cells in leaf are long squiggles, but cells at outside corners of leaf base are square.

Wet shoots are bushy and fuzzy-looking, like a smashed paintbrush

Dry shoots are short, shiny, stringy and curl upward, against gravity

Curled dry
P. selwynii branches

Wet *P. selwynii* shoots open and straighten;
P. polyantha shoots are straight wet or dry

Capsule
with lid

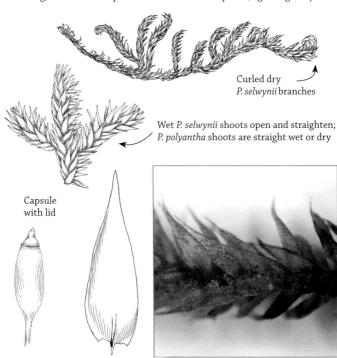

224

Pylaisia selwynii

PAINTBRUSH MOSS

APPEARANCE: Dry patches of this small moss growing on tree trunks are shiny, olive-tinged light green, with crowded, short, irregularly dividing, stringy branches that curl upward, against gravity. Dry leaves are pressed tight to the branches except for wispy leaf tips that curve off to the side. Wet branches are dull green, fuzzy and bushy as the crowded leaves spread out 45 degrees. Leaf tips tend to point in the same direction.

LEAVES: Lance- to egg-shaped, about 1 mm long, slightly cupped, tapering to a long, narrow tip. Midrib is lacking and edges are smooth.

CAPSULES: Upright cylindrical, 1–2 mm long, lid is cone-shaped. Stalk is 6–16 mm tall.

HABITAT: Tree trunks of hardwood trees and junipers.

SIMILAR SPECIES

Pylaisia polyantha, **STIFF PAINTBRUSH MOSS**: Leaves are straight, not tightly drawn to stems when dry; dry branches are not as tightly curled.

Leskea gracilescens (p. 265) Forms long, fine, stringy branches covered sparsely with leaves cupped even when dry, looking like tiny necklace chains.

Leucodon andrewsianus (p. 277) Produces tiny, fuzzy branchlets amid leaves near branch tips, is larger in scale, with longer branches. Leaves are 2 mm long and pleated.

Platygyrium repens (p. 223) Has an "oily" golden cast; produces tiny fuzzy branchlets amid leaves near branch tips. Leaves tend to be straight when dry.

MICROSCOPIC FEATURES

Ten or more small square cells in outside corners of leaf base. Otherwise, cells are long squiggles. Bases of inner capsule teeth are attached to outer capsule teeth.

Glossy, slender shoots look like hair combed over tree bark
Plants branch irregularly; some tips are like stringy tails

P. tenuirostris

P. tenuirostris capsules have a narrow-beaked lid

S. fabronia capsules have a conical lid (lacking below)

P. tenuirostris leaves are lance or gently sickle-shaped

Tiny leaves lack midrib and are crowded and overlapping

S. fabronia

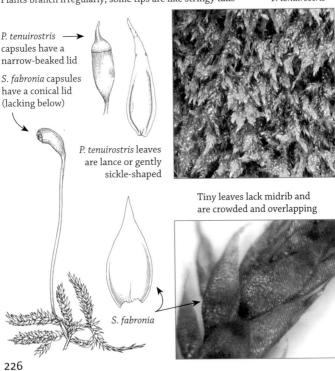

Schwetschkeopsis fabronia

RAPUNZEL MOSS

APPEARANCE: Plants form stringy, flat, irregularly branching mats, with the branches running parallel to each other like strands of combed hair. Shoots are small, slender, and green with a gentle golden sheen; some taper to a long thin tip bearing tiny leaves. Branches are densely covered in leaves that are drawn together, scale-like when dry. Wet leaves are still overlapping and upright with only their wispy tips spreading outward.

LEAVES: Lance-shaped with bowed sides to egg-shaped, tapering gradually to a slender point, shorter than 1 mm. Midrib is lacking and edges are smooth.

CAPSULES: Oblong-cylindrical, with a conical lid, 1 mm long. Stalk is orange red, 4–8 mm long. Uncommon.

HABITAT: Bark toward the base of hardwood trees, also rocks; more common in the southern part of this guide's range.

SIMILAR SPECIES

***Pylaisiadelpha tenuirostris*, GENTLE MOSS**: Similarly small and shiny, but with leaves curved off to either side of branch. Lid is slenderly beaked.

Hypnum pallescens (p. 183) Shoots are more regularly branching, feather-like. Leaf tips curl off to one side like sickles. Capsules are very common.

Pylaisia polyantha and *P. selwynii* (p. 225) Wet leaves flare out up to 45 degrees, giving shoots a bushy appearance. Dry leaves of *P. selwynii* are drawn in tightly but branch tips curl upward. *P. polyantha* shoots lack upward curl when dry but their leaves are not drawn tightly to stems.

MICROSCOPIC FEATURES

Leaves are finely toothed. Leaf cells are long diamond-shaped and have a single bump projecting from end nearest the point of the leaf. Leaf cells of *Pylaisiadelpha* are long and narrow, except they are enlarged and clear or yellowish in the lower outside corners of leaves.

Wet

Dry

Wiry, threadlike mats are formed from creeping shoots covered in tiny leaves

P. subtilis upright capsule, with lid

P. confervoides bent capsule, with lid

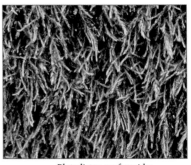

Platydictya confervoides

228

Platydictya subtilis

ALGAL THREAD MOSS

APPEARANCE: Small creeping moss that forms patches of stiff, thin threads with tiny green leaves. When wet, they appear dull green and flare out at 75 degrees; when dry they are slightly shiny and pressed to stems except for their wispy tips.

LEAVES: Tiny lances, 0.2–0.5 mm long with narrow tips. Midrib is lacking, but too small to verify with hand lens. Edges are smooth.

CAPSULES: Short-cylindrical, about 1 mm long, upright, with a conical lid. Stalk is 7–12 mm tall.

HABITAT: Tree trunk bases and bare roots, sometimes on fallen logs.

SIMILAR SPECIES

***Platydictya confervoides*, ALGAL ROCK MOSS**: Grows on calcareous rocks rather than tree bark. Capsules bent or curved.

Hygroamblystegium varium (p. 211) Is a similarly stringy, small creeping moss, but its leaves have a midrib and are about twice the size, 1–2 mm long.

Leskea gracilescens (p. 265) Leaves are pointed egg-shaped without a drawn-out narrow tip. They also have a midrib.

Leskeella nervosa (p. 215) Stem leaves are about 1 mm long, branch leaves 0.5 mm. Some branches end in fuzzy clusters of branchlets.

MICROSCOPIC FEATURES

Leaf edges are free of even minute teeth. Cells near tip of leaf in *P. subtilis* are relatively long, being 3–5× longer than wide versus at most 2–3× in *P. confervoides*. Cells in outside corners of leaf are clusters of small squares. Rusty-colored, smooth rhizoids sprout from the underside of leaves where they join the stems and branches.

F. sphagnifolia, note differing leaf sizes

Aquatic moss tethered in flowing water like limp, irregularly branching seaweed

Orange capsules hidden among leaves

F. dalecarlica, note tight branch tips, which would be absent in *F. hypnoides*

F. dalecarlica

F. hypnoides   *F. sphagnifolia*

Fontinalis dalecarlica

CUPPED WATER MOSS

APPEARANCE: Aquatic moss with long-tapering, slender, floppy stems that run and ripple in the flowing water, reminiscent of seaweed with tight, budlike tips. Stems are 10–50 cm long or more and are dark olive green, tinged with orange, yellow, or red. Wet leaves are deeply cupped, not much spread from stems and appearing to sheath stems in dense spikes. Dried leaves flatten to stem and edges curl back, giving a messy and scraggly appearance to the plants.

LEAVES: Tapering lance shape, 2–4 mm long, strongly cupped and thus appearing even more narrowed and pointy. Stem and branch leaves of similar size. Midrib is lacking. Edges are smooth and reflexed when dry.

CAPSULES: Egg-shaped, 2 mm long, hidden among leaves on nearly nonexistent stalk.

HABITAT: Attached to rocks in flowing water of streams.

SIMILAR SPECIES

***Fontinalis sphagnifolia*, ROLLED WATER MOSS**: Leaves of main stem and branches differing in size, 3–6 and 2–4 mm respectively. Some leaves are wide and softly cupped, others tightly cupped and needle-like. Lacks reflexed leaf edges when dry. Grows in streams that are often seasonally dry.

***Fontinalis hypnoides*, LAX WATER MOSS**: Branch tips tend to be short-tapered and loose. Leaves are sparse and spread wide, 3–7 mm long, and tend to be flat or only gently cupped near base.

Fontinalis antipyretica (p. 233) Leaves are larger, often 4–8 mm long, and sharply keeled rather than cupped, thereby often making branches triangular in cross-section.

MICROSCOPIC FEATURES

Leaf cells are irregular long polygons with thin walls. In outside lower leaf corners, cells are more inflated, especially in *F. hypnoides*.

231

Aquatic moss tethered in flowing water, with long, robust, floppy branches that are triangular in cross-section

Plants look shiny and synthetic when wet, satin when dry

Leaves sharply keeled and often with fin along back

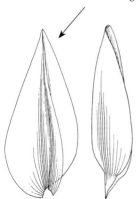

Fontinalis antipyretica

KEELED WATER MOSS

APPEARANCE: Large aquatic moss with long, floppy branches, 10–40 cm, that ripple in the flowing water, reminiscent of seaweed. The leaves are sparse but held close, especially when dry, thereby filling in space between points of leaf insertion on branches, and making shoots triangular in cross-section. Stems are rusty colored. Many dirt particles are trapped in the sharply folded, brown or green leaves. They are shiny when wet, looking synthetic; satin when dry.

LEAVES: Spearhead shape, 4–8 mm long, deeply keeled, or folded lengthwise, occasionally some leaves are cupped, others forming a separate fin along back of leaf. All leaves are of similar size. Midrib is lacking, though the keel fins and folds can be misleading. Edges are smooth.

CAPSULES: Uncommon, egg-shaped, 2–3 mm long, hidden among leaves on nearly nonexistent stalk.

HABITAT: Tethered to rocks, sticks, logs, and tree roots in running water of streams, submerged at least part of the year.

SIMILAR SPECIES

Fontinalis dalecarlica (p. 231) Leaves are smaller, 2–4 mm long, and cupped rather than keeled. Stems lack the triangular aspect and are more long-tapered and slender.

Fontinalis hypnoides (p. 231) Leaves sparse, flat and limp, forming blunt and loose branch tips.

Fontinalis sphagnifolia (p. 231) Leaves of main stem and branches differing in size, 3–6 and 2–4 mm respectively. Some leaves are wide and softly cupped, others tightly cupped and needle-like, but not keeled. Grows in streams that are often seasonally dry.

MICROSCOPIC FEATURES

Cells in center of "earlobe" of lower leaf are clear, thin-walled, and enlarged.

Stiff, bushy, regularly dividing branches
arch out and upward from tree trunks

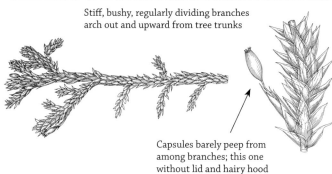

Capsules barely peep from
among branches; this one
without lid and hairy hood

Cupped and
pleated leaves are
densely packed
and overlapping,
like scales

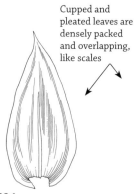

APPEARANCE: Creeping primary stems attached to the tree trunk are hidden under the downward-growing, outwardly curved, and sometimes upwardly curved secondary stems, which hang free and divide abundantly and regularly into straight branches. When dry, the densely packed, overlapping leaves are drawn inward; wet leaves flare outward 60 degrees, making the branches appear bushy.

LEAVES: Ovate, 1–2 mm long, coming to an abrupt short tip, cupped and pleated. Smooth edges appear dark and folded, more prominent than the narrow midrib, which runs to about midleaf or is sometimes absent.

CAPSULES: Cylindrical, 1–2 mm long, upright with a stoutly beaked lid and a sparsely hairy hood. Capsules barely peep from among leaves that surround the short, 1–4-mm stalks.

HABITAT: Tree trunks and sometimes rocks in humid, shady spaces, often near streams.

SIMILAR SPECIES

Heterophyllium affine (p. 221) Leaves lance-shaped, gradually tapered to a slender point, not pleated, sometimes curved in the same direction. Capsules on stalks 2–4 cm long.

Leucodon andrewsianus and *L. julaceus* (p. 277) Plants are darker green and branches curl markedly upward like coat hooks, especially when dry. Stems are sparsely branched and in *L. andrewsianus* often bear tiny fuzzy branchlets among normal leaves.

MICROSCOPIC FEATURES

Outside lower corners of leaf have many rows of small square cells, markedly different from the long diamond-shaped cells of the rest of leaf.

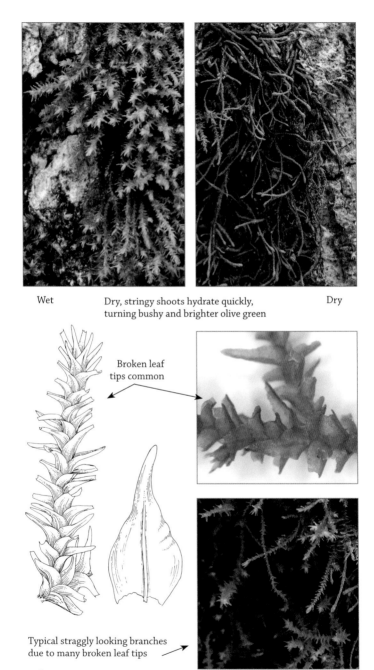

Wet

Dry, stringy shoots hydrate quickly, turning bushy and brighter olive green

Dry

Broken leaf tips common

Typical straggly looking branches due to many broken leaf tips

236

Anomodon tristis

THREADBARE MOSS

APPEARANCE: Slender, irregularly branched, creeping shoots form delicate, stiff mats of dull, dark olive green to brown. Densely crowded leaves draw in like scales when dry, causing branches to look like tight chains with blunt ends. Wet leaves spread outward 80 degrees, but often the tips are broken off and only the clasping bases remain.

LEAVES: Up to 1 mm long with an ovate base that narrows abruptly into a tongue-shaped blade with a pointed apex; tips are often broken off. Midrib ends below apex, but is too fine to see. Edges are smooth.

CAPSULES: Not found in North America.

HABITAT: Tree trunks.

SIMILAR SPECIES

Anomodon attenuatus (p. 239) Some branches are blunt-tipped and rounded; others end like stringy rat tails. Leaves are 1–2 mm long and have intact tips and an obvious midrib.

Anomodon rostratus (p. 217) Leaves are triangular with a fine, sharp, unbroken tip.

Leskea gracilescens (p. 265) Leaves are ovate with a triangular, unbroken tip; branch tips are tapered and stringy.

Leskeella nervosa (p. 215) Branches often end in clusters of tiny branchlets, like pom-poms. Leaves have gradually tapering, unbroken tips and a prominent midrib.

MICROSCOPIC FEATURES

Cells are covered in several bumps. Capsule teeth are also covered in bumps.

Wet, close-up, showing flattened branches

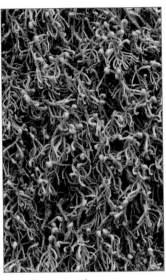

Dry, distant view showing characteristic thick-thin, pinnately forked branches, with balled-up ends

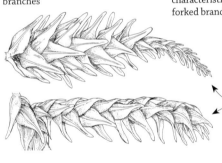

Some branches taper to stringy tails, others blunt-tipped

Leaf tip rounded with tiny teeth

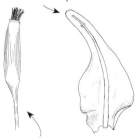

Capsules upright, cylindrical; this one without beaked lid

Anomodon attenuatus

POODLE MOSS

APPEARANCE: Plants form dull olive green, loose, irregularly thick-and-thin mats when dry. Some branches taper to a stringy tail; others are blunt-tipped and when dry curl under into a knobby pom-pom. Dry leaves fold around stem, wrapping it into chains. Wet leaves turn brighter green and are angled to the side at 45 degrees, making the plants look bushier and the branches a bit flattened.

LEAVES: Triangular with a rounded base coming to a rounded tip with a hint of a short tooth at the apex, 1–2 mm long. The thick, pale midrib ends just below apex. Edges are smooth except at tip.

CAPSULES: Upright, cylindrical, tan, 2–3 mm long, with a beaked lid. Stalk is 1–3 cm tall.

HABITAT: Tree trunk bases and soil banks, also on dry rocks, especially calcareous cliffs and boulders.

SIMILAR SPECIES

Anomodon rostratus (p. 217) Forms denser, more golden mats. Leaves are less than 1 mm long and gradually taper to a tiny, white, hairlike tip.

Anomodon rugelii (p. 315) Leaves taper more abruptly at shoulders into narrow, tongue-shaped top. Leaves are somewhat crumpled when dry; midribs are dark rust colored, at least near leaf base.

Anomodon minor (p. 315) Leaves taper gradually to broad tongue-like blade, rounded at tip and lacking tiny tooth.

Anomodon viticulosus (p. 191) Leaves are 2–4 mm long, not appressed to stems when dry.

Leskea gracilescens (p. 265) Stringy and thin; some branches with tapered tips but none with pom-pom tips.

MICROSCOPIC FEATURES

Upper cells are round and densely obscured by small bumps. Lower cells are longer, clear and thick walled.

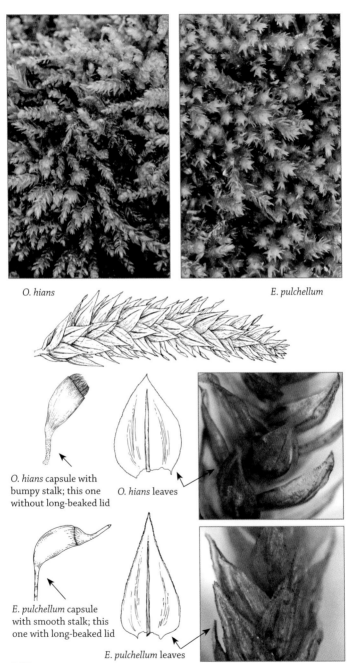

O. hians

E. pulchellum

O. hians capsule with bumpy stalk; this one without long-beaked lid

O. hians leaves

E. pulchellum capsule with smooth stalk; this one with long-beaked lid

E. pulchellum leaves

Eurhynchiastrum pulchellum

RUG MOSS

APPEARANCE: Plants form large mats of creeping stems that divide irregularly or pinnately into stubby, creeping or often upright branches, resembling strands of shag carpet. Fairly shiny, yellow green or half-dead-looking brown. Leaves are crowded and spread outward 50–80 degrees when wet, less when dry. Branches are cylindrical or somewhat flattened; their ends more blunt than long tapering.

LEAVES: Triangular, straight-sided above ovate base, coming to a blunt or slender point. Leaves up to 1 mm long, stem leaves are bigger and more sharply pointed than branch leaves. Midrib reaches just below tip. Edges are minutely toothed, though difficult to discern with a hand lens.

CAPSULES: Cylindrical, 2 mm long, bent over to horizontal with a long-beaked lid. Stalk is reddish when mature, 1–2 cm tall and smooth.

HABITAT: Mounds of forest soil and well-rotted stumps or logs in damp woodlands or dry spots in conifer swamps, also on bark of tree trunk bases or on rocks.

SIMILAR SPECIES

Oxyrrhynchium hians, **SPARE RUG MOSS**: Leaves are more egg-shaped, all coming to a short point; capsule stalk is rough.

Brachythecium rutabulum (p. 245) Leaves are egg-shaped triangular, sometimes quite wide at base, 2–3 mm long. Branches taper at ends. Capsule stalk is bumpy.

Brachythecium salebrosum (p. 205) Leaves are much longer-pointed and usually around 2 mm long.

MICROSCOPIC FEATURES

Leaf tip cells are 2× as long as wide and diamond-shaped; otherwise leaf cells longer and narrower except for small squares in lower outside corners of leaf. Cells smooth, without bumps. Teeth along leaf edge run from leaf tip to base.

Plants form loose mats of irregularly branching shoots of shiny yellow or bright green

Capsules are bent over and have a distinctive, long-beaked lid

Stalk smooth, lacking tiny bumps →

Sparse leaves reveal brown fuzz on lower stems

Leaf tip often twisted

Finely toothed edge

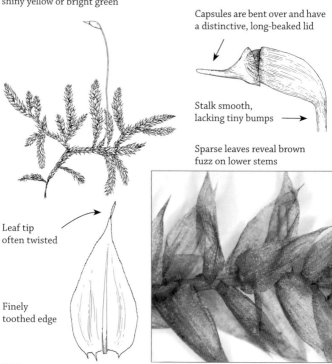

242

Rhynchostegium serrulatum

BEAKED COMB MOSS

APPEARANCE: Plants form loose, shiny, flat patches of yellow green or bright green. Stems branch irregularly and are covered with brown fuzz here and there. Branches are somewhat flattened, with leaves not crowded and spreading outward 70 degrees. Not much changed wet or dry.

LEAVES: Narrowly ovate, 1–2 mm long, coming to a fine, often twisted point. Midrib ends below tip. Blade is slightly cupped, not pleated. Edges are finely toothed much of length.

CAPSULES: Cylindrical, 2 mm long, bent over and curved, with a long-beaked lid. Stalk is 1–3 cm tall, smooth, yellow to red brown.

HABITAT: Soil, bark at tree bases, rotting logs, and rock in dry or moist forests, open pastures, or along roads.

SIMILAR SPECIES

Brachythecium rivulare (p. 247) Stems are sprawling, and branches are upright. Capsules are not long-beaked.

Oxyrrhynchium hians (p. 241) Leaves come to a short point, about 1 mm long. Capsule stalk is finely bumpy.

Rhynchostegium aquaticum (p. 251) Old growth is blackish; new growth is bright green, leaves trap dirt particles. Grows on rocks in stream beds or waterfall spray.

MICROSCOPIC FEATURES

Cells in lower outside corners of leaf are not much different from long, narrow neighboring cells. Midrib often ends in a small tooth.

Plants form a jumbled mat of shaggy, irregularly dividing foxtail-like shoots; shiny when dry

Stubby, bent capsule, with a bumpy stalk; this one without lid

Wide ovate-triangular leaves are not or weakly pleated, wet or dry

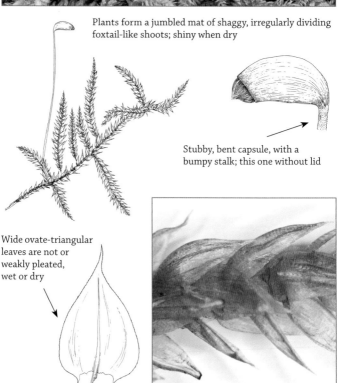

Brachythecium rutabulum

ROUGH FOXTAIL MOSS

APPEARANCE: Shaggy, glossy mats of large plants with creeping to arching stems and upright branches that divide irregularly and resemble bright green or yellow foxtails. Leaves closely spaced and spreading at various angles from the stem, not much different wet or dry.

LEAVES: Ovate-triangular, sometimes quite wide at base, 1–3 mm long, with a long tapering tip. Midrib ends well below tip. Not or weakly pleated. Edges lacking teeth.

CAPSULES: Horizontally bent-over, stubby macaroni shape, 2–3 mm long. Mouth is capped by a conical lid while developing. Stalk is 1–3 cm high, rust-colored, and roughened with tiny bumps from top to bottom.

HABITAT: Moist areas on soil, rock, rotting logs, or tree trunk bases, both in shade of forest and in open among grasses.

SIMILAR SPECIES

Brachythecium salebrosum and *B. oxycladon* (p. 205) Leaves are pleated, especially when dry, not as wide at leaf base. Capsule stalk is smooth.

Brachythecium rivulare (p. 247) Leaves are short-tapered to tip and have large clear cells in lower corners of stem leaves.

Callicladium haldanianum (p. 289) Similar size and shagginess but its leaves lack a midrib.

MICROSCOPIC FEATURES

Leaf margin is finely toothed. Few cells in lower leaf corners are enlarged.

Robust branches stand upright from sprawling stems, forming loose mats of white or yellow green

Chubby, tilted capsules have a bumpy stalk and a conical lid

Leaves have a short-tapered tip and are not pleated

Strip a leaf off stem to see clear, balloon-like cells in lower corners

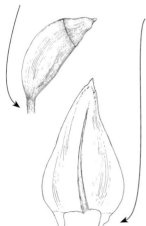

Brachythecium rivulare

RIVER FOXTAIL MOSS

APPEARANCE: Plants are robust, whitish green to yellow green, forming loose mats composed of sprawling to erect-arching stems with irregular to pinnate branching, sometimes vaguely treelike. Leaves are not crowded along branches and spread 30–90 degrees when wet; held at same angle when dry, but then looking spikey rather than soft.

LEAVES: Stem leaves are 2–3 mm long, egg-shaped coming to a short, sharp tip, cupped, unpleated, with discernible midrib. Strip a few leaves from stem to see large, balloon-like cells visible in the lower corners of the leaves. Branch leaves are narrower, 1–2 mm, cupped and barely pleated, with a very short midrib. Edges are smooth.

CAPSULES: Chubby macaroni shape, bent like a field hockey club, 2–3 mm long, lid conical. Stalk is maroon, 12–25 mm tall, and rough all along length.

HABITAT: On rocks and soil in shady, soggy habitats, such as around springs, on seepy slopes, and in or along streams.

SIMILAR SPECIES

Brachythecium rutabulum (p. 245) Leaves taper to longer tip.

Bryhnia novae-angliae (p. 249) Similar growth habit but smaller; leaves are only 1 mm long and twisted at the tip.

Rhynchostegium aquaticum (p. 251) Plants are dark green or blackish except bright new growth at branch tips. Leaves are more ovate than triangular. Capsule lid is long-beaked and stalk is smooth.

Sciuro-hypnum plumosum (p. 207) Leaves tend to point in one direction and are often yellow or brown, 1–2 mm. Stems and branches creep along ground rather than standing upright.

MICROSCOPIC FEATURES

Lower outside leaf corners run down stem beyond base of center of leaf as triangular lobes. Stem leaves have large, balloon-like cells in lower corners.

Wet   Shoots irregularly branch and arch to form loose mats,   Dry
appearing cylindrical when wet and scraggly when dry

Capsules with
and without lid

Bumpy stalks

Leaf tips are
often twisted

Wide branch and stem leaves

248

Bryhnia novae-angliae

BONSAI MOSS

APPEARANCE: Irregularly branching, horizontal, and arching stems, 2–10 cm long, form pale green, loose mats. Wet leaves cup away from stems and then curve upward, creating airy wormlike branches. When dry, leaves still spread from stem, but shrivel and lose their cup shape; thus branches look scraggly rather than cylindrical.

LEAVES: Broadly ovate, about 1 mm long and nearly as wide, with a short sharp tip that is often twisted. Fine midrib ends below leaf tip. Leaves are cupped like a spoon. Edges are smooth.

CAPSULES: Short, chubby macaroni, 2 mm long, inclined to horizontal, dark rust-colored; lid is conical. Stalk is 10–20 mm tall and finely bumpy.

HABITAT: On a variety of substrates in seepage and along shady streams, especially on wet rocks.

SIMILAR SPECIES

Brachythecium rivulare (p. 247) Larger in scale; stem leaves are 2–3 mm long and lacking twisted tips.

Sciuro-hypnum plumosum (p. 207) All leaves tend to point in one direction and are often yellow or brown. Shoots all creep along ground rather than tending to stand upright.

Rhynchostegium aquaticum (p. 251) Leaves are 2–3 mm long, with a shorter leaf tip. Plants are bright green in new growth, otherwise, dark brownish green.

MICROSCOPIC FEATURES

Cells have a bump at end nearest leaf tip. Midrib is not toothed along back of leaf. Leaf edge is finely toothed.

Stiff, irregularly branching, blackish shoots with olive green tips sprawl over wet rocks

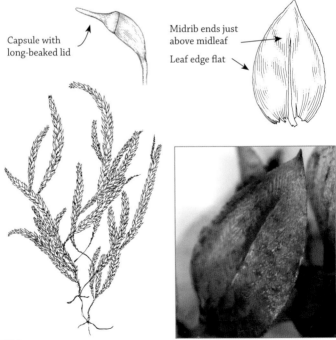

Capsule with long-beaked lid

Midrib ends just above midleaf

Leaf edge flat

Rhynchostegium aquaticum

BLACK BROOK MOSS

APPEARANCE: Dark green, somewhat shiny, prostrate moss with blackish old growth and bright green branch tips. Short branches divide irregularly from stems, and leaves trap dirt particles. Leaves are held 40–60 degrees from stem. Not much changed wet or dry, though leaves are not as regularly cupped when dry and are instead swiped to the side.

LEAVES: Stem leaves are 2–3 mm long, branch leaves up to 2 mm long. Ovate, coming to a short point, cupped, and leaf bases flare out from stem, making leaves seem even wider. Midrib ends just above midleaf. Edges are smooth.

CAPSULES: Cylindrical, 1–2 mm long, bent over, with a long-beaked lid. Stalk is 10–23 mm long, smooth, and chestnut-colored.

HABITAT: Wet rocks in stream beds or waterfall spray, often under water.

SIMILAR SPECIES

Brachythecium rivulare (p. 247) Has sprawling to erect-arching stems and a pale green color. Capsule stalks are finely bumpy.

Bryhnia novae-angliae (p. 249) Leaves are only 1 mm long and very cupped, with a longer, often twisted tip. Plants are usually a pale green color.

Hygrohypnum duriusculum (p. 279) All leaves are 1–2 mm long, squat-ovate; midrib is variable, often double. Capsule lids are convex.

Hygrohypnum eugyrium (p. 281) Leaves are ovate, 1–2 mm long, usually with tips curving to one side; midrib is absent or extending to midleaf. Capsule lid is conic, without a beak.

MICROSCOPIC FEATURES

Leaf edge is faintly toothed. Cells in lower outside corners of leaf are squarer, but not dramatically different from neighboring cells. Midrib often ends in a small tooth.

Stiff, irregularly branching, dark brown shoots with olive green tips sprawl over wet rocks

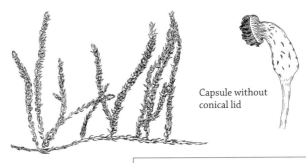

Capsule without conical lid

Very prominent midrib reaches apex

Leaf border thickened

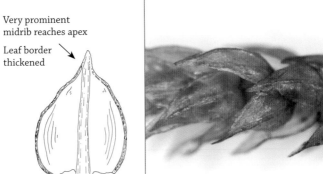

BORDERED BROOK MOSS

APPEARANCE: Plants form stiff mats of prostrate, scruffy, dark brown stems that divide irregularly but frequently into trailing or arching olive green branches. Leaves are not at all crowded and spread 30–70 degrees wet or dry; when dry the leaf tips curve back toward the stem and twist slightly. Neither shiny nor dull.

LEAVES: Egg-shaped, 1 mm long, coming to a triangular point. Midrib is prominent to apex. Edges are smooth and with a thickened border, like a hem running around the blade.

CAPSULES: Macaroni-shaped to curved-cylindrical, 2 mm long, with a conical lid and yellow-brown teeth. Strongly contracted below mouth when dry. Stalk 1–3 cm, yellow, orange, or red brown.

HABITAT: Rocks in streams or on dripping cliffs, either acidic or calcium-enriched.

SIMILAR SPECIES

Hygroamblystegium varium (p. 211) Leaves 1–2 mm, variously lance- to egg-shaped but without a thickened border.

Hygrohypnum luridum and *H. eugyrium* (p. 281) Leaves 1–2 mm long, oval, cupped, scale-like with an abrupt sharp point.

Leptodictyum riparium (p. 211) Leaves are 2–5 mm long, lance-shaped, midrib ends well below tip, edges lack border.

MICROSCOPIC FEATURES

Typical leaf cells are oblong-oval with thick walls. Border is formed by two rows of linear, thick-walled cells.

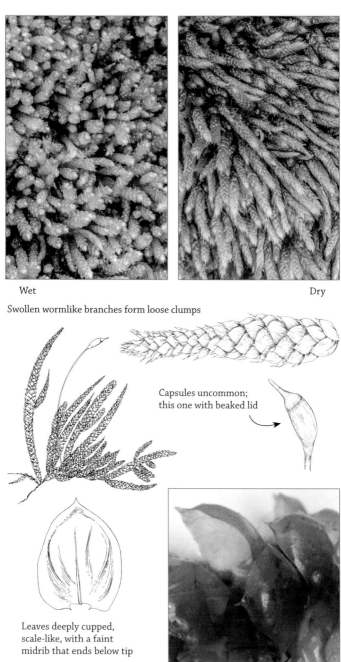

Wet

Dry

Swollen wormlike branches form loose clumps

Capsules uncommon;
this one with beaked lid

Leaves deeply cupped,
scale-like, with a faint
midrib that ends below tip

Bryoandersonia illecebra

WORM MOSS

APPEARANCE: Cylindrical, plump, olive or golden green shoots branch irregularly and arch upward, forming loose clumps. Leaf bases angle out widely from stem and then curve upward; leaves are very dense near branch tops, less so at base. Not much changed wet or dry. Somewhat shiny.

LEAVES: Broadly ovate or lentil shape, 1–2 mm long, with a short, often twisted, wispy tip, deeply cupped like a spoon. Midrib is very fine and ends below tip. Edges are smooth.

CAPSULES: Rare; short-cylindrical, 1–2 mm long, bent over. Lid is long-beaked. Stalk is 13–25 mm long, red.

HABITAT: Forest soil, especially basic and shady soils, also on rocks or tree bases, and in grassy fields and lawns.

SIMILAR SPECIES

Brachythecium rivulare (p. 247) Shoots are loose, trailing to upright-arching, not smoothly cylindrical, especially when dry. Branch leaves are narrower than stem leaves.

Myurella julacea and *M. sibirica* (p. 273) Like miniature versions of *Bryoandersonia*, often with a white metallic sheen. Tiny cylindrical branches are composed of leaves less than 1 mm long. Prefer to grow on basic, moist rocks and in calcium-enriched wetlands.

Rhynchostegium aquaticum (p. 251) Plants on wet rocks in streams, often submerged, or in spray of waterfalls. Leaves 2–3 mm, without a wispy, twisted tip. Midrib is easy to see.

MICROSCOPIC FEATURES

Leaf edge has short teeth. Cells of leaf smooth, lacking bumps.

Plants stiffly upright, forming short, dense mounds of yellow green or brown

Capsules with lid atop stalks that arise midstem

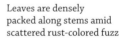

Leaves are densely packed along stems amid scattered rust-colored fuzz

Cratoneuron filicinum

FURRY FERN MOSS

APPEARANCE: Pinnately branching stems that creep or arch stiffly upward and crowd together to form deep cushions 4–10 cm deep, green or yellow green to brownish with age. Reddish brown fuzz is matted or at least scattered along stems. Leaves are densely packed and are held stiffly upright or flare out slightly from stems and branches.

LEAVES: Egg-shaped triangular, 1–2 mm long, coming to a slender tip that curves gently to side, often more strongly curved on branches than stem. Midrib is strong to tip. Edges are smooth.

CAPSULES: Cylindrical, curving, and bent over to horizontal, 2–3 mm long, lid is conical with a nib. Stalk is 3–5 cm tall, and reddish.

HABITAT: Grows on rock or soil in seeps and soggy spaces that are calcium-enriched, such as in drainage ditches, by springs, or along rivulets.

SIMILAR SPECIES

Calliergonella cuspidata (p. 285) Stems are not matted with rusty fuzz. Leaves are egg-shaped, cupped, with more rounded tip, not curved to one side.

Helodium blandowii (p. 197) Similarly hairy, but leaves are longer tapered, pleated, and their edges are rolled down.

Tomentypnum nitens (p. 199) Leaves are long, narrow, tapering triangles, very pleated and 3–4 mm long.

MICROSCOPIC FEATURES

Leaf cells are smooth, lacking minute bumps, 3–6× as long as wide, though longer near leaf tip. Cells of basal corners of leaf are dramatically inflated compared with neighboring cells. Leaf edge has shallow teeth from tip to base.

Plants have upright stems and regularly dividing, horizontal branches; both are red beneath dense leaves

Capsules with lid atop stalks that arise midstem

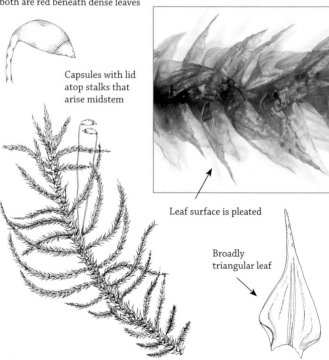

Leaf surface is pleated

Broadly triangular leaf

Rhytidiadelphus triquetrus

PLEATED SHAGGY MOSS

APPEARANCE: Creeping to upright stems like shaggy "trees" form bushy mats 5–20 cm tall. Stems are regularly or irregularly pinnately branched; branches taper at tips, and are horizontal or arch down toward the ground. Leaves are green and close together, but not hiding the reddish brown stems and branches beneath. Leaves flare out nearly 90 degrees from stem. Not much changed wet or dry.

LEAVES: Stem leaves are 3–5 mm long and branch leaves are 2–3 mm long. Triangular egg-shaped, gradually tapering from base to pointed tip. Tip of leaf is flat, and base of leaf clasps stem. Midrib is weak and forked, to about midleaf. Surface is pleated. Edges are smooth.

CAPSULES: Egg-shaped, 2–3 mm long, bent over, rust-colored, with a conical lid. Stalk is 2–4 cm tall.

HABITAT: Forest soil in conifer forests or openings in hardwood forests, woods enriched with calcium or along streams.

SIMILAR SPECIES

Rhytidiadelphus subpinnatus (p. 309) Tends to be more sprawling and less upright. Leaves are not pleated, tip is rolled lengthwise forming a U-shaped channel.

Loeskeobryum brevirostre (p. 311) New stems are upright-arching from creeping older stems; leaves are pleated, stem leaves 2–3 mm, branch 1–2 mm long, abruptly narrowed from ovate base to slender tip.

Pleurozium schreberi (p. 287) Irregularly branched and less treelike, more shag-carpet-like. Leaves are rounded, egg-shaped, and cupped.

MICROSCOPIC FEATURES

As viewed from underside of leaf, each cell has a bump at the top. Cells in "lobes" at base of leaf are not much different from nearby cells. Leaves have tiny teeth along edges.

Shoot tips are budlike points of tightly clustered leaves

Rounded leaf tip

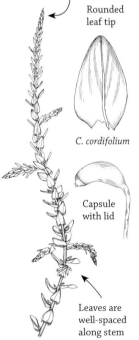

C. cordifolium

Capsule with lid

Leaves are well-spaced along stem

C. giganteum leaves (above) have a cluster of clear bubble cells in lower lobes, lacking in *C. cordifolium* (below)

Calliergon cordifolium

HEART-LEAVED SPEAR MOSS

APPEARANCE: Sprawling to upright moss forms soft green mounds up to 15 cm high of loosely clustered stems that are spindly and sparsely covered in leaves, reminiscent of a sprig of thyme. Stems branch sparingly and irregularly; shoot tips come to blunt, budlike points of tightly clustered leaves. Wet leaves are flat and spread widely from stems. Dry leaves shrivel, thus causing plants to look more jagged and skimpy.

LEAVES: Egg-shaped, 2–3 mm long, with little earlobes or bulges at base where they attach to stem and a bluntly pointed tip which is sometimes cupped like a hood. Midrib runs to tip. Edges are smooth.

CAPSULES: Cylindrical, 2–3 mm long, horizontal, curved; lid is conical with a nib. Stalk is 4–7 cm tall and orange brown.

HABITAT: Wetlands such as marshes, swamps, and boggy forests, often standing with its feet wet.

SIMILAR SPECIES

***Calliergon giganteum*, BUBBLE-LOBED SPEAR MOSS**: Leaves are more densely packed and stems divide regularly into opposite branches. Clear bubble cells are obvious in lower lobes of leaf.

Calliergonella cuspidata (p. 285) Leaves are crowded and cupped close to stems, lacking a midrib.

MICROSCOPIC FEATURES

Lower outside corners of leaf in *C. cordifolium* gradually transition from the long, narrow, rectangular shape typical of most of the leaf to large, inflated, and clear cells. In *C. giganteum*, cells in lower lobes are very large, inflated, and clear, like balloons, and abruptly different from other cells.

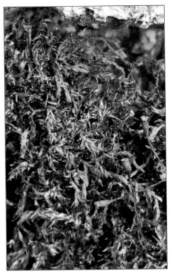

Wet   Starry, tiny, dark green plants creep out   Dry
of knotholes on hardwood tree trunks

Sparse leaves spread widely from
shoots and are angled in all directions

Upright capsule
without lid, showing
reflexed teeth

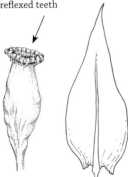

Anacamptodon splachnoides

KNOTHOLE MOSS

APPEARANCE: Tiny, dark green, creeping plants form dense, thin mats in moist spots on tree trunks. Branches divide irregularly and have a prickly, starry aspect due to the sparse leaves that flare out 90 degrees from stems and point upward rather than angle in all directions. Not much changed wet or dry.

LEAVES: Arrowhead shape with evenly tapered tip, 1 mm long. Midrib ends below leaf tip. Edges are smooth.

CAPSULES: Upright, urn-shaped, 1–2 mm long; while developing, mouth is covered by a cone-shaped lid, when dry, puckered below mouth with reflexed teeth. Stalk is orange and around 1 cm tall.

HABITAT: Tree trunks, in moist nooks, such as knotholes, cracks, and rain channels.

SIMILAR SPECIES

Hygroamblystegium varium (p. 211) Small and often dark green, but more stringy and lacking the starry charisma of *Anacamptodon*. Capsules are curved and 2–4 mm long.

Leskea gracilescens (p. 265) Forms long, fine, stringy branches covered sparsely with leaves that are cupped even when dry, looking like tiny necklace chains.

Platygyrium repens (p. 223) Has an "oily" golden cast, produces tiny, fuzzy branchlets amid leaves near branch tips. Leaves are crowded on branches.

Pylaisia selwynii (p. 225) Its densely packed leaf tips are wispy fine and swept to the side in gentle curls.

MICROSCOPIC FEATURES

Cells are shaped like long diamonds, with small square cells in the lower outside corners of leaf.

Tidy, chainlike branches, like fuzzy sewing threads, form thin mats on tree trunks

L. gracilescens leaves at branch ends are straight

L. gracilescens capsule upright; this one with lid

L. polycarpa leaves at branch ends all curl in one direction

L. polycarpa capsule curved; this one without lid

L. polycarpa

L. gracilescens

Leskea gracilescens

NECKLACE CHAIN MOSS

APPEARANCE: Dark green, slender, creeping moss, looks like thin mats of fuzzy sewing threads stuck to tree bark. Leaves are sparse along irregular branches and at branch tips they are tiny, giving ends a tapered, stringy aspect. When wet, leaves spread from stem. When dry, leaves are drawn parallel to stems, but still cupped, looking like a necklace chain.

LEAVES: Ovate with a triangular tip, cupped at base. Stem leaves are slightly larger than branch leaves, but both are less than 1 mm long. Very faint midrib ends below tip. Leaf edges are smooth.

CAPSULES: Upright, cylindrical, 1–2 mm long; lid is short-conical. Stalk is brown, 5–8 mm tall.

HABITAT: Tree trunks, especially near tree trunk base, also rocks and logs.

SIMILAR SPECIES

Leskea polycarpa, **CURLED CHAIN MOSS**: Leaves at ends of branches mostly curl in one direction. Capsules are curved.

Anacamptodon splachnoides (p. 263) Leaves spread up to 90 degrees from stem when wet and are not as cupped. Capsules are strongly constricted below the mouth when dry.

Hygroamblystegium varium (p. 211) Small and often dark green, but more stringy. Leaves are not usually cupped. Capsules are curved, 1–3 mm long, and contracted below mouth when dry.

Pylaisia selwynii (p. 225) Leaf tips are wispy fine and swept to the side. Branches curl gently and are densely covered with leaves.

MICROSCOPIC FEATURES

Leaf cells are roundish, each with one central bump, especially as seen from undersurface of leaf. Lower leaf edges are slightly curled under. Base of leaf is twice-pleated.

Plants are 1× pinnate with tightly cylindrical shoots that creep over tree trunks

Capsules are upright, with beaked lid over white teeth

T. hirtella stem leaves bigger than branch leaves (below); same size in *T. asprella*

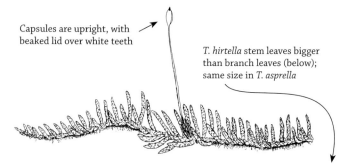

Cupped, scale-like leaves are held close to shoots and are so tiny it is difficult to see their midrib or teeth

Thelia hirtella

TRAIN TRACKS MOSS

APPEARANCE: Small, pale green to grayish green, regularly pinnate plants creep over bark, forming dull mats. Long trailing stems are sparsely covered with leaves but densely matted with brown fuzz attaching plants to bark, and give rise to numerous short branches of similar length. Branches are spreading or erect, densely covered in leaves, and thereby cylindrical. Wet leaves are cupped; dry leaves are flat but still tightly pressed to branches.

LEAVES: Stem leaves are clearly bigger than branch leaves, but both are only about 1 mm long. Wide egg-shaped coming to a narrow tip. Very cupped and scale-like. Midrib is present but mostly not discernible with a hand lens. Teeth along leaf edge are not easily visible; under plenty of light, tilting stem down, it is possible to distinguish teeth on stem leaves.

CAPSULES: Cylindrical, about 2 mm long, upright, with white teeth and a beaked lid. Stalk 5–12 mm.

HABITAT: Tree trunk bases and tree trunks.

SIMILAR SPECIES

***Thelia asprella*, ALLIGATOR MOSS**: Similar species except its stem and branch leaves are about the same size.

Entodon seductrix (p. 291) Also has cylindrical branches with scale-like leaves, but is very shiny. Wet leaves are translucent. When dry, the moss looks like glossy embroidery floss.

Myurella spp. (p. 273) Plants lack regular pinnate branches, but branches are similar in color and cylindrical shape; leaves are 0.3–0.6 mm long, lack a midrib. Grow on rock and in crevices.

MICROSCOPIC FEATURES

Leaves have long jagged teeth along margins. Weak midrib ends around midleaf. Cells of *T. hirtella*, except along transparent margins, each have a tall, unbranched bump in center of cell. Cells of *T. asprella* have tall bumps with 2–4 tips.

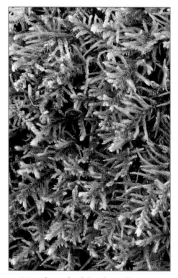

Wet plants look bushy as leaves spread slightly

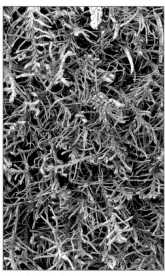

Dry plants look like thin, wiry threads

Shoots divide regularly, 1× pinnate, looking like dull olive green or golden brown, miniature ferns

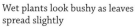

Capsule with lid

Leaves pleated

Stem leaves 2× size of branch leaves

Abietinella abietina

WIRY FERN MOSS

APPEARANCE: Plants in dull, dark olive green to golden brown mats, stiff and wiry when dry but more pliable and bushier when wet. Stems up to 12 cm long, with ends arching upright, once pinnate, resembling a miniature fern leaf. When dry, the leaves are drawn in tight, making the branches look like threads. Wet leaves spread slightly so the plants look fuller.

LEAVES: Stem leaves are 1–2 mm long, twice the size of branch leaves, and therefore easier to examine. Triangular with pleats parallel to the strong midrib that reaches at least ¾ of the way to tip. Leaf edge not toothed but often rolled down.

CAPSULES: Very rare, like curved macaroni, 2–3 mm long, with a short-beaked lid. Stalk is 2–3 cm tall.

HABITAT: On calcium-enriched dry rocks and soils, on sand dunes and the floor of conifer forests.

SIMILAR SPECIES

Thuidium delicatulum (p. 271) Stems are twice to three-times pinnately divided and look like tiny, lacy fern fronds. Common in acidic habitats.

Thuidium recognitum (p. 271) Twice pinnately branched, with pleated stem leaves that curve away from stems when dry. Prefers moist, calcium-enriched soil and rock.

MICROSCOPIC FEATURES

Leaf cells each have a bump on both the upper and lower surfaces. When leaves are removed, tiny threadlike projections called paraphyllia can be seen growing on the stems and branches.

Shoots finely and regularly divided like fern fronds;
T. delicatulum shoots are 2–3× pinnate (above) vs. 2× in *T. recognitum* (lower left)

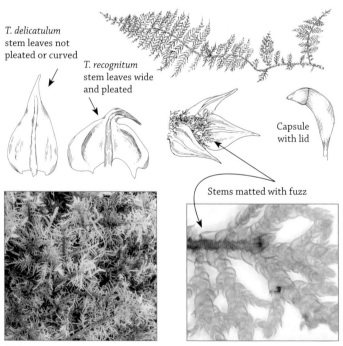

T. delicatulum stem leaves not pleated or curved

T. recognitum stem leaves wide and pleated

Capsule with lid

Stems matted with fuzz

Thuidium delicatulum

DELICATE FERN MOSS

APPEARANCE: Plants resemble delicate, miniature ferns, forming mats of dull green to yellow green over the forest floor. Stems are 3–10 cm long and regularly twice to three times pinnate. Leaves are sparse revealing green fuzz on stems and big branches, but are very densely clustered and overlapping on the small (terminal) branches. Leaves are held close to stem when dry, and spread out somewhat when wet.

LEAVES: Stem leaves are about 1 mm long, egg-shaped triangular, tapering to a strong pointed tip, unpleated. Midrib extends to tip. Edges are smooth and rolled down. Branch leaves are similarly shaped but much smaller.

CAPSULES: Long cylindrical, inclined to horizontal, curved gently, 2–4 mm long; lid is long-beaked. Stalks are 2–4 cm tall and rust-colored.

HABITAT: Forest soil, rotting logs, and rocks; prefers damp shady sites.

SIMILAR SPECIES

Thuidium recognitum, **KILT FERN MOSS**: Plants are yellow green to yellow brown; stems are twice-pinnate. Stem leaves are pleated, come to an abrupt point, and curve away from stem when dry. Prefers calcareous habitats.

Abietinella abietina (p. 269) Stems are once-pinnate and wiry, with tips arching upright; capsules are very rare.

Hylocomium splendens (p. 313) Sprays grow in airy stair-step tiers, each year's growth arching-ascending from top of the previous. Stem leaves are 2–3 mm long, abruptly narrowed to a long point.

MICROSCOPIC FEATURES

The midrib peters out just below the tip of leaf. Each cell has at least one bump. Tiny, green, threadlike paraphyllia cover the stems and branches between the leaves.

Tiny, cylindrical, lime or mint green shoots with a metallic sheen

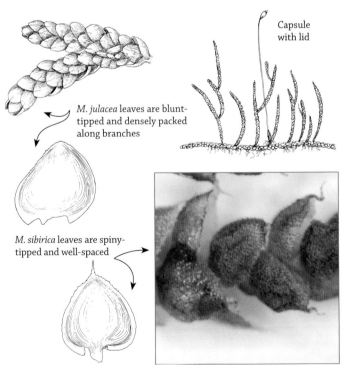

Capsule with lid

M. julacea leaves are blunt-tipped and densely packed along branches

M. sibirica leaves are spiny-tipped and well-spaced

Myurella sibirica

VERDIGRIS MOUSETAIL MOSS

APPEARANCE: Small, cylindrical, mousetail-like threads of lime, pale mint, or blue green with a white metallic sheen, either creeping or arching upright. When wet, the leaves spread 90 degrees from stems and are not much changed when dry. Leaves have a pebbly texture. Leaves are well spaced, often with the green stem visible between them.

LEAVES: Broadly ovate to rounded, 0.5 mm long, scale-like, deeply cupped, abruptly narrowed to a delicate point. Midrib is lacking. Edges are smooth.

CAPSULES: Oblong, almost upright, 1 mm long, mouth covered in a conical lid while developing. Stalk is reddish and 7–12 mm tall.

HABITAT: Moist rock outcrops, in crevices, and beneath overhanging ledges, usually calcium enriched.

SIMILAR SPECIES

Myurella julacea, **STUBBY MOUSETAIL MOSS**: Branches with leaves crowded and overlapping thus hiding stem; leaves less than 0.5 mm long, tip rounded, pressed close to stem when dry, spreading 45 degrees when wet.

Thelia spp. (p. 267) Pale green to grayish plants, regularly pinnate; leaves about 1 mm long, densely crowded on spreading to erect, cylindrical branches. Grows on bark.

Leskea gracilescens (p. 265) Dark green plants prefer to grow on tree bark; leaves gradually tapered to triangular apex.

MICROSCOPIC FEATURES

Cells of *M. sibirica* each have one bump in the middle, whereas those of *M. julacea* are either smooth or the end of the cell toward the leaf top projects upward. Leaves of *M. julacea* are 0.3 mm long, and the edges are smooth or have regular shallow teeth. In comparison, the leaves of *M. sibirica* are 0.4–0.6 mm long, and their edges are irregularly deeply toothed, even spiny.

Very different in appearance wet and dry; wet above, dry below

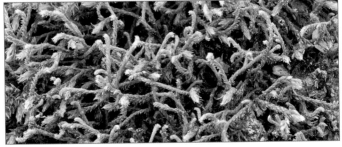

Wet leaves flare outward, turn bright olive green and reveal orange stems beneath

Dry plants look like clusters of stiff, frosty worms due to tightly drawn-together, scale-like leaves

Pale leaf tips

Egg-shaped, orange capsules are hidden among shoots and surrounded by fringed leaves; with lid below

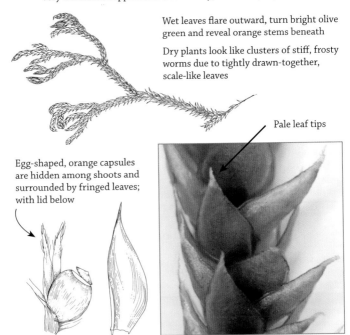

Hedwigia ciliata

MEDUSA MOSS

APPEARANCE: When dry, the dull, silver-tipped, olive green to grayish leaves are closely pressed to branches, causing plants to looking like frosty, wormy strings. The stiff stems branch irregularly to form cushions 1–3 cm tall. When moistened, leaf color brightens to yellow green or brown, and leaves flare out up to 90 degrees from bright red-orange to brownish stems, looking bushy.

LEAVES: Ovate, 1–2 mm long, cupped. The white portion of the sharp tips is highly variable in length from one patch to another. Lacking midrib. Edges are smooth.

CAPSULES: Ball or cup-shaped, orange, with a flat-conic lid. Capsules are hidden among leaves on very short stalks and surrounded by triangular, fringed leaves.

HABITAT: Dry rocks in both sunny and shady habitats.

SIMILAR SPECIES

Anomodon tristis (p. 237) Usually grows on trees. Leaves are more pear-shaped and often have broken off tips.

Bucklandiella microcarpa (p. 117) Stems with numerous, stubby side branches; leaves 2–3 mm long with a midrib.

Codriophorus acicularis (p. 115) On wet rocks rather than dry and often submerged. Leaves are 2–3 mm long with a midrib.

Leucodon andrewsianus (p. 277) Leaves are triangular, pleated. Branches curl upward like a hook when dry and often produce fuzzy clusters of tiny branchlets near shoot tips.

MICROSCOPIC FEATURES

Tips of leaves are roughened by small teeth. Lower leaf edges are rolled under and made of small square cells. Cells are covered in tiny bumps.

Wet Branches curl upward, note frizzy brood branch clusters Dry

Leucodon andrewsianus sprouts frizzy brood branches near shoot tips, but rarely produces capsules

Leucodon julaceus shoots lack brood branches but commonly produce capsules

Egg-shaped capsules on short stalks

Leucodon andrewsianus

FRIZZY HOOK MOSS

APPEARANCE: Olive green stringy moss grows in clumps on tree trunks. Stems are orange brown, densely covered by leaves but revealed when wet leaves flare out 75 degrees; plants thus looking like pipe cleaners, starlike from above. When dry, branch tips are blunt and curl upward, and leaves are overlapping and appressed to stem like scales. Clusters of messy, tiny branchlets (called brood branches) frizz out from amid leaves near tops of some branches.

LEAVES: Triangular, around 2 mm long, with a broad base, coming to a long tapered tip; pleated wet or dry. Midrib is lacking, but the pleats can be deceiving! Sometimes the leaves appear cupped and have slightly inrolled edges, especially when dry. Edges are smooth.

CAPSULES: Very rare. Usually reproduces vegetatively via brood branches amid leaves.

HABITAT: Tree trunks, occasionally on rock.

SIMILAR SPECIES

Leucodon julaceus, **SMOOTH HOOK MOSS**: Lacks tiny frizzy branchlets near shoot tips. Leaves are ovate, with shorter tips, and not pleated. Capsules are more common, egg-shaped, 1–2 mm long, on short stalks, 3–8 mm long.

Pylaisia selwynii (p. 225) Has branches that curve up when dry, but it is smaller, with leaves about 1 mm long. Its leaves are not pleated and have a narrow base.

Platygyrium repens (p. 223) Produces fuzzy branchlets amid leaves near branch tips, but is smaller with leaves about 1 mm long, and has an "oily" golden cast.

MICROSCOPIC FEATURES

Cells near top of leaf are long-diamond shaped, longer in the middle of leaf. There are several rows of short square cells at leaf base. Cells are smooth. Leaf tip cells of *L. julaceus* are short-diamond shaped.

Soft, irregularly branching, brown and green shoots sprawl over wet rocks like ruffled crepe-paper chains

Capsule with lid

Nearly circular leaves with a broad, blunt tip are very tightly packed together

Midrib short or lacking

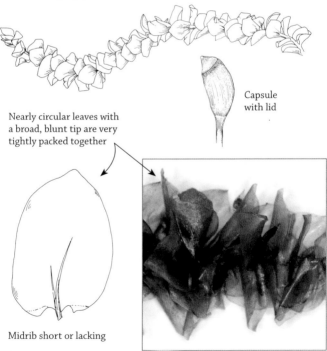

278

Hygrohypnum duriusculum

RUFFLED BROOK MOSS

APPEARANCE: Plants form soft mats of green or yellowish green, prostrate, irregularly branching stems. Older growth is brown, shoot tips are olive green. Plants are shiny when dry but encrusted with dust and dirt. Leaves are densely packed and spread wide up to 70 degrees from shoots, looking ruffled. Dry leaves also spread out, but are slightly crumpled.

LEAVES: Wide oval or circular, 1–2 mm long, with a clasping base and broad, blunt point, slightly cupped. Midrib is variable: usually one fork reaching midrib, but sometimes completely lacking; check several leaves. Edges are smooth.

CAPSULES: Cylindrical, about 2 mm long, curved over, teeth are brownish with a conical lid. Stalk 9–25 mm, reddish.

HABITAT: On wet, acidic rocks in stream bed.

SIMILAR SPECIES

Hygrohypnum eugyrium and *H. luridum* (p. 281) Leaves overlapping, with abrupt sharp tips.

Hygrohypnum ochraceum (p. 281) Leaves long egg-shaped, tips curl to alternating sides of branch, bubble-like.

Brachythecium rivulare (p. 247) Pale green plants. Stem leaves are 2–3 mm long, with a single midrib; branch leaves are smaller, with a less apparent midrib.

MICROSCOPIC FEATURES

Leaf corner cells are square or somewhat larger than neighboring cells and in small lobes that clasp the stem. Leaf edges are toothless.

Plants form soft, cylindrical, brown and green mats over wet rocks

Dry shoots are shiny despite being encrusted with dirt

Capsule without lid

Hygrohypnum ochraceum leaves less crowded, more sickle-curved

Leaves scale-like, midrib presence and length variable

H. eugyrium   *H. luridum*

Hygrohypnum eugyrium

SWOLLEN BROOK MOSS

APPEARANCE: Plants form soft mats of prostrate, irregularly branching stems; older growth is brown, shoot tips are olive green and budlike. Plants are shiny when dry but encrusted with dust and dirt. Leaves are densely packed and overlapping, scale-like. Leaf bases angle out about 30 degrees from branches, but cup back inward, giving shoots a swollen, cylindrical aspect.

LEAVES: Oval, 1–2 mm long, abruptly coming to a sharp, short point that is sometimes tipped to one side, deeply cupped. Midrib is variable: sometimes completely lacking, in other leaves reaching midleaf. Edges are smooth.

CAPSULES: Cylindrical, about 2 mm long, curved over, teeth brownish with a conical lid. Stalk 13–25 mm, reddish.

HABITAT: On wet rocks, either in or beside a stream bed.

SIMILAR SPECIES

***Hygrohypnum luridum*, STIFF BROOK MOSS**: Smaller plants. Leaves 0.7–1.5 mm. Prefers calcium-enriched habitats.

***Hygrohypnum ochraceum*, BUBBLE BROOK MOSS**: Leaves are less crowded and not scale-like, leaf tips curl to alternating sides of branch, bubble-like due to cupped blade. Midrib usually reaches midleaf. Prefers acidic habitats.

Rhynchostegium aquaticum (p. 251) Stem leaves are 2–3 mm long, midrib ends above midleaf.

Sciuro-hypnum plumosum (p. 207) Grows near streams but out of water. Leaves with midribs to midleaf; capsule stalks are smooth at base but rough with tiny bumps above.

MICROSCOPIC FEATURES

Leaf edges are toothless. Leaf corner cells of *H. luridum* are small, square, and not much different from neighboring cells. Those of *H. ochraceum* are dramatically inflated and colorless. In *H. eugyrium* they are abruptly enlarged and orange.

Shiny, reddish gold, green-tipped plants grow standing
in water and are often encrusted with dirt

Leaves are strongly cupped
and often wrinkly

Curved capules
with lid

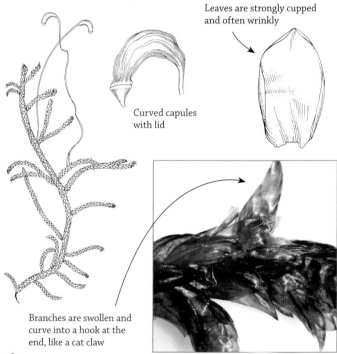

Branches are swollen and
curve into a hook at the
end, like a cat claw

Scorpidium scorpioides

SWOLLEN SCORPION MOSS

APPEARANCE: Robust aquatic and wetland plants, usually more than 10 cm long, with thick wormlike stems that can be creeping or erect-ascending. Younger plants are a beautiful shiny green, yellow green, or reddish gold, but older parts are often brown or black, and the plants commonly are encrusted with marl or slime. The crowded leaves are curved to one side and give a hooked appearance to the ends of stems.

LEAVES: Ovate, 2–3 mm long, strongly cupped and often wrinkled, with a blunt to sharp tip. Especially toward the ends of stems the leaves curve with the tips pointing in one direction and look something like cats' claws. Leaves lack both a midrib and teeth.

CAPSULES: Curved-cylindrical, 2–3 mm long, bent over at the tip of 3–5-cm-long wavy stalks. Lids are conical.

HABITAT: Calcareous fens and beach pools, submerged or emergent from shallow water with high pH and calcium bicarbonate content.

SIMILAR SPECIES

Hygrohypnum eugyrium/luridum/ochraceum (p. 281) Similar in color and leaf curvature, but plants are much smaller and inhabit wet rocks in and near mountain streams and waterfalls.

Rhytidium rugosum (p. 175) Grows in dry habitats, and its leaves have a midrib extending to midleaf.

Scorpidium revolvens (p. 173) Leaves are narrower, more strongly curved to one side like a sickle, and have a midrib.

MICROSCOPIC FEATURES

Short, double midrib. Basal cells are shorter than those at midleaf and have thick, pitted walls; a few cells in the basal corners are enlarged and thin-walled.

Upright shoots branch like a feather, look flat, and are densely covered in shiny, scale-like leaves

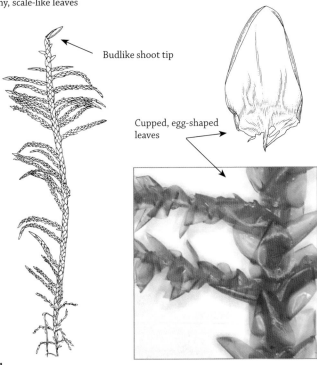

Budlike shoot tip

Cupped, egg-shaped leaves

Calliergonella cuspidata

BEECH BUD MOSS

APPEARANCE: Green to yellow-green plants form loose tufts of upward-arching stems, 3–10 cm tall, which branch pinnately in one plane. The shiny leaves are very densely packed together and overlapping like scales. Branch leaves spread out slightly when wet, stem leaves stay cupped close to the green stems; neither is much changed when dry. Tips of the flattened sprays end in long budlike points composed of tightly rolled leaves.

LEAVES: Egg-shaped, with a very short point at tip, cupped, 2 mm long. Midrib is lacking. Edges are smooth.

CAPSULES: Cylindrical, curved, and well bent over, 3–4 mm long; lid is conical. Stalk is reddish, smooth, and 3–5 cm tall.

HABITAT: Wetlands, especially open, calcium-enriched, grass and sedge meadows; usually growing with its feet wet on soggy soils or in shallow pools.

SIMILAR SPECIES

Tomentypnum nitens (p. 199) Plants are similar in size and form but stems are matted with rusty fuzz. Leaves are long lance-shaped, strongly pleated, 3–4 mm long.

Pleurozium schreberi (p. 287) Has similar shaped, cupped, yellow-green leaves that lack a midrib, but has reddish stems and grows in dry to wet sites.

Calliergon cordifolium and *C. giganteum* (p. 261) Have hooded blunt leaves with a midrib.

MICROSCOPIC FEATURES

Leaf cells are long and narrow except at base of leaf. Outside basal corner cells are large and inflated, and immediately adjacent cells are yellow and thick-walled. Large, clear cells from the stem strip off with leaf in dissection.

Large, feathery, cylindrical shoots sprawl or stand upright and form loose mats

Red stems easily visible through wet leaves

Capsule
with lid

Leaves deeply cupped

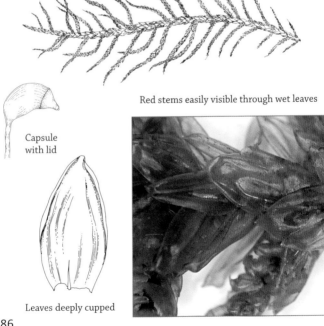

Pleurozium schreberi

PHOENIX FEATHER MOSS

APPEARANCE: Evoking a deep, shag carpet, the light green to yellowish plants form feathery, sprawling to ascending-upright sprays, 7–16 cm long. Stems divide irregularly or more commonly are once-pinnate, with the cylindrical branches diverging at a right angle to the stem in one plane. The bright red-orange stems show through the translucent leaves when wet, even though leaves are densely crowded and overlapping.

LEAVES: Ovate to elliptic, 1–3 mm long, and very cupped. Upper leaf edges curl inward, creating a peaked tip. Outside lower corners of the leaves are tinged with orange brown. Midrib is lacking and edges are smooth.

CAPSULES: Short-cylindrical, curved and tipped over to horizontal, about 2 mm long; lid is conical. Stalks 2–4 cm, reddish orange.

HABITAT: On soil, humus, and rock in a variety of forest types from dry to wet; also in bogs, fens, and among grasses in semi-open woodlands and road banks. Often carpeting large areas.

SIMILAR SPECIES

Brachythecium salebrosum (p. 205) Lacks red stems, its leaves have a short midrib and are more long-triangular, pleated, and feather out from the branches like foxtails.

Callicladium haldanianum (p. 289) Lacks red stems and its loosely overlapping leaves are less scale-like, giving the branches a more feathered or flattened, less wormlike shape.

Calliergonella cuspidata (p. 285) Grows only in basic wetlands, has green rather than red stems, and stem tips with tightly rolled leaves.

MICROSCOPIC FEATURES

Cells in outside lower corners of leaves are thick walled and orange brown.

Shiny, irregularly branching shoots loosely carpet growing surface

Ends of branches are flattened and pointed like the tip of a sword

Leaves loosely overlapping

Capsule upright at base but curved above; this one with lid

Callicladium haldanianum

SWORD MOSS

APPEARANCE: Yellow green and brown, somewhat shiny, irregularly branched but frequently untidy moss loosely carpets growing surface. Its branches tend to be short, tapered, and flattened at ends, like swords. Leaves are dense along branches, but only loosely overlapping, not scale-like, and flare out about 45 degrees. Similar wet and dry.

LEAVES: Narrowly ovate, 1–2 mm long, gradually tapering to a pointed tip, cupped. Tips are occasionally gently curved to one side. Midrib is lacking; edges are smooth.

CAPSULES: Cylindrical, erect at base then gently curved above, brown, 2–3 mm long; lid is short-beaked. Stalk is 1–3 cm and rust-colored.

HABITAT: Rotting logs and stumps, especially in dry and shady brushy areas. Also on acidic rocks or on tree bases and soil in moist forests.

SIMILAR SPECIES

Brachythecium salebrosum (p. 205) Leaves have a midrib, are somewhat pleated and more triangular, less rounded. Branches are not flattened at tips. Chubby capsules.

Brotherella recurvans (p. 185) Very shiny, with tightly overlapping leaves, the tips curling down, giving a tidy embroidered look to branches. Short capsules with a long-beaked lid while developing.

Entodon cladorrhizans (p. 293) Very shiny, leaves densely packed along stems, overlapping and strongly flattened together like scales. Capsules are upright.

Heterophyllium affine (p. 221) Stem leaves are 2–3 mm long; restricted to the Southern Appalachians.

MICROSCOPIC FEATURES

Cells in outside lower corners of leaf, the "earlobes," are large, square, and orange, differing from other cells in leaf, which are long and narrow.

Very shiny, cylindrical branches form patches that look like silky embroidery floss

Capsule with lid

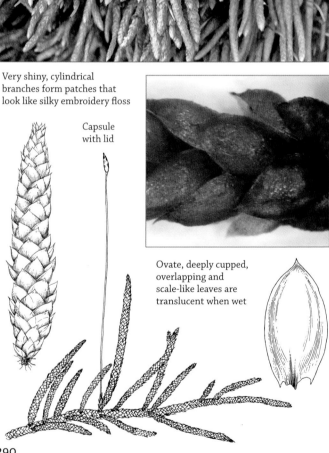

Ovate, deeply cupped, overlapping and scale-like leaves are translucent when wet

Entodon seductrix

CORD GLAZE MOSS

APPEARANCE: Very shiny, green or yellowish, wormlike moss that creeps horizontally, forming flat silky patches. Leaves are densely crowded, overlapping, scale-like, and form tightly cylindrical, or sometimes slightly flattened branches. Wet leaves are translucent, revealing the green to brown stems beneath. Dried, the moss looks like glossy embroidery floss.

LEAVES: Ovate-elliptic, 1–2 mm long, coming to an abrupt sharp point, very cupped. Midrib is lacking. Edges are smooth.

CAPSULES: Cylindrical, 2–4 mm long, upright to barely tilted, with a beaked lid. Stalk is 5–16 mm tall and rusty red.

HABITAT: Rocks, rotting logs, at base of trees in airy, dry woods or thickets.

SIMILAR SPECIES

Entodon cladorrhizans (p. 293) Similarly shiny but its branches are strongly flattened, not cylindrical.

Hypnum imponens (p. 181) Shiny with an orange cast, its leaves are long triangular with long narrow tips, and all curl down to the side, like a sickle.

Brotherella recurvans (p. 185) Similar oval-shaped leaves with abrupt tips, but the tips curl off to either side of stem, like a fringe of tiny sharp hairs, just escaping from the tight flat stems. Leaves about 1 mm long.

Thelia hirtella and *T. asprella* (p. 267) Cylindrical branches and scale-like leaves, but the plants are dull, not shiny.

MICROSCOPIC FEATURES

Many small, square cells at lower outside corners of leaf; otherwise cells are long and skinny.

Very shiny and flattened shoots
taper at the ends like satin swords

Upright capsule
with lid

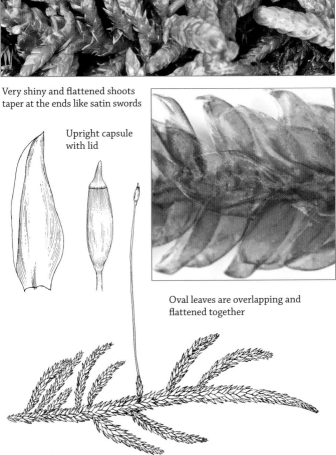

Oval leaves are overlapping and
flattened together

Entodon cladorrhizans

FLAT GLAZE MOSS

APPEARANCE: Stems are creeping, divide irregularly, and are densely covered in very shiny, overlapping, closely appressed leaves, thus forming flattened shoots that taper at either end, like satin swords. Stems sometimes are orange-tinged and fade into yellow or bright green branches. Leaf tips are sometimes curved down toward the ground. Not much changed wet or dry, though the shine and smooth flatness are more exaggerated when dry. Red-brown fuzz scattered along the undersides of the shoots attaches them to the substrate.

LEAVES: Oval, about 2 mm long, coming to a short, sharp tip, cupped. Midrib is lacking. Edges are smooth.

CAPSULES: Cylindrical, 2–3 mm long, upright, brown, with a blunt-beaked lid. Stalk is 7–20 mm tall and orange brown.

HABITAT: Rotting logs and tree trunk bases, sometimes also on soil, rocks, or old stone walls in dry shrubby woodlands.

SIMILAR SPECIES

Callicladium haldanianum (p. 289) Shoots are not as strongly flattened and tidy, leaves are not flattened and scale-like. Capsules are bent over.

Entodon seductrix (p. 291) Shiny shoots are cylindrical or slightly flattened, rather than strongly flat.

Brotherella recurvans (p. 185) Oval-shaped leaves with abrupt tips that are not held compressed to stem; instead they curl off, like a fringe of tiny sharp hairs, just escaping from the tight, flat stems. Leaves are about 1 mm long.

MICROSCOPIC FEATURES

Some leaves are notched or rounded, rather than coming to a short, sharp tip. Most leaf cells are long and skinny. Those in outer corners of leaf base are small and square.

Shoots are shiny and cylindrical (left) or flat (right);
comb-like when wet and crumpled when dry

Capsule
with lid

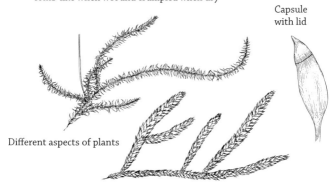

Different aspects of plants

Symmetrical egg-shaped leaves

Tip flares
outward

Base is cupped

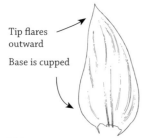

Plagiothecium cavifolium

ROUND SILK MOSS

APPEARANCE: Plants form mats of bright or olive green with a yellow cast. This species has two forms: one with cylindrical shoots bearing crowded, overlapping, cupped leaves held close to stem, just their tips wide-spreading; less commonly with flattened shoots bearing well-spaced, wide-spreading leaves. Some plants have shoots flattened at the tip but cylindrical below. Dry plants are shiny and more flattened, sometimes with slightly crumpled leaves.

LEAVES: Symmetrically ovate, 1–3 mm long, tapering gradually or abruptly to a short point, often cupped at base with curled tips when wet. Lacking midrib. Edges are smooth.

CAPSULES: Tubby cylindrical, 1–3 mm long, upright to somewhat curved and tilted, golden with a beaked lid. Stalk is 9–20 mm long. Capsules are infrequent.

HABITAT: Soil or humus, often overlying rock, or on rotting wood or tree bases, usually in moist, shady places.

SIMILAR SPECIES

Plagiothecium denticulatum (p. 297) Plants are strongly flattened; shoots are up to 5 cm long. Leaves are 2–3 mm long and asymmetrically ovate. Capsules are common, curved and bent to horizontal on 15–35-mm-tall stalks. Prefers wet habitats.

Plagiothecium laetum (p. 297) Plants are strongly flattened; shoots are up to 2 cm long. Leaves are 1–2 mm long, asymmetrically ovate-elliptic. Capsules are common.

Pseudotaxiphyllum elegans (p. 299) Leaves are 1–2 mm long with tiny branchlets scattered along stem at base of leaves.

MICROSCOPIC FEATURES

Lower outside corners run down stem and are narrow-triangular and made of rectangular cells.

Shoots are very flat and shiny, as if the patch were ironed to the ground

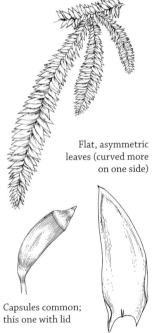

Flat, asymmetric leaves (curved more on one side)

Wet   *P. denticulatum*   Dry

Capsules common; this one with lid

Plagiothecium laetum

PRESSED SILK MOSS

APPEARANCE: Very shiny, flat, bright green to golden mats that look as though someone ironed them to the ground. Shoots are up to 2 cm long, not or irregularly branching. Leaves are loosely overlapping and spreading outward 45–90 degrees in one plane; similar in aspect wet or dry. Leaf tips are sometimes pointed down toward the substrate.

LEAVES: Ovate-elliptic, 1–2 mm long, tapering gradually to a sharp tip; surface is not cupped. One side of leaf is longer and more rounded than the other, giving an asymmetric tilt to the leaf. Lacking a midrib. Edges are smooth.

CAPSULES: Cylindrical, upright or barely tilted, 1–2 mm long, not wrinkled or pleated when dry; lid is beaked. Stalk is 8–16 mm long. Capsules are common.

HABITAT: On bases of trees, rotten logs, humus, steep soil banks, and sides of rocks and cliffs in dry to moist forests.

SIMILAR SPECIES

***Plagiothecium denticulatum*, WET SILK MOSS**: Shoots are up to 5 cm long; leaves are 2–3 mm long. Capsules are curved and bent to horizontal, usually wrinkled-pleated when dry, common; stalks are 15–35 mm long. Prefers wet habitats.

Plagiothecium cavifolium (p. 295) Leaves are symmetrical-ovate, 1–3 mm long. Plants with two forms: one with cylindrical shoots bearing crowded, cupped leaves held close to stem; less commonly with flattened shoots bearing well-spaced, wide-spreading leaves. Capsules are infrequent.

Pseudotaxiphyllum elegans (p. 299) Leaves are 1–2 mm long with tiny branchlets scattered along stem at base of leaves.

MICROSCOPIC FEATURES

Very tip of leaf is toothed in *P. denticulatum*. Lower outside corners of *P. laetum* leaves run down stem and are narrow-triangular and made of rectangular cells. In *P. denticulatum,* clusters are lobe-shaped and made of at least a few inflated round cells in addition to the rectangular ones.

Shoots are very shiny, flattened like a two-sided comb, and look as though plastered to growing surface

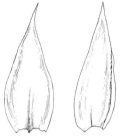

P. elegans (left) and *T. deplanatum* (right) leaves are symmetric

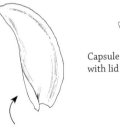

Capsule with lid

P. distichaceum leaves are asymmetric (curved more on one side than the other)

Tiny wormlike branchlets sprout from leaf bases along stems of *P. elegans* but are found only near stem tips in *P. distichaceum*

Pseudotaxiphyllum elegans

SPROUTING SILK MOSS

APPEARANCE: This shiny moss is flattened and creeping along the growing surface. Leaves flare outward from stem 80 degrees, opposite each other, like teeth of a two-sided comb. Not much changed wet or dry, with the leaves staying straight, rather than wavy. Leaves are uncrowded on stems, becoming sparser toward branch tips. Tiny, slender, wormlike branchlets with minute leaves sprout in clusters at leaf bases scattered here and there along length of stem.

LEAVES: Egg-shaped, symmetrical, 1–2 mm long, coming to an abruptly narrow little tip that flicks to the side in a gentle curl. Leaf bases wrap around stem, giving leaves an irregularly folded, asymmetric profile. Midrib is lacking. Edges are smooth.

CAPSULES: Cylindrical, 2 mm long, bent over; lid is conical. Stalk is 12–18 mm tall and orange red.

HABITAT: Moist, shady rocks, especially on acidic ledges. Sometimes also on forest soil.

SIMILAR SPECIES

Pseudotaxiphyllum distichaceum, **SCIMITAR SILK MOSS**: Its tiny branchlets are found only at leaf bases at tips of stems, like a frizzy pom-pom. Also its leaves tend to be wavy when dry and are asymmetrical and somewhat curved.

Taxiphyllum deplanatum, **COMBED SILK MOSS**: Lacks tiny branchlets. Leaves are more crowded and flatter.

Plagiothecium laetum and *P. denticulatum* (p. 297) Tend to look more plastered down and lack the stringy baby plantlets that help distinguish *Pseudotaxiphyllum*. Also, *P. denticulatum* has slightly longer leaves, 2–3 mm long.

MICROSCOPIC FEATURES

Cells in lower outside corners of leaf are not different in *Pseudotaxiphyllum* but small and square in *Taxiphyllum*. Tiny lance-shaped projections are found along stems of *T. deplanatum* when leaves are stripped off in dissection.

Branches arch away from tree trunks like shaggy shingles

Leaves are rippled and flattened together

Capsules nestled amid branches; these without lid

Asymmetric leaves, flat on one side, curved on the other

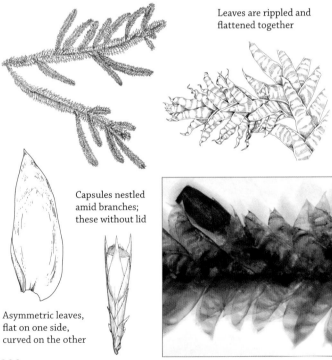

Neckera pennata

SHINGLE MOSS

APPEARANCE: Very flat branches of shiny, wavy leaves hang free from tree trunks like arching, shaggy shingles, 4–10 cm long. The bare and wiry stems clinging to the bark are easy to overlook, while the flat, irregularly dividing branches look like two-sided combs, densely covered in leaves angled 45 degrees to the side. New leaves are light green and older growth is olive brown.

LEAVES: Narrowly ovate, 2–3 mm long, asymmetric (curved on one side, flat on the other), gradually coming to a short, sharp point. Midrib is lacking. Leaves are clasping and flattened together to stem, and their surfaces are horizontally rippled, especially when dry. Edges are smooth.

CAPSULES: Urn-shaped capsules, 1–2 mm long, nearly stalkless and tightly surrounded by leaves on short side branches. Lid is short-beaked.

HABITAT: Tree trunks, especially old hardwoods in moist woods, occasionally on moist cliffs in gorges.

SIMILAR SPECIES

Homalia trichomanoides (p. 303) Leaves are rounder, lack ripples, and when dry, curve gently downward from branch, giving the plants an arching, ruffled look. Surface evokes moist frog skin: both shiny and dull.

Plagiothecium denticulatum and *Plagiothecium laetum* (p. 297) Leaves are not horizontally rippled, and branches don't fan up from growing surface. Mats look like shiny flat green waterfalls.

MICROSCOPIC FEATURES

Edges of upper leaf are finely toothed.

Drooping shoots look like scalloped, ruffled ribbons of frog skin

This moss looks quite like a liverwort

Capsule without lid

Leaves are plastered together, making it difficult to see the negligible midrib

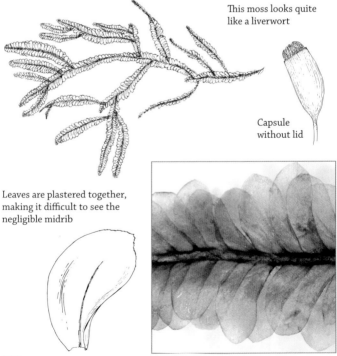

Homalia trichomanoides

FROG SKIN MOSS

APPEARANCE: Plants form mats of light olive green; their leaves are very densely packed, overlapping and flattened together along irregularly forked, sheetlike branches, 3–7 cm long. Leaves spread out 45 degrees from branches, but are plastered together, making it hard to distinguish individual leaves. When dry, the leaves curl gently downward from branches, giving the plants an arching, round-ruffled look. Leaf surface evokes moist frog skin, at once both shiny and dull. This moss could be easily mistaken for a leafy liverwort.

LEAVES: Oval, 1–2 mm long, with a rounded to bluntly pointed tip. Asymmetrical (convex curve on one side, flat to concave curve on the other). Midrib is fine, reaching midleaf at most and is often hard to see. Edges are smooth.

CAPSULES: Cylindrical, upright or slightly tilted, 1–2 mm long; lid is beaked. Stalk is 1–2 cm, red to yellow brown.

HABITAT: Rocks, acidic or basic; also found on tree bases and rotting logs.

SIMILAR SPECIES

Neckera pennata (p. 301) Branches and leaves similarly flattened, but sprays arch and fan upward, rather than curling under like wet ruffles. Leaves are more gradually pointed and horizontally rippled or wavy.

MICROSCOPIC FEATURES

Edge of upper leaf has tiny teeth. Upper leaf cells are hexagonal, middle cells are long and narrow, and cells in lower outside corners of leaf are short-rectangular.

Leaves spread widely, looking airy despite being crowded along creeping, irregularly branching shoots

Capsule without lid

Leaves abruptly narrow to tip

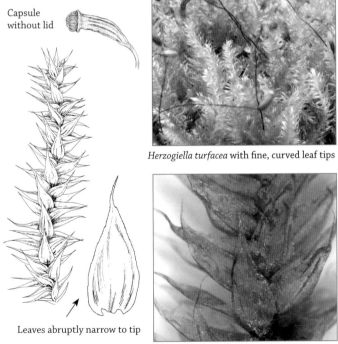

Herzogiella turfacea with fine, curved leaf tips

Herzogiella striatella

TASSEL MOSS

APPEARANCE: Forms shiny, bright green or yellowish mats. The horizontally creeping stems divide irregularly into upright branches that are densely packed with leaves. In spite of the crowded leaves, wet shoots seem airy as the leaf tips flare outward up to 90 degrees from erect leaf bases. Dry leaves are drawn in closer, stand upright, and sometimes are slightly pleated; shoots can be gently flattened.

LEAVES: Oval, 1–2 mm long, abruptly tapered to a long narrow tip, cupped. Midrib is lacking. Edges are smooth.

CAPSULES: Cylindrical, 1–2 mm long, horizontal, contracted below mouth and pleated when dry, with a short-beaked lid. Stalk is 9–20 mm long and reddish to light brown.

HABITAT: Forest floor, on soil, humus, base of trees, tree roots, rock, and logs in moist shady sites.

SIMILAR SPECIES

Herzogiella turfacea, **FLAT TASSEL MOSS**: Branches are somewhat flattened; leaves spreading widely to either side of branch with their tips curved downward. Typically on decaying wood.

Pseudotaxiphyllum elegans (p. 299) Shoots are strongly flattened, looking like two-sided combs. Tiny wormlike branchlets sprout in clusters at leaf bases along stem. Usually on moist rocks.

Plagiothecium spp. (pp. 295–297) Plants are strongly flattened or flattened at shoot tips and cylindrical below. Leaves are more gradually tapering to short point.

MICROSCOPIC FEATURES

Upper half of leaf edge is toothed. Compared to other cells in the leaf, cells in basal outside corners of *H. striatella* are dramatically larger, transparent, and thin-walled. These corners run down onto the stem. Both of these characters are lacking in *H. turfacea*, whose corner cells are square and not inflated. Stems lack tiny projections beneath leaves.

Tiny, threadlike, trailing stems look spiky or starry due to crowded leaves with wide-flaring tips

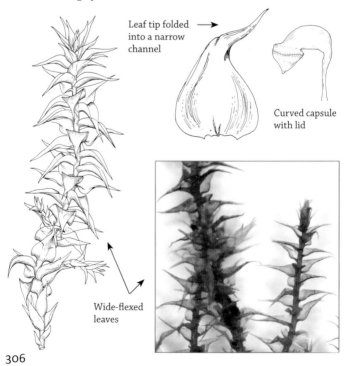

Leaf tip folded into a narrow channel

Curved capsule with lid

Wide-flexed leaves

Campylophyllum hispidulum

TINY STAR MOSS

APPEARANCE: Grass green plants form mats of tiny, bristly, threadlike trailing stems that branch irregularly. Leaves are crowded with their bases held close to stems but the tips flex outward 90 degrees, giving shoots an airy, spiky aspect. Similar wet or dry.

LEAVES: Ovate, less than 1 mm long, the wide base abruptly narrowing to a very fine, arching tip that is furrowed to form a U-shaped channel. Leaves are cupped, lack a midrib, and have smooth edges.

CAPSULES: Cylindrical, curved, 1–2 mm long, drawn in below mouth; lid is conical. Stalk is orange, 8–15 mm.

HABITAT: Soil, rocks, logs, and tree bases, preferring calcium-enriched and damp hardwood forests.

SIMILAR SPECIES

Campylium stellatum (p. 195) A much larger plant with upright branches; leaves 1–3 mm long. Common in wetlands.

Campyliadelphus chrysophyllus (p. 193) Leaves are 1–2 mm long with midrib that reaches midleaf.

Platydictya confervoides and *P. subtilis* (p. 229) Tinier leaves, 0.2–0.5 mm long, are narrowly triangular and spread 30 degrees when wet and are upright and pressed to stems when dry.

Pylaisia selwynii (p. 225) Stringy branches that curl upward, against gravity. Dry leaves are pressed tight to the branches except for their wispy leaf tips that all curve off to the side.

MICROSCOPIC FEATURES

Leaf edges are shallowly toothed. Cells in lower corners of leaves are square and gradually transition from surrounding long oval-shaped cells.

Scruffy-looking shoots stand upright from trailing mats. Plants branch regularly or irregularly, and their red stems and branches show between crowded leaves

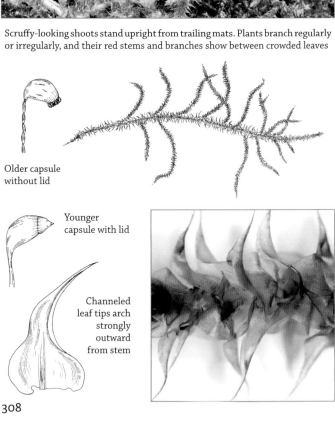

Older capsule
without lid

Younger
capsule with lid

Channeled
leaf tips arch
strongly
outward
from stem

Rhytidiadelphus subpinnatus

CHANNELED SHAGGY MOSS

APPEARANCE: Scruffy loose mats with stiff stems trailing to ascending, up to 15 cm long, irregularly branched to pinnate. Yellow green to green leaves are close but not so tightly packed as to hide red branches and stems. Leaves flare away from stem and the tips arch even farther downward. Not much changed wet or dry.

LEAVES: Stem leaves are 2–4 mm long; branch leaves are 1–3 mm long. Triangular, wide and rounded but not clasping at base, coming to a narrow, long point. Tip edges are folded upward into a channel exaggerating the sharpness of point. Midrib is weak, forked, no longer than ⅓ leaf length. Leaf surface and edges are smooth.

CAPSULES: Short macaroni shape, 1–2 mm long, bent over to horizontal, with a conical lid. Stalks 2–3 cm.

HABITAT: On soil, humus, logs, and tree roots in moist shady forests, often along streams or in spray of waterfalls.

SIMILAR SPECIES

Rhytidiadelphus triquetrus (p. 259) Tends to be more upright and its leaves are pleated, more gradually taper to a point, and lack the channeled tip.

Loeskeobryum brevirostre (p. 311) New stems are upright-arching from creeping older stems; stem leaves are moderately pleated with base clasping stem, especially obvious near base of new stem innovations.

Pleurozium schreberi (p. 287) Leaves are more densely packed so that stem is visible through but not between the leaves, oval to egg-shaped with a blunt tip and very cupped.

MICROSCOPIC FEATURES

Leaves, especially near tips, have tiny teeth along edges. Cells, as seen from back of leaf, are smooth, bumpless. Cells in lower corner leaf lobes are rounded, clear, and thin-walled compared to nearby cells in leaf base.

Arching stems divide into irregular feather-like branches and form loose mats in cool, moist forests.

Branch leaf   Stem leaf

Leaves pleated, tip finely toothed

Capsule with lid

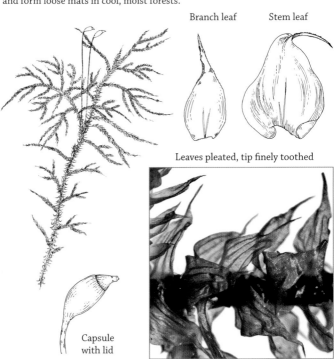

Loeskeobryum brevirostre

PINCHED SHAGGY MOSS

APPEARANCE: Robust yellow green, golden, or dark green mosses forming airy mats with new stems upright-arching from the older ones. Stem leaves are not crowded, their bases clasp the dark red stems; the rest of the leaf curves outward away from the stem. Branch leaves are not clasping, but spread outward and then curve upward toward the branch tip. Not much changed upon drying.

LEAVES: Stem leaves are 2–3 mm long, ovate, abruptly narrowed to a slender, elongate, sometimes rumpled tip, moderately pleated. Branch leaves are 1–2 mm long, cupped, and gradually tapered to a sharp tip. Midrib is variable: lacking or double and extending no further than midleaf. Edges are smooth except at apex where teeth are visible with good lighting.

CAPSULES: Bent over or horizontal, 2–3 mm long, egg-shaped. Lid is conical with stout beak. Stalk 1–4 cm.

HABITAT: Over soil, humus, rotten logs, and rocks in humid mixed hardwood-hemlock forests of the Appalachian Mountains, especially near waterfalls and along streams in deep ravines; also in moist oceanic forests of the Northeast.

SIMILAR SPECIES

Hylocomium splendens (p. 313) Sports new stems arching from the old in a distinctive stair-step pattern with each "step" a flat fernlike spray.

Rhytidiadelphus subpinnatus (p. 309) Unpleated stem leaves that do not clasp the stem. Stem and branch leaves differ in size but are otherwise similar.

Rhytidiadelphus triquetrus (p. 259) Larger, triangular stem leaves, 3–5 mm long, that gradually taper to a broad apex.

MICROSCOPIC FEATURES

Tiny, green hairs, called paraphyllia, clothe the stems and branches. Cells across base of stem leaves are golden brown with strongly pitted walls.

Plants form loose mats of arching, fernlike shoots growing in a stair-step habit

3×-pinnate branches in one plane

Midrib faint, short or absent

Stem leaves wider and at least 2× as long as branch leaves; often pleated

Capsule with lid

Hylocomium splendens

STAIR-STEP MOSS

APPEARANCE: Olive green, fernlike, thrice-pinnate moss; each year's growth is a flat, horizontal spray arising from the back of the previous year's growth, like ascending stair steps. Close inspection of the wiry, rust-colored stems reveals a covering of tiny, green hairs (easiest to see when dry). Branches taper to slender tips. Leaves cling tightly to branchless portion of stems, but spread up to 45 degrees on upper stem and on branches when wet; not much altered upon drying. The arching stair-step growth form is unique and distinctive to this species.

LEAVES: Stem leaves are 2–3 mm long, ovate, cupped, sometimes pleated, abruptly narrowed to a long, crimped point. Branch leaves are similar except only around 1 mm long and narrower. Midrib is lacking and edges of leaf are smooth.

CAPSULES: Stubby cylindrical, bent over to horizontal, 2–3 mm long, with a beaked lid. Stalk is 1–3 cm tall, rust colored.

HABITAT: Forest floor of cool, moist coniferous and hardwood forests of the north and at higher elevations in the southern mountains; on soil, humus, rotten logs, and rocks.

SIMILAR SPECIES

Thuidium delicatulum (p. 271) Another fernlike, regularly 2–3×-divided moss; however, it lacks the raised stair-step growth form of *Hylocomium splendens*, and its leaves have a midrib.

Pleurozium schreberi (p. 287) A spreading to ascending-upright, yellowish moss that resembles an ill-formed, irregularly branched *Hylocomium splendens*. Its leaves are deeply cupped and lack the abrupt, long narrow point of *Hylocomium*.

MICROSCOPIC FEATURES

Higher magnification reveals fine teeth along upper edges of leaves and a short double midrib.

Wet shoots look bushy
(*A. rugelii* above)

Dry plants form patchy mats like
shriveled shag carpet with upward-
curved branches (*A. minor* above)

A. rugelii has
narrow-tipped leaves
that become quite
crumpled when dry

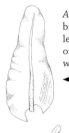

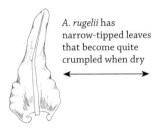

A. minor leaves have
broad and rounded
leaf tips and become
only slightly curled
when dry

Anomodon minor

ROUNDED TONGUE MOSS

APPEARANCE: Plants form mats of dark olive to yellow green that adhere very loosely to their growing surface, and when dry, look like shriveled shag carpet. The main stems are creeping and nearly bare, producing leafy branches that arch upward and curl when dry to form a hook. Wet plants are bushy, as their dense, straight leaves spread out 75 degrees from somewhat flattened branches. When dry, the leaves are scale-like, drawn in around the stem, only slightly curled, the tips remaining flat.

LEAVES: Oval at base, gradually tapering to a broad tongue-like blade, rounded at top, about 1–2 mm long. Leaf base clasps the stem with a wide ruffle-like collar. Midrib ends just shy of leaf tip and is pale compared to surrounding blade. Edges of leaves are smooth.

CAPSULES: Cylindrical urn-shaped, upright, about 2 mm long on a 4–16-mm-high stalk.

HABITAT: Tree trunks and bases, also on calcium-enriched rocks.

SIMILAR SPECIES

***Anomodon rugelii*, RUFFLED TONGUE MOSS**: Pear-shaped leaves are more narrowed at tip, somewhat crumpled when dry with the margins incurved, making the tips look sharply pointed. Midrib is dark brown, at least near leaf base.

Anomodon attenuatus (p. 239) Much more branched, ends of branches are of two types, either rounded and curled under, like kitten paws, or narrowed and stringy, like a rat tail.

Anomodon viticulosus (p. 191) Leaves are 2–4 mm long, and curve to the side and crumple when dry.

MICROSCOPIC FEATURES

Leaf cells are round and covered in several small, craggy bumps, except cells along bottom edge of leaf, which are long and clear. *A. rugelii* leaves have small earlobe-shaped extensions in the lower outside corners, lacking in *A. minor*.

Leafless plants, at first glance resembling a fungus, a seed, or a "bug on a stick" rather than a moss

Capsules with lid

Capsules have a flat, long lentil shape with a nose-like lid

Bumpy stalk ends in collar

Capsule leaves fringe base of capsule stalk

Plants lack typical leaves, and their brown threadlike protonema blend in with soil

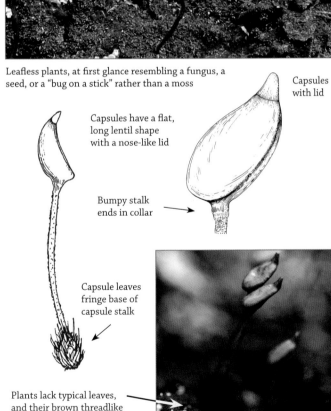

Buxbaumia aphylla

ALADDIN'S LAMP MOSS

APPEARANCE: Leafless moss; its stalked capsules, like lentils with an upturned nose, appear to arise directly from a dark green to blackish crust on the ground. New, bright green capsules form in early winter, making this the easiest season to search for this moss, which looks more like a fungus than a plant.

LEAVES: Only a few tiny leaves at base of capsule stalk. Gametophyte is almost entirely protonema, a mat of brown and green algal-like threads.

CAPSULES: Flattened, asymmetric egg-shape, like a satellite dish, 3–6 mm long, with a rounded beak at the top. Inclined at a 45–90-degree angle. Bright green when young, turning copper-colored and shiny when mature, the base of beak ringed by dark red. Stalk is 4–11 mm tall, thicker than most stalks and expanded into a collar just below capsule.

HABITAT: Disturbed, acidic soil, such as along roads and woodland trails, also on humus, well-decayed logs and stumps; partially shaded to open sites. Often associated with black algal-protonemal crust on soil. This is not a common moss, but it is unique and easy to identify in the field.

SIMILAR SPECIES

No other species has similar capsules, and since the leaves are so minute they are not likely to be noticed on their own, this moss is unmistakable. This species has also been called Bug-on-a-stick.

SPECIAL ECOLOGICAL NOTE

Similar to *Diphyscium foliosum* (p. 163), the flat-topped capsule faces the angle with maximum sunlight. Raindrops striking the capsules expel spores like puffball fungi.

The filamentous protonema is the juvenile stage of leafy moss gametophytes, which in this case never amount to much.

Capsule stalks arise from
bright green algal-like mat

Capsules without lid,
with hairy hood, and
with lid but without hood
(from left to right)

Developing capsule

Brown lance-shaped
leaves form
inconspicuous clusters
at base of capsule stalks

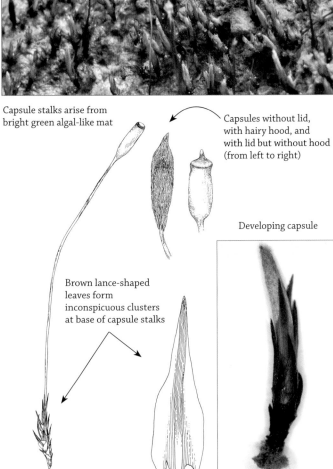

Pogonatum pensilvanicum

ALGAL HAIRCAP MOSS

APPEARANCE: The upright, cylindrical capsules of this moss rise on long stalks from a mat of bright green algal-like filaments, called protonema, covering the soil. Closer inspection reveals small clusters, 2–6 mm high, of upright, overlapping, green to brownish leaves scattered amid the protonema. These leaves curl slightly when dry.

LEAVES: Oval at the base, tapering to a lance-shaped tip, 2–4 mm long and brown. Leaves have a dull, waxy surface due to the midrib being several layers thick. Midrib is pale yellow near base of leaf and dark red at tip. Edges are smooth.

CAPSULES: Upright to slightly inclined cylinders, 2–4 mm long, with a hairy hood over the short-beaked lid. Stalk is 1–3 cm tall.

HABITAT: Bare, disturbed soil, especially in shady moist spots. It is a common pioneer of woodland road cuts, eroding river banks, and muddy bottoms of overturned trees.

SIMILAR SPECIES

The persistent protonema and tiny leafy shoots differentiate this species from others of *Pogonatum, Polytrichastrum,* and *Polytrichum*. Furthermore, capsules of *Polytrichastrum* and *Polytrichum* are mostly angled, like a box, rather than smoothly cylindrical, as in *Pogonatum*.

MICROSCOPIC FEATURES

Leaves are toothed at a microscopic level. Midrib is covered by parallel strips of cells stacked about 4–5 cells high (never more than 8).

SPECIAL ECOLOGICAL NOTE

The protonema are the juvenile stage of leafy moss gametophytes. Usually transitory and inconspicuous, the protonema and capsules are the most distinctive features of this moss. The bright green filaments aid the photosynthetic needs of the moss beyond the capacity of the small leaves.

Stiff plants with large pom-pom heads

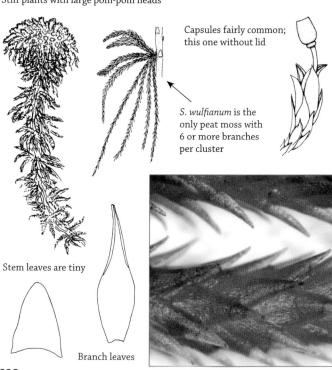

Capsules fairly common; this one without lid

S. wulfianum is the only peat moss with 6 or more branches per cluster

Stem leaves are tiny

Branch leaves

Sphagnum wulfianum

POM-POM PEAT MOSS

APPEARANCE: Robust plants with a large apical head resembling a pom-pom or a dry head of clover. Plants are dull green to brownish green, growing scattered in loose tufts (rather than in mats or carpets typical of other peat mosses). With their stiff, almost woody, upright stems and oversized shaggy heads, the plants suggest British royal guards with their bearskin hats. *S. wulfianum* is one of the easiest peat mosses to recognize because it is the only *Sphagnum* with 6 or more branches per cluster.

LEAVES: Branch leaves are 1 mm long, lance-shaped with long, narrow tips that are reflexed when dry, giving the branches the look of frizzy foxtails. Stem leaves are tiny, less than 1 mm long, oblong-triangular, with blunt tips. Margins are without teeth. No midrib.

CAPSULES: Fairly common, brown to black, spherical, about 2 mm in diameter.

HABITAT: Usually in wet, nutrient-rich conifer forests such as white cedar swamps or forested fens with tamarack and black spruce, but also found under alder and poison sumac. Nearly always shaded, growing on damp soil, humus, or on well-rotted logs and stumps. *S. wulfianum* inhabits the driest sites of all our peat mosses.

SIMILAR SPECIES

No other species of *Sphagnum* has 6 or more branches per cluster and such a dominant shaggy apical head.

MICROSCOPIC FEATURES

Green cells of branch leaves are more or less equally exposed on both surfaces. Strongly ringed pores are common on convex surface with a few small pores on the concave surface.

Plants with large heads and open, spiky branches

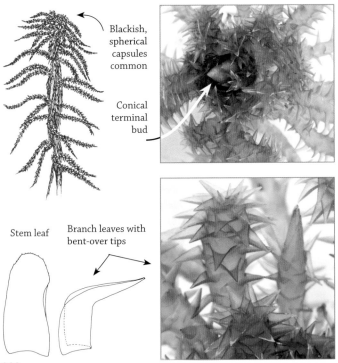

Blackish, spherical capsules common

Conical terminal bud

Stem leaf

Branch leaves with bent-over tips

322

Sphagnum squarrosum

SPIKY PEAT MOSS

APPEARANCE: Plants are robust, upright, 8–20 cm tall, forming loose carpets, bright to pale green, with a spiky appearance due to branch leaves pointing outward from the branches. The conical terminal bud in the center of the apical head is large and conspicuous when viewed from above; when viewed from the side it is overtopped by nearby branches.

LEAVES: Branch leaves are 2–3 mm long, with an oval broad base clasping the branch and the apical half abruptly narrowed to a half-tubular tip that is bent outward away from the branch at a 45–90-degree angle. Stem leaves are 1–2 mm long, oblong, with broadly rounded tips. Margins are without teeth. No midrib.

CAPSULES: Common, brown to black, spherical, about 2 mm in diameter.

HABITAT: Nutrient-rich, wet conifer forests, such as white cedar swamps, forested fens with tamarack, and stream sides under alders and willows. Usually found in shade.

SIMILAR SPECIES

Sphagnum palustre (p. 325) Similar in size and sometimes has branch leaves that bend away from the branch, but the plants often have brown or pink splotches and leaves with hooded tips.

MICROSCOPIC FEATURES

Green cells of branch leaves are exposed more broadly on the convex surface. Pores are common on both surfaces, ringed on the concave surface and unringed on the convex surface.

Sphagnum palustre

Sphagnum papillosum

Plump, wormlike branches
with tapered ends

Sphagnum magellanicum

Stem leaf (cells
not fully drawn in)

Branch leaves
with blunt,
hooded tips

Sphagnum palustre

BLUNT-LEAVED PEAT MOSS

APPEARANCE: Plants are large, upright, 8–25 cm tall, forming carpets and hummocks; green to yellowish brown, sometimes with a pink blush (but never purplish red). Apical head with plump wormlike branches with tapered ends.

LEAVES: Branch leaves are 2–3 mm long, egg-shaped, margins inrolled above, forming a blunt hooded apex, sometimes with the tips bent away from the branch at up to a 45-degree angle. Stem leaves are 1–2 mm long, tongue-shaped. Margins are without teeth. No midrib.

CAPSULES: Uncommon, brown to black, spherical, about 2 mm in diameter.

HABITAT: Swampy coniferous and hardwood forests, forested fens, sedge meadows, and at the margins of streams, bogs, and ponds; more typically shaded than in full sun.

SIMILAR SPECIES

Sphagnum magellanicum, **MAGENTA PEAT MOSS**: Very similar in structure but is commonly purplish red and grows in open acid bogs.

Sphagnum papillosum, **OCHRE PEAT MOSS**: Another similar species of open acid bogs but is commonly golden brown and has shorter branches with blunt ends.

Green plants could be any of these three as well as several other species of *Sphagnum*. Precise species determination usually requires the use of microscopic characters.

MICROSCOPIC FEATURES

Outer cells of stems and branches have delicate spiral wall thickenings visible with staining. Green cells of branch leaves in *S. palustre* and *S. papillosum* are triangular and exposed more broadly on the concave surface. In *S. magellanicum*, they are elliptical, lie midway between the concave and convex surfaces, unexposed. Pores are numerous and large on the convex surface in *S. palustre*, fewer on concave. In the other two species pores are few to none on both surfaces.

Small, yellowish green plants with short, curved branches

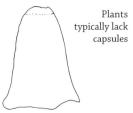

Stem leaf

Plants typically lack capsules

Apical head appears twisted because of curved branches

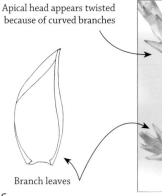

Branch leaves

Sphagnum subsecundum

COW-HORN PEAT MOSS

APPEARANCE: Plants small, slender, upright, forming small mounds or loose carpets, 6–12 cm tall, sometimes submerged in water; green, yellow green, or golden brown. The apical head is domed and appears twisted when viewed from above; the branches are short and curved. Terminal bud is not visible.

LEAVES: Branch leaves are about 1 mm long, egg-shaped, usually with their tips curved in the same direction. Stem leaves are less than 1 mm long, triangular to tongue-shaped, tips rounded. Margins are without teeth. No midrib.

CAPSULES: Rare, brown to black, spherical, 2 mm in diameter.

HABITAT: In open to semi-open wet sites with moderate to high nutrient enrichment, such as sedge meadows and margins of fens. Sometimes submerged or in shady swamps or alder thickets.

SIMILAR SPECIES

Sphagnum cuspidatum (p. 331) Branch leaves are 2–4 mm long and lance-shaped.

Sphagnum fallax (p. 329) Apical head is star-shaped with straight branches.

MICROSCOPIC FEATURES

Green cells of branch leaves are exposed equally on both surfaces to somewhat more broadly on the convex surface. Branch leaf colorless cells have numerous small pores looking like strings of beads on convex surface, few or none on concave.

Note capsules in upper left corner

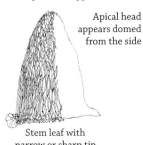

Stem leaf with narrow or sharp tip (cells not fully drawn in)

Apical head appears domed from the side

Viewed from above, head is starlike with short, spreading branches

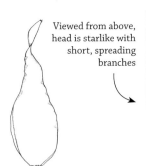

Branch leaf

Sphagnum fallax

TRICKY PEAT MOSS

APPEARANCE: Plants medium-sized to large, 8–20 cm tall, commonly upright and forming carpets, sometimes submerged in water; green, yellow green to yellowish brown. Apical head is domed and usually star-shaped as viewed from above, with leaves weakly to clearly arranged in five rows on the branches.

LEAVES: Branch leaves are 1–2 mm long, lance-shaped, wavy, and spreading away from the branch when dry. Stem leaves are about 1 mm long, triangular with tip pinched into a sharp point. Margins are without teeth. No midrib.

CAPSULES: Uncommon, brown to black, spherical, about 2 mm in diameter.

HABITAT: Abundant in open bogs and fens, especially in wetter areas at or near water level, sometimes submerged; also in shaded habitats and on seepage over rock outcrops.

SIMILAR SPECIES

Sphagnum cuspidatum (p. 331) Apical head is messy, with poor differentiation of spreading and hanging branches. Branch leaves are 2–4 mm long.

MICROSCOPIC FEATURES

Green cells of branch leaves are exposed more broadly on the convex surface. Pores on both surfaces are few and inconspicuous.

Delicate, feathery plants float in the water; when removed from water, they collapse like a tangle of matted fur

Plants have a poorly developed apical head

Stem leaves have sharp tips (cells not fully drawn in)

Capsule with lid

Branch leaves

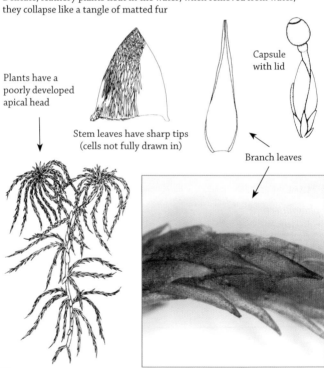

Sphagnum cuspidatum

LONGLEAF PEAT MOSS

APPEARANCE: Plants are medium-sized to large, submerged in water, trailing when stranded, or upright forming carpets, 10–20 cm tall or even longer in water; green to yellow, some branches in the head may be tinged brown. The aquatic plants have a feathery appearance, the head floating at the water's surface. When pulled from the water, the flaccid stems and branches collapse, giving the wet tangled mass the appearance of matted fur. The apical head may be poorly differentiated, and branches scarcely noticeable as spreading and hanging. Emergent plants are more typical of peat mosses and bear weakly star-shaped heads as seen from above.

LEAVES: Branch leaves are 2–4 mm long, lance-shaped with long pointed tips, often curved, especially at branch tips where the leaves all curve in the same direction. Stem leaves are 1 mm long, triangular with pointed tips. Margins are without teeth. No midrib.

CAPSULES: Infrequent, brown to black, spherical, about 2 mm in diameter.

HABITAT: Submerged near margins of acidic lakes, in shallow pools and wet hollows of peatlands; emergent at the margin of bog mats and forming carpets over areas just above water level. One of our most aquatic peat mosses.

SIMILAR SPECIES

Sphagnum fallax (p. 329) Apical head is well-differentiated and star-shaped with pairs of young hanging branches between the rays. Branch leaves are no longer than 2 mm.

MICROSCOPIC FEATURES

Green cells of branch leaves are exposed more broadly on the convex surface. Pores on both surfaces are few, small, and inconspicuous.

Sphagnum warnstorfii

Characteristic red-green growth

Sphagnum russowii

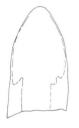

Stem leaf, notched at tip in *S. russowii*

Branch leaf

Sphagnum capillifolium

Starlike and flat-topped apical head; note lack of terminal bud

Sphagnum warnstorfii

RED-GREEN PEAT MOSS

APPEARANCE: Plants small to medium-sized, upright, 6–15 cm, loosely packed to form soft carpets and small hummocks; purplish red in bright sunlight to dark green in shade, but typically a mixture of red and green. Apical head is flat-topped, star-shaped when viewed from above, lacking a visible terminal bud. Stems are slender; upper spreading branches extend at right angles to the stem, with leaves clearly arranged in five rows.

LEAVES: Branch leaves average 1 mm long and are lance-shaped; when dry the tips are reflexed. Stem leaves are 1 mm long, tongue-shaped with rounded to broadly pointed tips. Margins are without teeth. No midrib.

CAPSULES: Uncommon, spherical, about 2 mm in diameter.

HABITAT: Restricted to nutrient-rich sites, such as open fens and white cedar swamps.

SIMILAR SPECIES

Sphagnum capillifolium, **DOMED PEAT MOSS**: Grows in more acidic, nutrient-poor habitats. Its apical head is domed rather than star-shaped, and the branch leaves are not in rows.

Sphagnum russowii, **STARRY PEAT MOSS**: Has small but visible terminal bud, and its stem leaves have a small notch at the tip. Plants are often tinged with pink. Found in bogs, on banks, or in seepage over rocks in conifer forests.

MICROSCOPIC FEATURES

Stem cortical cells are without pores or fibrils. Green cells of branch leaves are exposed more broadly on the concave surface. Colorless cells toward tip of branch leaf have tiny, ringed pores on convex surface in *S. warnstorfii*; few or no pores on concave surface. *S. capillifolium* and *S. russowii* have larger pores. Stem leaf colorless cells of *S. capillifolium* have fibrils, whereas the colorless cells of *S. russowii* and *S. warnstorfii* are without fibrils and are once or not divided.

Brownish plants, commonly with capsules, are crowded together into a smooth carpet on drier patches of a wetland.

Capsule with lid

Broad, tongue-shaped stem leaf

Branch leaf

Terminal bud lacking at center of flat apical head

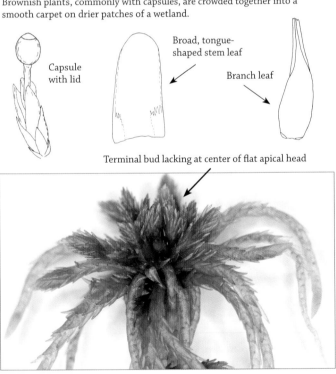

Sphagnum fuscum

TAWNY PEAT MOSS

Appearance: Small, slender, upright, 7–15 cm, densely packed plants forming large, firm hummocks; deep ruddy brown or occasionally greenish brown; never any trace of red or pink. The flat-topped apical heads crowded closely together give the hummock a rather smooth surface. No terminal bud is visible at the center of the head.

Leaves: Branch leaves are about 1 mm long, lance-shaped. Stem leaves are about 1 mm long, tongue-shaped, with broadly rounded tips. Margins are without teeth. No midrib.

Capsules: Common, brown to black, spherical, about 2 mm in diameter.

Habitat: Open, acid bogs on tops of hummocks; relatively high above the water level, in the driest and most acidic microhabitats of the bog.

Similar Species

No other small brown hummock-forming peat mosses are common in the region; other brownish species are significantly larger and closer to water level.

Microscopic Features

Green cells of branch leaves are exposed more broadly on the concave surface. Pores are few on convex surface, very few to none on concave. Stem leaves are broadly bordered with narrow cells at the base; colorless cells are commonly divided near the leaf apex. Cells of the stem cortex lack pores.

Starlike head with a small but visible terminal bud and long, spreading branches

Stem leaves with ragged tips cover wiry stems that snap crisply when bent

Capsules uncommon

Branch leaves

Sphagnum girgensohnii

GRACEFUL PEAT MOSS

APPEARANCE: Plants are large, 8–20 cm tall, stiff, in extensive loose carpets; green, or occasionally yellowish or brownish green, never with any hint of red or pink. The wiry stem snaps crisply like a celery stalk when bent double. The apical head is flat-topped, distinctly star-shaped as viewed from above, and has a visible but small terminal bud. The spreading branches extend laterally at right angles to the stem and then curve downward with long, slender tips.

LEAVES: Branch leaves are 1–2 mm long, lance-shaped, margins without teeth. Stem leaves are 1 mm long, tongue-shaped with a broadly rounded fringed apex. No midrib.

CAPSULES: Uncommon, brown to black, spherical, about 2 mm in diameter.

HABITAT: Common and widespread in our region; a shade-loving species found on moist soil and humus in a variety of forest types.

SIMILAR SPECIES

Sphagnum fimbriatum (p. 339) Apical head is smaller with a conspicuous terminal bud; plants usually have capsules. Stem leaves are broadest above the middle and tattered partway down the sides.

Sphagnum russowii (p. 333) Plants typically show at least some red; stem leaves have a small notch at the tip.

MICROSCOPIC FEATURES

Green cells of branch leaves are exposed more broadly on the concave surface. Pores are abundant on convex surface, fewer on concave. Stem leaves have broad borders of narrow cells on either side of a sieve-like area of enlarged cells at the base.

Loose, flexible plants with gracefully curving branches commonly produce capsules (with lid above)

Oversized terminal bud dwarfs small apical head

Stem leaf with ragged tip

Branch leaves

Sphagnum fimbriatum

FRINGED PEAT MOSS

APPEARANCE: Medium-sized plants, upright, 7–20 cm tall, in loose carpets or soft mounds; grayish green, or occasionally yellowish or brownish green, never with any hint of red or pink. Atop the rather flexible, slender stem, the center of the small apical head is accented by an oversized terminal bud. The very long, slender spreading branches arch gracefully out and downward.

LEAVES: Branch leaves are 1–2 mm long, egg- to lance-shaped, margins without teeth. Stem leaves are 1–2 mm long, often as broad as long, fan-shaped (widest above the middle); margin is tattered across the upper third of the leaf. When the apical head is pulled off the stem, the clasping stem leaves project as an erect "ruff" surrounding the torn end of the stem. No midrib.

CAPSULES: Common, brown to black, spherical, about 2 mm in diameter. More commonly found with sporophytes than any other peat moss.

HABITAT: In both shaded and open fens with good nutrient availability. Often at the shrubby margin where open bog meets bog forest.

SIMILAR SPECIES

Sphagnum girgensohnii (p. 337) Stem is much more rigid, head has less conspicuous terminal bud and usually lacks capsules. Stem leaves are fringed only across the apex.

Sphagnum russowii (p. 333) Plants typically show at least some red; terminal buds are visible but small. Stem leaves have a small notch at the tip.

MICROSCOPIC FEATURES

Green cells of branch leaves are exposed more broadly on the concave surface. Pores are abundant on convex surface, fewer on concave. Stem leaves have broad borders of narrow cells on either side of a sieve-like area of enlarged cells at the base.

How to Use the Identification Keys

An identification key is a tool, a systematic, step-by-step approach to identify a plant. Our keys are dichotomous, which means they are made of paired descriptions, called couplets. Always begin with couplet 1 and read both of the contrasting descriptions, called leads. Which of the two best describes your plant? It need not match every detail of your specimen perfectly; choose whichever lead is a more accurate description of the moss you wish to identify. In some critical places, we have provided illustrations to help you visualize what is being described.

At the end of each lead, you will find either the scientific name of a plant (in italics) or a number directing you to the next pair of contrasting statements. If it is a number, go to that number (skip all the intervening numbers and descriptions) and read the two leads of that couplet, again choosing the better of the two descriptions. The process of keying continues from one couplet to another until you reach a name rather than a number at the end of the lead. When you arrive at a name, turn to the indicated page. Compare your plant with the photographs and drawings; read the description. Be sure to check the section listing "Similar Species," and perhaps check those pages as well. Assess how well your moss matches the illustrations and description. If you are satisfied with the match, you have identified your plant.

If you don't like the match, consider couplets in the key where you were uncertain which lead to follow. Return to the key and choose the lead not followed to see if you arrive at a better match on your second try. As with all tools, the more experience you have in using the tool, the better the results.

If you have tried several routes through a particular key and seem no closer to a good match, consider the possibility that we may have interpreted leaf shape differently. Or, perhaps you have overlooked a faint midrib, or misinterpreted a pleat as a midrib when the leaf actually lacks a midrib. If that is possible, switch keys and begin again. Finally, our keys cover the 200 common mosses that we describe in the book. If you look at enough mosses, surely you will find some of the less common species that we had to omit. In this case you will need to use the more comprehensive professional literature.

KEY I

ACROCARPS WITH HAIRLIKE LEAVES

1. Plants usually less than 1 cm tall; common on disturbed soils **2**

   Plants larger than 1 cm tall; usually in forests on soil, rock, logs, or trees **3**

2. Leaves 2–3 mm long, not much changed when wet or dry, with gentle brushlike curve to one side; capsule ≤1.5 mm long, inclined (Fig. 1a) .... *Dicranella heteromalla* (p. 37)

   Leaves 3–5 mm long, curled when dry; capsule ≥ 1.5 mm long, upright to somewhat inclined (Fig. 1b) .... *Ditrichum pallidum* (p. 35)

   Fig. 1 a & b

3. Leaves swept to one side of stem with tips more or less pointing in one direction **4**

   Leaves irregular in orientation with tips pointing in various directions **5**

4. Plants dark green; entire clump windswept to one side; capsule 3–4 mm; stalk 2–4 cm .... *Dicranum scoparium* (p. 47)

   Plants gray green or whitish green; individual plants with leaves swept to one side, but not all plants swept the same direction; capsule 2–3 mm; stalk 1–2 cm
   .... *Paraleucobryum longifolium* (p. 43)

5. Plants small, usually 0.5–3 cm tall; leaves up to 3 mm long
   .... *Dicranum montanum* (p. 41)

   Plants medium-sized, 1–6 cm tall; leaves 3–7 mm long **6**

6. Leaves finely toothed; capsule spherical when wet but short cylindrical and deeply furrowed when dry (Fig. 2) .... *Bartramia pomiformis* (p. 33)

   Leaf edges smooth or so finely toothed that the teeth are difficult to see; capsule elongate or macaroni-shaped **7**

   Fig. 2

7. Capsules upright, no bump where capsule joins
    stalk (Fig. 3a) . . . . *Dicranum fulvum* (p. 45)

    Capsules inclined, tiny to small bump where
    capsule joins stalk (Fig. 3b) **8**

Fig. 3 a & b

8. Leaf tips crisped in all directions; capsule ≤ 1.5 mm,
    slender, with small but obvious bump at connection to stalk
    . . . . *Oncophorus wahlenbergii* (p. 39)

    Leaf tips tend to curve toward one side of stem; capsule
    ≥ 1.5 mm, stout, with tiny bump at connection to stalk
    . . . . *Dicranum fuscescens* (p. 45)

KEY II

ACROCARPS WITH LANCE-SHAPED LEAVES

1. Plants gray or whitish green (dry) to light green (wet); shoots
    very densely packed together forming domed mounds; leaves
    tubular in upper half and seemingly without midrib **2**

    Plants darker green, yellow green, or brownish black, shoots
    loosely associated or if densely packed then not in domed
    mounds; leaves flat or folded but not tubular, with midrib
    usually visible at least at base of leaf **3**

2. Stems 1–9 cm tall; leaves 4–8 mm long; rarely with capsules
    . . . . *Leucobryum glaucum* (p. 123)

    Stems <1 cm tall; leaves 2–4 mm long; often with capsules
    . . . . *Leucobryum albidum* (p. 123)

3. Plants submerged in water attached to rocks, sticks,
    logs; leaf bases folded so as to appear to have a small
    pocket at base (Fig. 1) . . . . *Fissidens fontanus* (p. 213)

    Plants on soil, rocks, trees, or logs in dry areas, or if in
    wetter areas, not submerged in water; leaves not folded at
    base **4**

Fig. 1

4.   Leaf surface rippled or wavy when wet **5**
     Leaf surface not rippled or wavy when wet **9**

5.   Leaf midrib conspicuous to leaf tip (extra strips of
     tissue running along their length, visible as green
     and white stripes under 20× hand lens) (Fig. 2a) .. **6**
     Leaf midrib obvious in lower leaf but hard to see in
     long tapered tips (Fig. 2b) **8**

Fig. 2 a & b

6.   Midrib fills ≥⅓ width of upper leaf; leaves 0.4–0.8 mm wide
     .... *Atrichum angustatum* (p. 67)
     Midrib fills ≤¼ width of upper leaf; leaves 0.7–2 mm wide **7**

7.   Plants 3–7 cm tall; lower stems often matted with white fuzz
     .... *Atrichum crispulum* (p. 69)
     Plants 1–3 cm tall; lower stems often matted with rust-colored
     fuzz .... *Atrichum altecristatum* (p. 69)

8.   Leaves 7–10 mm long, barely contorted when dry
     .... *Dicranum polysetum* (p. 49)
     Leaves 3–6 mm long; somewhat to strongly contorted when dry
     .... *Tortella tortuosa* (p. 77)

9.   Leaves mostly ≥ 4 mm long (some at base or tip of stem may be
     shorter) **10**
     Leaves < 4 mm long **21**

10. Wet leaves flexible, thin, and translucent when held up to light;
     midrib obvious **11**
     Wet leaves stiff, thick, and opaque when held up to light
     (reminiscent of conifer needles); midrib difficult to see except
     at leaf base **14**

11. Leaf tips frequently broken off; midrib difficult to see because
     entire leaf is so narrow .... *Dicranum viride* (p. 53)
     Leaf tips ending in tapered point; midrib apparent **12**

12. Leaf base sheathing stem, blade lance-
shaped with parallel sides from the base to
midleaf then tapering to the apex (Fig. 3a)
.... *Timmia megapolitana* (p. 71)

Leaf base not sheathing stem, blade oval, tapering
equally at base and apex (Fig. 3b) **13**

Fig. 3 a & b

13. Leaves spreading widely from stem when wet,
giving plants a rose-like appearance from above; capsules
upright to inclined, lid long-beaked .. *Atrichum crispum* (p. 131)

Leaves not spreading as widely from stem and plants without a
rose-like appearance; capsules hanging upside down, lid not
beaked but conical .... *Mnium hornum* (p. 133)

14. Leaf margin smooth except along needle tip; capsules
with separate disk at connection to stalk (Fig. 4) .. **15**

Leaf margin toothed except along clasping leaf base;
capsules with or without disk **17**

Fig. 4

15. Stem covered with abundant fine white hairs
appearing almost woolly; grows on hummocks in bog
.... *Polytrichum strictum* (p. 63)

Stem covered with brown hairs or not hairy; grows in drier,
often sandy soils **16**

16. Needle tip of leaves white; plants <2 cm tall
....*Polytrichum piliferum* (p. 65)

Needle tip of leaves rusty or reddish; plants >2 cm tall
.... *Polytrichum juniperum* (p. 63)

17. Capsules cylindrical (Fig. 5) **18**
Capsules 4-sided like a box (Fig. 4, above) **19**

Fig. 5

18. Plants 4–10 cm tall, resembling conifer
seedlings; leaves 8–10 mm long; capsules 3–5 mm long
.... *Polytrichastrum alpinum* (p. 55)

Plants 2–5 cm tall, resembling mini yucca plants; leaves 3–7
mm long; capsules 2–3 mm long .. *Pogonatum urnigerum* (p. 61)

19. Capsules with a disk at attachment to stalk
    (Fig. 6a) .... *Polytrichum commune* (p. 57)
    Capsules lacking disk, attached directly to stalk
    (Fig. 6b) **20**

Fig. 6 a & b

20. Plants typically >5 cm tall, common in the North in
    coniferous forests and at high elevations; leaves sheathing
    capsule stalks with tips like those of other leaves
    .... *Polytrichastrum pallidisetum* (p. 59)

    Plants usually <5 cm tall, common in the South
    and oak-hickory forests; leaves sheathing capsule
    stalks with tips different in color from other leaves
    .... *Polytrichastrum ohioense* (p. 59)

21. Leaves gently curving to one side when
    wet; plants commonly with stiff brood
    branchlets standing upright from tips of stems
    (resembling mini asparagus shoots) (Fig. 7)
    .... *Dicranum flagellare* (p. 51)

Fig. 7

    Leaves spreading in various directions or barely diverging from
    stem when wet; plants lacking brood branchlets **22**

22. Plants 2–10 cm tall (or sprawling and stems 2–10 cm long) ... **23**
    Plants 0.2–2 cm tall **34**

23. Leaf margins toothed .... *Mnium hornum* (p. 133)
    Leaf margins smooth **24**

24. Plants whitish, pale green, or bluish green **25**
    Plants yellow green, dark green or reddish **26**

25. Leaves triangular, widest at base, often pleated
    (Fig. 8a), spreading up to 35° from stem
    when wet; capsules inclined to horizontal
    .... *Philonotis fontana* (p. 125)

    Leaves elliptical, widest above base, not
    pleated (Fig. 8b), spreading up to 80° from
    stem when wet; capsules drooping upside
    down .... *Pohlia wahlenbergii* (p. 125)

Fig. 8 a & b

345

26. Stems matted with red-brown hairs ...*Aulacomnum palustre* (p. 73)
    Stems without hairs or few scattered near base only **27**

27. Stems reddish **28**
    Stems brown or green (not reddish) **29**

28. Leaves spread <30° from stem when wet, leaf margin flat,
    lacking border ....*Pohlia nutans* (p. 89)
    Leaves spread >50° from stem when wet; leaf margin curled
    under, forming darker border
    .... *Ptychostomum pseudotriquetrum* (p. 127)

29. Plants green to purplish, always upright, growing on
    rock sometimes but more commonly on soil or a variety
    of manmade substrates; capsule stalks 1–3 cm long
    ....*Ceratodon purpureus* (p. 87)
    Plants olive green with older growth brown or blackish,
    sometimes sprawling, growing on rock; capsule stalks
    0–1.5 cm long **30**

30. Capsules lifted above leaves on stalks
    3–15 mm tall (Fig. 9a) **31**
    Capsules hidden among leaves on
    stalks ≤1 mm tall (Fig. 9b) **32**

Fig. 9 a & b

31. Plants on dry rocks; leaf tips sharp, often with
    white pricks ....*Bucklandiella microcarpa* (p. 117)
    Plants on wet rocks; leaf tips blunt, without white pricks
    ....*Codriophorus acicularis* (p. 115)

32. Leaves without hair points, though sometimes
    pale at tip (Fig. 10a) ... *Schistidium rivulare* (p. 113)
    Leaves (at least at tips of branches) ending in
    pale or white hair points (Fig. 10b) **33**

Fig. 10 a & b

33. Leaves 1–2.5 mm long, midrib difficult to see; capsules
surrounded by enlarged leaves ... *Schistidium apocarpum* (p. 111)

    Leaves 2.5–4 mm long, midrib prominent; capsules surrounded
by undifferentiated leaves .... *Grimmia pilifera* (p. 119)

34. Plants growing on bark of trees (above tree base) **35**

    Plants growing on rock, soil, rotting wood, tree base, or other
substrate **39**

35. Shoots grow in lines, connected by creeping stems
.... *Drummondia prorepens* (p. 101)

    Shoots in clusters, not connected by creeping stems **36**

36. Capsules surrounded by leaves, stalks not or barely visible
(Fig. 9b, above) **37**

    Capsules on stalks well above leaves, stalks clearly visible
(Fig. 9a, above) **38**

37. Plants 3–5 mm tall; capsule hoods hairless
.... *Orthotrichum stellatum* (p. 103)

    Plants 6–10 mm tall; capsule hoods hairy
.... *Orthotrichum sordidum* (p. 105)

38. Leaves tightly curled and contorted when dry;
capsules cylindrical, with 8 ribs when dry, mouth
as broad as capsule (Fig. 11a) . *Ulota crispa* (p. 99)

    Leaves not much contorted when dry (slightly
twisted); capsules pear-shaped, not or irregularly
ribbed when dry, mouth much smaller than
width of capsule (Fig. 11b) ... *Ulota coarctata* (p. 97)

    Fig. 11 a & b

39. Scattered tiny, budlike shoots surrounded by persistent
protonema (bright green algal-like film covering the
ground); leaves thick, needle-like, opaque hiding midrib
.... *Pogonatum pensilvanicum* (p. 319)

    Shoots not surrounded by persistent protonema (no green
film); leaves various **40**

40. Leaves pale blue green, covered with a white cobwebby or waxy film (look somewhat moldy when dry) ....*Saelania glaucescens* (p. 75)

Leaves not at all bluish and not cobwebby or moldy in appearance **41**

41. Leaves strongly contorted when dry, twisted and curled, sometimes into corkscrews **42**

Leaves not or slightly contorted when dry, sometimes tips slightly twisted or leaf folded like keel **48**

42. Capsules inclined to horizontal, somewhat curved and grooved when dry ....*Ceratodon purpureus* (p. 87)

Capsules upright, nor curved or grooved when dry **43**

43. Capsules cylindrical, 1–3 mm long, stalks 6–30 mm tall (Fig. 12a) **44**

Capsules goblet- or egg-shaped, up to 1 mm long, stalks 2–8 mm tall (Fig. 12b) **45**

Fig. 12 a & b

44. Plants reddish brown at base; leaf margins rolled under, forming border (Fig. 13a) .... *Bryoerythrophyllum recurvirostrum* (p. 85)

Plants darker at base but not reddish; leaf margins flat, lacking border (Fig. 13b) *Tortella humilis* (p. 79)

45. Leaves 2–4 mm long . *Rhabdoweisia crispata* (p. 83)

Leaves 1–2 mm long **46**

Fig. 13 a & b

46. Capsule rim lacking teeth (Fig. 14a) .... *Gymnostomum aeruginosum* (p. 83)

Capsule rim with tiny teeth (Fig. 14b) **47**

Fig. 14 a & b

47. Plants olive to blackish green; capsule stalks 2–3 mm long; capsule hoods torn into shreds at bottom edge ....*Ptychomitrium incurvum* (p. 93)

Plants pale green or yellow green; capsule stalks 3–8 mm; capsule hoods not torn .... *Weissia controversa* (p. 81)

48. Plants whitish or pale green .... *Pohlia wahlenbergii* (p. 125)
    Plants not whitish or pale green **49**

49. Capsule stalks 1–4 cm; plants growing mostly on soil but also
    on rock and other substrates, green to yellowish green **50**
    Capsules stalks <1 cm; plants growing on rock, green to dark
    green, brown, or blackish **53**

50. Leaves evenly distributed on short brown
    stems, rounded or short-pointed (Fig. 15a);
    capsules 1–2 mm long on yellow stalks
    .... *Barbula convoluta* (p. 161)
    Leaves more densely clustered toward
    tips of red stems, long-pointed (Fig. 15b);
    capsules 2–4 mm long on orange to red stalks **51**   Fig. 15 a & b

51. Capsule stalks orange like shiny copper .... *Pohlia nutans* (p. 89)
    Capsule stalks scarlet red **52**

52. Leaf margins flat, lacking a border
    .... *Gemmabryum caespiticium* (p. 91)
    Leaf margins rolled under, forming a border
    .... *Ptychostomum creberrimum* (p. 91)

53. Capsules football-shaped, opening by 4
    lengthwise slits to resemble a Chinese paper
    lantern when dry (Fig. 16 a & b) **54**
    Capsules goblet-shaped to cylindrical,
    opening by lid at top to leave open mouth
    when dry (Fig. 12, 14 above)................... **55**   Fig. 16 a & b

54. Leaves narrowly lance-shaped, midrib present
    .... *Andreaea rothii* (p. 121)
    Leaves triangular to fiddle-shaped, midrib absent
    .... *Andreaea rupestris* (p. 155)

55. Capsules held above leaves on stalks 3–4 mm long **56**
    Capsules barely visible among leaves, stalks 0–1 mm long ... **57**

56. Leaves edges curled back, making edges look dark; capsules (when dry) with 8 long and 8 short ribs (alternating), teeth held upright; capsule hood sparsely hairy
.... *Orthotrichum anomalum* (p. 107)

Leaf edges flat with no obvious border; capsules (when dry) with 8 ribs, teeth fold downward over lip of mouth; capsule hood densely hairy ....*Ulota hutchinsiae* (p. 95)

57. Plants 5–10 mm; capsules cylindrical, 1–2 mm long, with 8 ribs when dry (Fig. 17a)
.... *Orthotrichum strangulatum* (p. 109)

Plants ≥10 mm; capsules goblet- to egg-shaped, 1 mm long, not ribbed when dry (Fig. 17b) **58**

Fig. 17 a & b

58. Leaves without hair points, though sometimes pale at tip (Fig. 10a, above) ....*Schistidium rivulare* (p. 113)

Leaves (at least at branch tips) end in pale hair points (Fig. 10b, above) **59**

59. Leaves 1–2.5 mm long, midrib faint; capsules surrounded by enlarged leaves ....*Schistidium apocarpum* (p. 111)

Leaves 2.5–4 mm long, midrib prominent; capsules surrounded by undifferentiated leaves .... *Grimmia pilifera* (p. 119)

KEY III

ACROCARPS WITH OVATE LEAVES

1. Plants ≤ 1 cm tall **2**
   Plants 1–15 cm tall **6**

2. Plants silvery pale green; leaves about 1 mm long, tightly packed so that stems appear wormlike *Bryum argenteum* (p. 149)

   Plants green, yellow green, or brown; leaves 1–4 mm long, either in basal clusters or loosely packed along stems; stems not wormlike **3**

3.   Leaves 1–2 mm long, sparse along upright stem, often forming a small nestlike cup at stem tip filled with small green "eggs" (Fig. 1); capsules upright with 4 teeth; found on rotting logs or stumps .... *Tetraphis pellucida* (p. 129)

Fig. 1

Leaves 2–4 mm long, clustered in basal rosette or toward the tip of stem but not as a nestlike cup; capsule upright and lacking teeth or capsule horizontal to drooping; found on tree bases, on soil or rocks in disturbed areas **4**

4.   Capsules upright, 1–2 mm long, on stalks 5–15 mm tall (Fig. 2) .... *Physcomitrium pyriforme* (p. 151)

Capsules drooping, 2–5 mm long, on stalks 12–50 cm tall **5**

Fig. 2

5.   Plants pale green; leaves without a border; capsules with mouth on side of capsule below the end (Fig. 3a) .... *Funaria hygrometrica* (p. 153)

Fig. 3 a & b

Plants dark green; leaves bordered with long clear cells; capsules with mouth at end (Fig. 3b) .... *Rosulabryum capillare* (p. 147)

6.   Leaf margins toothed at least near tip **7**

Leaf margins smooth throughout **16**

7.   All leaves clustered at top of stem in a circular flowerlike rosette (Fig. 4) .... *Rhodobryum ontariense* (p. 145)

Some leaves may be in terminal rosettes but many other leaves are attached along entire length of stem **8**

Fig. 4

8.   Leaf margin toothed from tip to near base **9**

Leaf margin toothed near tip but toothless in basal half of leaf **11**

9. Leaves pointed at apex, >2× longer than wide (Fig. 5a); creeping stems absent, only upright stems present; capsule upright to inclined, lid long-beaked............ *Atrichum crispum* (p. 131)

    Leaves rounded at apex with midrib extending as a short point, 1½–2× as long as wide (Fig. 5b); creeping and upright present; capsule nodding, lid without beak **10**

Fig. 5 a & b

10. Capsules one per stem tip; creeping stems abundant, often elongate .... *Plagiomnium ciliare* (p. 141)

    Capsules often 2–5 per stem tip; creeping stems few, short .... *Plagiomnium medium* (p. 141)

11. Leaves without thickened border **12**

    Leaves with pale or reddish thickened border **13**

12. Shoots somewhat flattened; leaves near shoot tip tending to point in same direction, coarsely toothed at apex .... *Arrhenopterum heterostichum* (p. 171)

    Shoots not flattened; leaves emerge in all directions, weakly toothed at apex .... *Mnium stellare* (p. 137)

13. Creeping stems often present along with upright stems; teeth along leaf margin single .. *Plagiomnium cuspidatum* (p. 139)

    Creeping stems absent, only upright stems present; teeth along leaf margin in pairs (Fig. 6)............ **14**

Fig. 6

14. Capsules often 2–3 per stem tip, teeth and rim of capsule mouth dark red brown; leaves only slightly contorted when dry .... *Mnium spinulosum* (p. 135)

    Capsules one per stem tip, teeth and rim of capsule mouth light brown; leaves crumpled and twisted when dry **5**

15. Leaves about 4× longer than broad; prefers acidic sites (Fig. 7a) .... *Mnium hornum* (p. 133)

    Leaves 2–3× longer than broad; prefers calcareous sites (Fig. 7b) .... *Mnium marginatum* (p. 135)

Fig. 7 a & b

16. Plants brownish or black; leaves without midrib; capsule
    opening by 4 longitudinal slits .... *Andreaea rupestris* (p. 155)

    Plants dark green, reddish, or light green; leaves with midrib;
    capsule opening by lid **17**

17. Leaves elliptic with rounded tips, widest at or above middle **18**

    Leaves triangular to egg-shaped with pointed tips, widest below
    the middle **19**

18. Plants 4–12 cm tall; leaves 7–13 mm long
    .... *Rhizomnium appalachianum* (p. 143)

    Plants 1–5 cm tall; leaves 3–6 mm long
    .... *Rhizomnium punctatum* (p. 143)

19. Plants 8–15 mm tall; leaves loosely spaced
    along upright stem, often forming a small
    nestlike cup at stem tip filled with small
    green "eggs" (Fig. 1, above); capsules upright
    with 4 teeth (Fig. 8a); growing on rotting
    logs or stumps .... *Tetraphis pellucida* (p. 129)

    Fig. 8 a & b

    Plants >15 mm tall; leaves variously spaced but not forming
    a nestlike cup; capsules horizontal to drooping with 16 teeth
    (Fig. 8b); growing on wet soil or rocks **20**

20. Stems green, with short branches coming out at right angle to
    main stem; leaf tips bluntly pointed **21**

    Stems red, not branching or if branching then branches in
    whorl at tip of stem or running parallel with main stem; leaf
    tips acutely pointed **22**

21. Stems sparsely and irregularly branched
    (Fig. 9a); cells at outer corners of leaf base
    not noticeably enlarged or clear as seen
    with hand lens *Calliergon cordifolium* (p. 261)

    Stems pinnately branched (Fig. 9b); cells
    at outer corners of leaf base enlarged
    and clear as seen with hand lens
    .... *Calliergon giganteum* (p. 261)

    Fig. 9 a & b

22. Plants dark green to reddish
    .... *Ptychostomum pseudotriquetrum* (p. 127)
    Plants yellow green to white green **23**

23. Leaves often pleated, rolled edges form a border;
    stems sometimes with whorls of branches at tip
    (Fig. 10a) .... *Philonotis fontana* (p. 125)
    Leaves not pleated, edges not rolled, borderless;
    stems without whorls of branches (Fig. 10b)
    .... *Pohlia wahlenbergii* (p. 125)

Fig. 10 a & b

KEY IV

ACROCARPS WITH TONGUE-SHAPED LEAVES

1. Leaves arranged neatly in two rows on
   opposite sides of stem; wet plants flat,
   resembling miniature fern fronds (Fig. 1a) ... **2**
   Leaves arranged in more than two rows and
   coming out all around stem; wet plants not flat
   or not resembling ferns (Fig. 1b) **6**

Fig. 1 a & b

2. Plants 3–11 mm tall; leaves ≤2 mm **3**
   Plants ≥10 mm tall; leaves ≥1.5 mm **4**

Fig. 2 a & b

3. Leaves without a border (Fig. 2a)
   .... *Fissidens osmundioides* (p. 167)
   Leaves with a border (at least on pocket portion if not all
   around) (Fig. 2b) .... *Fissidens bryoides* (p. 165)

4. Leaf margin same color shade as rest of blade, tip not toothed;
   "fronds" 2–3 mm wide; capsule stalks 2–7 mm long, arising
   from tip of leafy shoot .... *Fissidens osmundioides* (p. 167)
   Leaf margin paler than rest of blade, tip with tiny teeth;
   "fronds" 3–5 mm wide; capsule stalks 5–20 mm long, arising
   from middle of leafy shoot **5**

5. Plants usually >20 mm tall; growing in wet habitats
   .... *Fissidens adianthoides* (p. 169)

   Plants usually < 20 mm tall; growing in dry to moist habitats
   .... *Fissidens dubius* (p. 169)

6. Leaves keeled lengthwise like a kayak, ending in long white
   needle tip .... *Syntrichia ruralis* (p. 157)

   Leaves flat or cupped, lacking long needle tip.................... **7**

7. Plants ≤ 1.5 cm tall **8**

   Plants >2 cm tall **9**

8. Leaves with pointed tip ending in tiny prick
   (Fig. 3a); capsules 1–2 mm long, cylindrical,
   elevated on 1–2 cm stalk. *Barbula convoluta* (p. 161)

   Leaves with rounded tip (Fig. 3b); capsules 3
   mm long, shaped like a wheat kernel, stalkless
   .... *Diphyscium foliosum* (p. 163)

   Fig. 3 a & b

9. Leaf margins smooth; capsules upright **10**

   Leaf margins toothed; capsules inclined or drooping **11**

10. Plants 4–8 cm tall; with brown, threadlike asexual reproductive
    structures common on stems .... *Encalypta procera* (p. 159)

    Plants 0.5–2 cm tall; lacking brown, threadlike structures on
    stems .... *Encalypta ciliata* (p. 159)

11. Leaves 2–4 mm long, toothed in the apical half (Fig. 4a), little
    altered when dry; capsules curved and inclined; capsule stalk
    8–17 mm .... *Arrhenopterum heterostichum* (p.171)

    Leaves 5–10 mm long, toothed throughout (Fig. 4b), crumpled
    and twisted when dry; capsules straight and
    drooping; capsule stalk 18–50 mm **12**

12. One capsule per stem; creeping stems abundant,
    often elongate ...... *Plagiomnium ciliare* (p. 141)

    Capsules 2–5 per stem; creeping stems few,
    short .... *Plagiomnium medium* (p. 141)

    Fig. 4 a & b

KEY V

PLEUROCARPS WITH SICKLE-SHAPED LEAVES

1. Plants of wet habitats, submerged in water or kept constantly wet from seepage or spray from cascading brooks and waterfalls; leaves on one stem often variable in degree of leaf curvature, from sickle-shaped to straight **2**

   Plants of dry to very moist habitats, not submerged or kept constantly wet; leaves sickle-shaped on most of plant (curvature variable in *Rhytidium*) **7**

2. Mosses on wet rocks in or beside streams and waterfalls .... *Hygrohypnum ochraceum* (p. 281)

   Mosses of calcareous wetlands in seeps, swamps, or fens **3**

3. Leaves egg-shaped, midrib absent (Fig. 1a). **4**
   Leaves lance-shaped, midrib present (Fig. 1b) **5**

Fig. 1 a & b

4. Leaves not crowded, curved on most of stem (Fig. 2a) .... *Hypnum lindbergii* (p. 187)

   Leaves densely crowded, curved at stem tips but mostly straight elsewhere (Fig. 2b) .... *Scorpidium scorpioides* (p. 283)

5. Mosses reddish *Scorpidium revolvens* (p. 173)
   Mosses yellow green to brownish **6**

Fig. 2 a & b

6. Stems stiff, with red-brown fuzz on older parts; stem leaves 1–2 mm long .... *Cratoneuron filicinum* (p. 257)

   Stems flacid, without red-brown fuzz; stem leaves 2–5 mm long .... *Drepanocladus aduncus* (p. 173)

7. Leafy shoots 2–3 mm wide, appearing swollen due to very crowded leaves; leaf surfaces strongly wrinkled across the width .... *Rhytidium rugosum* (p. 175)

   Leafy shoots <2 mm wide, not appearing swollen; leaf surfaces flat or pleated lengthwise **8**

8.   Leaf bases spreading 60–90° from stems; leaf
     tips curving in various directions; leaves not
     appearing to be braided or forming ringlets
     (Fig. 3a) .... *Ctenidium molluscum* (p. 189)

     Leaf bases held more closely to stem, spreading
     <45°; leaf tips curving in the same direction to
     either side of the stem; leaves appearing to be
     braided or forming ringlets (Fig. 3b) **9**

Fig. 3 a & b

9.   Leaves strongly curved with the tips curled back
     toward the leaf base, nearly forming ringlets
     (Fig. 4a); branches not appearing braided;
     leaf surfaces pleated lengthwise **10**

     Leaves curved but not forming ringlets
     (Fig. 4b); branches appearing braided;
     leaf surfaces not pleated................. **11**

Fig. 4 a & b

10. Stems with regularly pinnate branches at
     right angles from stem, branch lengths
     becoming shorter toward stem tip in even
     progression; leaves 2–3 mm long (Fig. 5a)
     .... *Ptilium crista-castrensis* (p. 179)

     Stems with irregularly to regularly pinnate
     branches at various angles from stem,
     branch lengths variable toward stem tip; leaves
     2.5–4 mm long (Fig. 5b) .... *Sanionia uncinata* (p. 177)

Fig. 5 a & b

11. Plants small: leafy shoots ≤ 1 mm wide, 1–4 cm long; leaves 0.5–2
     mm long **12**

     Plants larger: leafy shoots > 1 mm wide and 2–10 mm long;
     leaves 1.5–2.5 mm long... **14**

12. Shoots somewhat flattened, extremely shiny like ironed satin;
     capsule lids long-beaked............ *Brotherella recurvans* (p. 185)

     Shoots not flattened, dull to glossy but not appearing ironed;
     capsule lids conical to short-beaked **13**

13. Leaves 0.5–1 mm long; capsule stalks 6–15 mm; capsules almost upright, somewhat curved, 1–2 mm long
.... *Hypnum pallescens* (p. 183)

    Leaves 1.4–2 mm long; capsule stalks 13–35 mm; capsules horizontal, strongly curved, 2–2.5 mm long
.... *Hypnum fauriei* (p. 183)

14. Plants branching irregularly and infrequently; shoots often standing upright, sometimes creeping; leaves appearing loosely braided to windswept (Fig. 6a) ...... *Hypnum lindbergii* (p. 187)

    Plants regularly branched in pinnate pattern; shoots creeping; leaves appearing tightly braided (Fig. 6b) ... **15**

Fig. 6 a & b

15. Capsules inclined to horizontal, strongly curved (Fig. 7a); capsule stalks 2–5 cm
.... *Hypnum curvifolium* (p. 181)

    Capsules nearly upright, only slightly curved (Fig. 7b); capsule stalks 1–3 cm .... *Hypnum imponens* (p. 181)

Fig. 7 a & b

KEY VI

PLEUROCARPS WITH LANCE-SHAPED LEAVES WITH MIDRIB

1. Plants with upright stems, top of plants 3–10 cm above substrate... **2**

    Plants creeping or creeping with ascending shoot tips, top of plants rarely more than 3 cm above substrate **7**

2. Stems unbranched for several centimeters at base, thus mimicking a tree trunk with crown of branches near tip of stem **3**

    Stems pinnately branched nearly to base, thus mimicking an upright feather.. **5**

3. Leaves not pleated; branches arching down from top of stem
.... *Thamnobryum alleghaniense* (p. 201)

Leaves pleated; branches spread outward and up from the top
of stem **4**

4. Base of leaf without lobes (Fig. 1a); capsules
1.5–3 mm long; common in northern part of
this guide's range   *Climacium dendroides* (p. 203)

Base of leaf with small lobes (Fig. 1b); capsules
3.5–6 mm long; common in southern part of
this guide's range   *Climacium americanum* (p. 203)

Fig. 1 a & b

5. Plants of dry habitats; stems
not matted with hairs; leaves at
stem tips curved in one direction
(Fig. 2a) *Rhytidium rugosum* (p. 175)

Plants of wet habitats; stems matted with
green or red-brown hairs; leaves at stem
tips straight (Fig. 2b) **6**

Fig. 2 a & b

6. Leaves well-spaced, 1–2 mm long.. *Helodium paludosum* (p. 197)
Leaves crowded, 3–4 mm long ..... *Tomentypnum nitens* (p. 199)

7. Plants submerged in water attached to rocks, sticks,
logs; leaf bases folded so as to appear to have a small
pocket at the base (Fig. 3) ..... *Fissidens fontanus* (p. 213)

Plants terrestrial on soil, rocks, trees, or logs, or if
submerged then leaves not folded at base to form
pocket.. **8**

8. Leaves ≤2 mm long **9**
Leaves 2–4 mm long **17**

Fig. 3

9. Plants grow in lines with upright clusters of branches along
creeping stems on tree bark .... *Drummondia prorepens* (p. 101)

Plants grow in tangled carpets or mats (not small clusters in
line) on various substrates **10**

10. Shoots often end with fuzzy cluster of tiny branchlets (Fig. 4a) .... *Leskeella nervosa* (p. 215)

Shoots lack cluster of tiny branchlets at tips (Fig. 4b) **11**

Fig. 4 a & b

11. Plants with crowded, short (<1 cm), erect branches arising from creeping stems (resembling carpet pile) **12**

Plants with creeping branches and stems **14**

12. Leaves spreading only slightly from stem, wet or dry (Fig. 5a); capsules erect .... *Anomodon rostratus* (p. 217)

Leaves spreading at least 45° from stem when wet (Fig. 5b); capsules bent over **13**

Fig. 5 a & b

13. Leaves crowded (Fig. 4b, above), ≤1 cm long; capsule not much arched, lid with long beak (Fig. 6a) ...... *Eurhynchiastrum pulchellum* (p. 241)

Leaves well-spaced (Fig. 5b, above), 1–2 mm long; capsule strongly arched, lid without beak (Fig. 6b) .. *Hygroamblystegium varium* (p. 211)

Fig. 6 a & b

14. Shoots look like bristly pipe cleaners; leaves spread widely from stem, wet or dry; leaf tip rolled lengthwise like a canoe hull .... *Campyliadelphus chrysophyllus* (p. 193)

Shoots look like threads or foxtails; leaves spread more widely from stem when wet; leaf tip not rolled lengthwise **15**

15. Plants on bark at base of trees, logs, or stumps .... *Sciuro-hypnum reflexum* (p. 207)

Plants on rock or soil **16**

16. Leaves 1–2 mm long, shiny green *Sciuro-hypnum plumosum* (p. 207)

Leaves ≤1 mm long, dull yellow green .*Bryhnia graminicolor* (p. 209)

17. Older shoots with blackish leaves; growing on rock; capsules erect on stalks from tips of shoots **18**

    Older shoots with green, yellow green, golden, or brownish green leaves; growing on various substrates; capsules usually bent over on stalks from short side branches .• **19**

18. Plants on wet rocks; leaf tips blunt, without white pricks (Fig. 7a) ...... *Codriophorus acicularis* (p. 115)

    Plants on dry rocks; leaf tips sharp, often with white pricks (Fig. 7b)
    .... *Bucklandiella microcarpa* (p. 117)

    Fig. 7 a & b

19. Leaf tips short and blunt; long branches curl when dry like a hook ....*Anomodon viticulosus* (p. 191)

    Leaf tips long and sharply pointed; long branches not curling like a hook when dry **20**

20. Leaves at stem tips curve in one direction
    .... *Rhytidium rugosum* (p. 175)

    Leaves at stem tips straight or curved in various directions . **21**

21. Leaf tips rolled lengthwise like a canoe hull   **22**

    Leaf tips flat, not rolled lengthwise **23**

22. Leaves abruptly narrowed to long straight tip (Fig. 8a) .... *Drepanocladus polygamus* (p. 195)

    Leaves more gradually narrowed to long, often gently curved tip (Fig. 8b)
    .... *Campyliadelphus chrysophyllus* (p. 193)

    Fig. 8 a & b

23. Leaves sparsely spaced, not pleated; capsules cylindrical and strongly arched, light brown ..... *Leptodictyum riparium* (p. 211)

    Leaves crowded, pleated (especially when dry); capsules stubby macaroni-shaped and gently curved, dark brown **24**

24. Leaves pleated when dry, less so when wet; capsules 2 mm long, inclined to horizontal (both sexes on one plant so frequently with capsules) .... *Brachythecium salebrosum* (p. 205)

    Leaves strongly pleated when wet or dry; capsules 2–3 mm long, nearly upright (separate sexed plants, so less frequently with capsules) ....*Brachythecium oxycladon* (p. 205)

KEY VII

PLEUROCARPS WITH LANCE-SHAPED LEAVES WITHOUT MIDRIB

1. Aquatic plants, submerged under water in streams or lakes part or all of year; shoots usually >10 cm long, flexible, rippling in flowing water; leaves 2–8 mm long **2**

   Terrestrial plants, usually not submerged under water; shoots mostly <10 cm and stiffer; leaves ≤3 mm long **5**

2. Leaves sharply keeled lengthwise (Fig. 1a); shoots triangular in cross-section .... *Fontinalis antipyretica* (p. 233)

   Leaves flat or rolled lengthwise (Fig. 1b); shoots circular or irregular in cross-section **3**

Fig. 1 a & b

3. Leaves of main stem and branches obviously differing in size ....*Fontinalis sphagnifolia* (p. 231)

   Leaves of main stem and branches not obviously differing in size...**4**

4. Leaves 2–4 mm long, strongly rolled lengthwise; branch tips long-pointed with tightly held leaves (Fig. 2a) .... *Fontinalis dalecarlica* (p. 231)

   Leaves 3–7 mm long, flat or only gently cupped near base; branch tips short-tapered with loose leaves (Fig. 2b) .... *Fontinalis hypnoides* (p. 231)

Fig. 2 a & b

5. Plants on wet rocks near or in streams, or on soil in calcium-enriched wetlands **6**

   Plants on dry rocks, tree trunks, tree bases, rotten logs or stumps **8**

6. Leaf tips curved outward and furrowed lengthwise like a canoe hull (Fig. 3a); branches often upright, look like spiky pipe cleaners .... *Campylium stellatum* (p. 195)

   Leaf tips straight or occasionally curved to side, not furrowed (Fig. 3b); branches creeping, look like brushes or bushy tails **7**

   Fig. 3 a & b

7. Leaves 1–1.2 mm long, edges rolled; branches curl slightly at ends .... *Sematophyllum demissum* (p. 219)

   Leaves 1.5–2 mm long, edges flat; branches straight .... *Sematophyllum marylandicum* (p. 219)

8. Plants large; stem leaves 2–3 mm long; capsule stalks 2–4 cm tall .... *Heterophyllium affine* (p. 221)

   Plants small; stem leaves ≤2 mm long; capsule stalks ≤2 cm tall **9**

9. Stem and branch leaves differ in shape, 1–2 mm long; stem leaves ovate, abruptly narrowed from a broad base; branch leaves lance, often with tips curved to one side .... *Ctenidium molluscum* (p. 189)

   Stem and branch leaves similar in shape, 0.2–1.3 mm long .. **10**

10. Plants grow radially, oily brown at center of disk to shiny green along the margins; branches often end with a fuzzy cluster of tiny branchlets (Fig. 4a) .... *Platygyrium repens* (p. 223)

    Plants grow in mats lacking obvious radial growth, shiny to dull green; branches without clusters of tiny branchlets (Fig. 4b) **11**

    Fig. 4 a & b

11. Branches thin, about 0.5 mm in diameter, curling outward
    away from substrate; plants on tree trunks **12**

    Branches very thin, ≤0.25 mm in diameter, creeping along
    substrate; plants on rocks, rotting logs, and tree bark
    (commonly near base of tree) **13**

12. Leaf tips curve to one side of branch;
    dry leaves pressed tight to branch
    (Fig. 5a) .... *Pylaisia selwynii* (p. 225)

    Leaf tips straight; dry leaves loosely
    spreading from branch (Fig. 5b)
    .... *Pylaisia polyantha* (p. 225)

    Fig. 5 a & b

13. Plants appear to have been combed, branches running parallel
    to each other; leaves upon wetting not spreading much
    .... *Schwetschkeopsis fabronia* (p. 227)

    Plants appear less orderly, branches running in various
    directions; leaves upon wetting spreading at least 45° **14**

14. Leaves 0.5–1.1 mm long, tips
    curved off to the side; branches
    somewhat flattened (Fig. 6a)
    ...... *Pylaisiadelpha tenuirostris* (p. 227)

    Leaves 0.1–0.5 mm long, tips straight;
    branches threadlike (Fig. 6b) **15**

    Fig. 6 a & b

15. Plants on bark; leaves 0.25–0.5 mm long
    .... *Platydictya subtilis* (p. 229)

    Plants on calcareous rock; leaves 0.1–0.3 mm long
    .... *Platydictya confervoides* (p. 229)

KEY VIII

PLEUROCARPS WITH OVATE LEAVES
WITH MIDRIB

1. Plants pinnately branched (like a feather or fern frond) (Fig. 1a) **2**

   Plants not pinnately, but sparsely or irregularly branched (not feather or fernlike) (Fig. 1b) **10**

Fig. 1 a & b

2. Stems 2–3× pinnate (Fig. 1a, above) .. **3**

   Stems once pinnate (Fig. 2) **4**

Fig. 2

3. Stem leaves not pleated, tip held close to stem when dry; plants often 3× pinnate, green to yellow green .... *Thuidium delicatulum* (p. 271)

   Stem leaves pleated, tip curves away from stem when dry; plants 2× pinnate, yellow green to yellow brown
   .... *Thuidium recognitum* (p. 271)

4. Plants on bark of trees, tree bases, or rotting logs **5**

   Plants on soil, humus, or rock **6**

5. Stem leaves distinctly larger than branch leaves
   .... *Thelia hirtella* (p. 267)

   Stem and branch leaves about the same size
   .... *Thelia asprella* (p. 267)

6. Plants large and shaggy (usually >10 cm long); leaves 3–5 mm long .... *Rhytidiadelphus triquetrus* (p. 259)

   Plants medium-sized (usually <10 cm long); leaves ≤3 mm long
   .... **7**

7. Leaf tips rounded or bluntly pointed; leaves 2–3 mm long
   .... *Calliergon giganteum* (p. 261)

   Leaf tips sharply pointed; leaves 1–2 mm long **8**

8. Plants of dry habitats; branches on dry plants thin and
    threadlike with leaves held tightly ..*Abietinella abietina* (p. 269)

    Plants of wet habitats; branches on dry plants bushy with
    leaves spreading at least a little **9**

9. Leaf tips long-tapering and often curved to
    side (Fig. 3a) .. *Cratoneuron filicinum* (p. 257)

    Leaf tips short-tapering and straight
    (not curved to side) (Fig. 3b)
    .... *Helodium blandowii* (p. 197)

    Fig. 3 a & b

10. Stems upright and unbranched for several centimeters at base,
    thus mimicking a tree trunk with crown of branches near tip
    of stem **11**

    Stems either branched nearly to base or sparsely branched, but
    without a "trunk and crown" **13**

11. Leaves not pleated; branches arching down from top of stem
    .... *Thamnobryum alleghaniense* (p. 201)

    Leaves pleated; branches spread outward and up from the top
    of stem.. **12**

12. Base of leaf without lobes (Fig. 4a); capsules
    1.5–3 mm long; common in northern part of
    this guide's range *Climacium dendroides* (p. 203)

    Base of leaf with small lobes (Fig. 4b);
    capsules 3.5–6 mm long; common in
    southern part of this guide's range
    .... *Climacium americanum* (p. 203)

    Fig. 4 a & b

13. Plants on wet rocks or soil, in or beside streams and waterfalls
    or in seepage, around springs, or in marshes or swamps
    (commonly moss is dripping wet when collected) **14**

    Plants on various substrates in moist to dry habitats (usually
    not dripping wet when collected)........................... **19**

14. Stems not or sparingly branched, sometimes
    sprawling but often upright (Fig. 5); leaf tips rounded
    to bluntly pointed .... *Calliergon cordifolium* (p. 261)

    Stems freely branched, creeping or erect-arching (Fig.
    1b, above); leaf tip sharply pointed **15**

Fig. 5

15. Plants on soil, humus, rock, or rotting logs in seepage
    or along streams in shady places, rarely submerged;
    capsule stalks roughened with tiny bumps
    (Fig. 6a) **16**

    Plants on wet rocks in streams or on dripping
    cliffs, sometimes submerged; capsule stalks
    smooth, without tiny bumps (Fig. 6b) **17**

Fig. 6 a & b

16. Leaves 1–3 mm long, gently cupped, tips not twisted
    .... *Brachythecium rivulare* (p. 247)

    Leaves 1 mm long, strongly cupped (especially on wet
    branches), tips twisted .... *Bryhnia novae-angliae* (p. 249)

17. Leaves 2–3 mm long, midrib thin and hard to see
    .... *Rhynchostegium aquaticum* (p. 251)

    Leaves 1–1.5 mm long, midrib thick and obvious **18**

18. Leaves with a thickened border (Fig. 7a)
    .... *Platylomella lescurii* (p. 253)

    Leaves without border (Fig. 7b)
    .... *Hygroamblystegium varium* (p. 211)

Fig. 7 a & b

19. Plants midsized to large (branches mostly longer than 2 cm
    and wider than 1 mm); leaves 1–3 mm long **20**

    Plants small (branches mostly shorter than 2 cm and thinner
    than 1 mm); leaves ≤1 mm long **25**

20. Leaves broadly ovate to almost circular, deeply
    cupped like a spoon; branches cylindrical and plump
    .... *Bryoandersonia illecebra* (p. 255)

    Leaves more elongate, not close to circular, not or gently cupped;
    branches cylindrical to somewhat flattened, not plump **21**

21. Leaf tips tongue-like and rounded *Anomodon attenuatus* (p. 239)

 Leaf tips pointed... **22**

22. Plants look rather different wet and dry (leaves drawn
 inward dry but spread 60° outward wet); leaves pleated
 .... *Forsstroemia trichomitria* (p. 235)

 Plants look similar wet or dry (leaves may spread slightly more
 when wet); leaves not pleated................................. **23**

23. Capsules with long-beaked lids; branches somewhat flattened;
 leaf edges finely toothed ... *Rhynchostegium serrulatum* (p. 243)

 Capsule with conical lid; branches not flattened; leaf edges
 smooth **24**

24. Capsules strongly contracted below
 mouth when dry; capsule stalk
 smooth, without tiny bumps (Fig. 8a)
 .... *Hygroamblystegium varium* (p. 211)

 Capsules not much contracted below mouth
 when dry; capsule stalk roughened with tiny bumps (Fig. 8b)
 .... *Brachythecium rutabulum* (p. 245)

Fig. 8 a & b

25. Leaf tips tongue-like and rounded, or commonly broken off
 ....*Anomodon tristis* (p. 237)

 Leaf tips pointed, not broken off **26**

26. Leaves when dry held close to stem and cupped so branches
 look like tiny necklace chains; leaves spreading when wet ... **27**

 Leaves when dry spreading somewhat, branches not looking
 like necklace chains; leaves not much altered when wet **28**

27. Leaves straight (Fig. 9a); capsules straight
 .... *Leskea gracilescens* (p. 265)

 Leaves curved to one side at ends of
 branches (Fig. 9b); capsules curved
 ....*Leskea polycarpa* (p. 265)

Fig. 9 a & b

━━━

28. Plants growing on tree trunks in knotholes or other moist nooks; capsules upright .... *Anacamptodon splachnoides* (p. 263)

Plants growing on soil, humus, rocks, rotting wood, or tree bases; capsules inclined to horizontal **29**

29. Capsules strongly curved and contracted below mouth when dry, lid conical .... *Hygroamblystegium varium* (p. 211)

Capsules gently curved and not or somewhat contracted below mouth when dry, lid long-beaked **30**

30. Leaf tips varying from short to long; capsule stalks smooth (Fig. 8a, above) .... *Eurhynchiastrum pulchellum* (p. 241)

Leaf tips all short; capsule stalks roughened with tiny bumps (Fig. 8b, above)....................... *Oxyrrhynchium hians* (p. 241)

KEY IX

PLEUROCARPS WITH OVATE LEAVES WITHOUT MIDRIB

━━━

1. Branches flattened; leaves appear to come off on either side of stem, more or less in one plane (Fig. 1a) **2**

Branches not flattened; leaves appear to come off all around stem, more or less 3-dimensional (Fig. 1b)...................... **12**

Fig. 1 a & b

2. Leaves angled out about 45° from stem, crowded and overlapping; stem rarely visible between leaves . **3**

Leaves wide-spreading 60–90° from stem, not crowded, not or loosely overlapping; stem mostly visible between leaves **5**

3. Plants on tree trunks; ends of branches curving outward and up away from trunk; leaves wrinkled across their width (Fig. 2); capsules nearly stalkless .... *Neckera pennata* (p. 301)

Fig. 2

Plants on tree bases, rotting logs, soil, or rock; ends of branches lying flat; leaves not wrinkled; capsules on stalks 7–20 mm tall **4**

4. Leaf tips rounded to bluntly pointed; leaves when dry curl downward on either side of branch, giving it a humpbacked ruffled look
.... *Homalia trichomanoides* (p. 303)

Leaf tips sharply pointed; leaves when dry not much changed
.... *Entodon cladorrhizans* (p. 293)

5. Stems often bearing tiny branchlets at base of leaves (Fig. 3) **6**

Fig. 3

Stems lacking tiny branchlets at base of leaves **7**

6. Tiny branchlets scattered along length of stem; leaves symmetric *Pseudotaxiphyllum elegans* (p. 299)

Tiny branchlets only at tips of stems; leaves asymmetric, shaped like a broad scimitar with one side curved and the other flat .... *Pseudotaxiphyllum distichaceum* (p. 299)

7. Plants rather weakly flattened with a fuzzy, airy appearance; leaves abruptly tapered to a long, narrow tip **8**

Plants quite flattened, looking as if they have been ironed..... **9**

8. Leaves spreading in various directions with straight tips; leaf bases running down stem .... *Herzogiella striatella* (p. 305)

Leaves spreading to either side of stem with tips curved downward; leaf bases not running down stem
.... *Herzogiella turfacea* (p. 305)

9. Capsules infrequent; leaves symmetric (Fig. 4a) **10**

 Capsules common; leaves asymmetric, shaped like a broad scimitar with one side curved and the other flat (Fig. 4b) **11**

Fig. 4 a & b

10. Leaves well-spaced, not much overlapping; leaf tips short-pointed (Fig. 4a)
 ....*Plagiothecium cavifolium* (p. 295)

Fig. 5

 Leaves fairly crowded and overlapping; leaf tips long-pointed (Fig. 5) *Taxiphyllum deplanatum* (p. 299)

11. Shoots to 2 cm long; leaves 1–1.5 mm long; capsules upright, not wrinkle-pleated when dry; capsule stalks 8–16 mm long ....*Plagiothecium laetum* (p. 297)

 Shoots to 5 cm long; leaves 1.5–3 mm long; capsules bent to horizontal, usually wrinkled-pleated when dry; capsule stalks 15–35 mm long ....*Plagiothecium denticulatum* (p. 297)

12. Leaves two-colored, gray green with white tips; capsules stalkless, surrounded by leaves with white, fringed tips
 .... *Hedwigia ciliata* (p. 275)

 Leaves mostly a single color; capsules either on stalks, or surrounding leaves not white-fringed **13**

13. Stems noticeably bright reddish orange to dark reddish brown in contrast to green or yellowish leaves (especially distinct on wet plants); large mosses with stems 5–16 cm long **14**

 Stems green to brown, not particularly contrasting with leaves; mosses of various sizes **17**

14. Plants 2–3 pinnate, each year forming a flattened spray ascending from the previous year's growth, the annual increments forming a stair-step pattern (Fig. 6a) . *Hylocomium splendens* (p. 313)

 Plants once pinnate or irregularly branched, not forming annual increments in a stair-step pattern (Fig. 6b) **15**

Fig. 6 a & b

15. Leaves strongly cupped; leaf tips broad but margins incurved to create a very short point .... *Pleurozium schreberi* (p. 287)

    Leaves not or gently cupped; leaf tips narrow with a long, sharp point **16**

16. Stem leaves clasping stem (Fig. 7a), moderately pleated; stems covered with tiny green hairs (best seen on dry stems with a few leaves stripped away) .... *Loeskeobryum brevirostre* (p. 311)

    Stem leaves not clasping stem (Fig. 7b), not pleated; stems without tiny green hairs .... *Rhytidiadelphus subpinnatus* (p. 309)

Fig. 7 a & b

17. Plants of wet habitats, submerged in water or kept constantly wet from ground water, seepage, or spray from cascading brooks and waterfalls **18**

    Plants of dry to very moist habitats, not submerged or kept constantly wet **23**

18. Mosses of calcareous wetlands in seeps, swamps, or fens **19**

    Mosses on wet rocks in or beside streams and waterfalls **20**

19. Stems branching pinnately in one plane; stem tips ending in long, budlike points with tightly rolled, straight leaves (Fig. 8a) . *Calliergonella cuspidata* (p. 285)

    Stems branching irregularly; stem tips ending in clawlike points with crowded leaves curved in one direction (Fig. 8b) .... *Scorpidium scorpioides* (p. 283)

Fig. 8 a & b

20. Leaves nearly circular, wide-spreading up to 70° from stem; leaf tip broad and blunt, not curved .... *Hygrohypnum duriusculum* (p. 279)

    Leaves ovate, held close to stems or spreading up to 30° from stem; leaf tips pointed, usually curved to one side of stem .. **21**

21. Plants growing on calcareous rock; leaves 0.7–1.5 mm long; capsule stalks 12–17 mm tall ..... *Hygrohypnum luridum* (p. 281)

    Plants on acidic rock; leaves 1.3–2.6 mm long; capsule stalks 17–33 mm tall **22**

22. Leaves narrowly ovate, midrib often extends to at least midleaf (Fig. 9a) .... *Hygrohypnum ochraceum* (p. 281)

    Leaves ovate, midrib absent or short (Fig. 9b) .... *Hygrohypnum eugyrium* (p. 281)

    Fig. 9 a & b

23. Branches appear fuzzy or bristly, wet or dry; leaves wide-spreading nearly at right angle to stem (Fig. 10a) **24**

    Branches appear cylindrical, at least when dry; leaves either held close to stem and overlapping when dry or if leaf bases wide-spreading then strongly cupped with tips curved back toward stem (some species with branches looking very different when wet) (Fig. 10b) **26**

    Fig. 10 a & b

24. Plants very small; leaves <1 mm long, tip furrowed to form U-shaped channel .... *Campylophyllum hispidulum* (p. 307)

    Plants midsized; leaves 1–2 mm long, tip flat **25**

25. Stem and branch leaves differ in shape (stem leaves ovate, abruptly narrowed from a broad base; branch leaves lance, often with tips curved to one side); stems branching pinnately (Fig. 11a) .... *Ctenidium molluscum* (p. 189)

    Stem and branch leaves similar in shape; stem branching irregularly (Fig. 11b) .... *Herzogiella striatella* (p. 305)

    Fig. 11 a & b

26. Leaves <1 mm long; plants very small **27**

    Leaves 1–2 mm long; plants midsized **29**

27. Plants appear to have been combed, branches running parallel to each other; leaves not cupped, gradually tapered to a long wispy tip .... *Schwetschkeopsis fabronia* (p. 227)

    Plants appear less orderly, branches running in various directions; leaves deeply cupped, blunt at tip or abruptly narrowed to a short point **28**

28. Leaves sparse, barely overlapping and spreading from stem, 0.4–0.6 mm long; leaf tip abruptly narrowed to short point (Fig. 12a) . *Myurella sibirica* (p. 273)

    Leaves crowded, overlapping and held tightly to stem, 0.3–0.4 mm long; leaf tip obtuse to rounded (Fig. 12b) .... *Myurella julacea* (p. 273)

Fig. 12 a & b

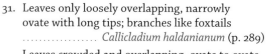

29. Plants growing on tree trunks; dry leaves overlapping and held tightly to stem, when wet spreading widely **30**

    Plants growing on soil, humus, rock, rotting wood, or tree bases; dry leaves overlapping and held tightly to stem or spreading outward up to 45°, when wet not much changed . **31**

30. Tiny branchlets frizz out from among leaves at ends of some branches; leaves pleated; capsules rare (Fig. 13, left) *Leucodon andrewsianus* (p. 277)

    Tiny branchlets lacking; leaves not pleated; capsules common on short stalks along sides of branches (Fig. 13, right) *Leucodon julaceus* (p. 277)

31. Leaves only loosely overlapping, narrowly ovate with long tips; branches like foxtails
    .... *Callicladium haldanianum* (p. 289)

    Fig. 13

    Leaves crowded and overlapping, ovate to ovate-elliptic with short tips; branches wormlike **32**

32. Capsules cylindrical, 2–3.5 mm long; leaves
     1–2 mm long, abruptly contracted to very
     short point (Fig. 14a) *Entodon seductrix* (p. 291)

     Capsules tubby-cylindrical 1.5–2.5 mm
     long; leaves 1.5–3 mm long, gradually
     tapered to acute point (Fig. 14b)
     .... *Plagiothecium cavifolium* (p. 295)

Fig. 14 a & b

KEY X

PLEUROCARPS WITH TONGUE-SHAPED LEAVES

1. Leaf margins toothed; midrib extends beyond leaf tip
    as short point (Fig. 1)...................................**2**

    Leaf margins not toothed; midrib ending just shy of
    leaf tip (Fig. 2a, below)................................**3**

Fig. 1

2. Leaves 5–8 mm long; creeping stems abundant,
    often elongate; capsules one per upright stem
    ....*Plagiomnium ciliare* (p. 141)

    Leaves 5–12 mm long; creeping stems few, typically short;
    capsules often 2–5 per upright stem *Plagiomnium medium* (p. 141)

3. Shoots very slender, like fine thread (<1 mm diameter
    when wet); leaves <1 mm long, tips often broken off
    ....*Anomodon tristis* (p. 237)

    Shoots bushy like yarn (1–3 mm diameter when wet); leaves >1
    mm long, tips intact **4**

4. Leaves only slightly curled with flat tips
    when dry; tongue-like upper half of leaf
    gradually tapered from slightly broader base
    (Fig. 2a) .... *Anomodon minor* (p. 315)

    Leaves somewhat crumpled with upper
    edges incurved when dry; tongue-like
    upper leaf abruptly tapered from obviously
    broader base (Fig. 2b) *Anomodon rugelii* (p. 315)

Fig. 2 a & b

KEY XI

LEAFLESS MOSSES

1. Capsules inclined, flattened, tick-shaped
   with a rounded beak at one end, on
   stout stalks up to 11 mm tall; leaves
   very small and rarely seen (Fig. 1a)
   .... *Buxbaumia aphylla* (p. 317)

   Fig. 1 a & b

   Capsules upright, cylindrical, on stalks
   10–35 mm tall; bright green film covering
   the ground around moss; leaves lance-shaped, clustered
   at base of stalk (Fig. 1b) *Pogonatum pensilvanicum* (p. 319)

KEY XII

PEAT MOSSES

1. Branch leaves with margins strongly incurved, forming a blunt
   hooded tip; stem cross-section with conspicuous cortex, about
   ⅓–½ diameter of stem; branches plump, wormlike **2**

   Branch leaves with margins flat to somewhat incurved,
   tip long-pointed, not hooded; stem cross-section without
   conspicuous cortex, less than ¼ diameter of stem; branches
   slender, stringy or spiky **5**

2. Plants purplish red, crimson, or at least red or pink tinged ... **3**

   Plants green, yellowish, or brownish; lacking any red, pink, or
   purple **4**

3. Plants purplish red or crimson, typically in acid bogs
   .... *Sphagnum magellanicum* (p.325)

   Plants green to yellowish brown, sometimes with pink
   highlights, typically in forests, sedge meadows, or at margin of
   ponds, streams, or bogs .... *Sphagnum palustre* (p. 325)

376

4. Plants green to yellowish brown, typically in forests, sedge meadows, or at margin of ponds, streams, or bogs; spreading branches usually with tapering ends *Sphagnum palustre* (p. 325)

    Plants yellowish green to golden brown, typically in acid bogs just above water level; spreading branches usually with blunt ends . . . . *Sphagnum papillosum* (p. 325)

5. Clusters of 6 or more branches attached at one point; apical head resembles a pom-pom or dry head of clover; stems stiff, woody; plants grow as scattered tufts in forests (Fig. 1a) . . . . *Sphagnum wulfianum* (p. 321)

    Fig. 1 a & b

    Clusters of 5 or fewer branches attached at one point; apical head large or small but not as dense as pom-pom; stems stiff to flexible; plants typically grow as cushions, mats, or carpets either in forests or open habitats such as bogs, fens, or sedge meadows (Fig. 1b) **6**

6. Branch leaves with apical half abruptly narrowed from clasping base and bent outward away from branch (Fig. 2a) . . . . *Sphagnum squarrosum* (p. 323)

    Branch leaves with apical half gradually narrowed and not bent outward from base (some species may have leaf tips reflexed outward when dry) (Fig. 2b) **7**

    Fig. 2 a & b

7. Plants typically red, red and green, or green with traces of red   **8**
    Plants green, yellowish, or brownish with no traces of red . . **10**

8. Apical head domed; plants often deep red, densely packed in firm hummocks with lumpy surface . . . . *Sphagnum capillifolium* (p. 333)

    Apical head flat-topped or slightly convex; plants a mixture of red and green, loosely packed in soft hummocks or carpets . . **9**

9. Terminal bud at center of apical head (viewed from above) visible but small; stem leaves with small notch at apex (Fig. 3a) ..... *Sphagnum russowii* (p. 333)

Terminal bud at center of apical head (viewed from above) not visible; stem leaves without notch or teeth at apex (Fig. 3b) .. *Sphagnum warnstorfii* (p. 333)

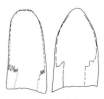

Fig. 3 a & b

10. Apical head with curved branches and thus appearing twisted when viewed from above .... *Sphagnum subsecundum* (p. 327)

Apical head with mostly straight branches and not appearing twisted when viewed from above **11**

11. Stem leaves triangular with pointed tips (Fig. 4a), much shorter than branch leaves, and spreading away from stem or lying flat against stem and pointing toward stem base; if apical head looks like a 5-pointed star, then developing branches between the rays in pairs . **12**

Stem leaves tongue- to fan-shaped with round tips (Fig. 4b), as long as branch leaves, and lying flat against stem and pointing toward stem tip; if apical head looks like a 5-pointed star, then developing branches between the rays solitary................................. **13**

Fig. 4 a & b

12. Branch leaves 2–4 mm, mostly ≥4× longer than broad; apical head weakly developed with messy appearance; developing branches between rays of head not visible; plants grow in water or very wet places, usually submerged or emergent
.... *Sphagnum cuspidatum* (p. 331)

Branch leaves 1–2 mm, <4× longer than broad; apical head well developed and neat; developing branches between rays of head in pairs; plants growing in moist to wet areas, occasionally submerged or emergent................... *Sphagnum fallax* (p. 329)

13. Plants brownish, densely packed in firm hummocks of acid bogs; stem leaves not or only slightly toothed across apex (Fig. 4b, above); terminal bud at center of apical head not visible
......................................*Sphagnum fuscum* (p. 335)

Plants greenish, loosely packed in carpets or small mounds of more shady and/or mineral-rich habitats; stem leaves fringed to tattered across apex (Fig. 5); terminal bud at center of apical head (viewed from above) clearly visible
....**14**

Fig. 5 a & b

14. Terminal bud conspicuous, appearing oversized compared to the small apical head; stem leaves fan-shaped, broader at tip than base, margin tattered across upper third of leaf (Fig. 5a); stem weak and flexible ....*Sphagnum fimbriatum* (p. 339)

Terminal bud visible but not conspicuous compared to the large apical head; stem leaves tongue-shaped, no broader at tip than base, margin fringed or notched just at apex (Fig. 5b); stem stiff ....*Sphagnum girgensohnii* (p. 337)

Peat moss and cranberry bog

Habitat Lists

Use these lists to learn which species you are likely to encounter growing in a given habitat. These groups are not comprehensive, but do suggest characteristic species of each habitat type.

Rotten Logs and Stumps

Brotherella recurvans 185
Callicladium haldanianum 289
Ctenidium molluscum 189
Dicranum flagellare 51
Dicranum fuscescens 45
Dicranum montanum 41
Dicranum viride 53
Entodon cladorrhizans 293
Entodon seductrix 291
Herzogiella turfacea 305
Heterophyllium affine 221
Hygroamblystegium varium 211
Hypnum curvifolium 181
Hypnum fauriei 183
Hypnum imponens 181

Hypnum pallescens 183
Leucobryum albidum 123
Leucobryum glaucum 123
Loeskeobryum brevirostre 311
Oncophorus wahlenbergii 39
Plagiomnium ciliare 141
Plagiomnium cuspidatum 139
Platygyrium repens 223
Pohlia nutans 89
Ptilium crista-castrensis 179
Sanionia uncinata 177
Sciuro-hypnum reflexum 207
Tetraphis pellucida 129
Thuidium delicatulum 271

Tree Bases

Anomodon attenuatus 239
Anomodon rostratus 217
Brotherella recurvans 185
Campyliadelphus chrysophyllus 193
Ctenidium molluscum 189
Dicranum fuscescens 45
Dicranum montanum 41
Entodon cladorrhizans 293
Entodon seductrix 291
Fissidens adianthoides 169
Fissidens dubius 169
Homalia trichomanoides 303
Hygroamblystegium varium 211
Hypnum pallescens 183
Leskea gracilescens 265
Leskea polycarpa 265
Leskeella nervosa 215

Mnium marginatum 135
Mnium stellare 137
Paraleucobryum longifolium 43
Plagiomnium ciliare 141
Plagiomnium cuspidatum 139
Plagiothecium laetum 297
Platydictya subtilis 229
Platygyrium repens 223
Pylaisiadelpha tenuirostris 227
Rhodobryum ontariense 145
Rhynchostegium serrulatum 243
Rosulabryum capillare 147
Sanionia uncinata 177
Sciuro-hypnum reflexum 207
Thelia asprella 267
Thelia hirtella 267
Tortella humilis 79

Tree Bark (trunks and branches)

Anacamptodon splachnoides 263
Anomodon minor 315
Anomodon rugelii 315
Anomodon tristis 237
Dicranum fuscescens 45
Dicranum montanum 41
Dicranum viride 53
Drummondia prorepens 101
Forsstroemia trichomitria 235
Leucodon andrewsianus 277
Leucodon julaceus 277
Neckera pennata 301
Orthotrichum sordidum 105
Orthotrichum stellatum 103
Platygyrium repens 223
Pylaisia polyantha 225
Pylaisia selwynii 225
Schwetschkeopsis fabronia 227
Ulota coarctata 97
Ulota crispa 99

Forest Floor (soil, humus, small rocks, well-rotted wood)

Abietinella abietina 269
Arrhenopterum heterostichum 171
Atrichum altecristatum 69
Atrichum angustatum 67
Atrichum crispulum 69
Bartramia pomiformis 33
Brachythecium rutabulum 245
Brachythecium salebrosum 205
Bryoandersonia illecebra 255
Campyliadelphus chrysophyllus 193
Campylophyllum hispidulum 307
Ctenidium molluscum 189
Dicranum polysetum 49
Dicranum scoparium 47
Diphyscium foliosum 163
Drepanocladus aduncus 173
Eurhynchiastrum pulchellum 241
Fissidens adianthoides 169
Fissidens dubius 169
Fissidens osmundioides 167
Herzogiella striatella 305
Heterophyllium affine 221
Hygroamblystegium varium 211
Hylocomium splendens 313
Hypnum curvifolium 181
Hypnum imponens 181
Hypnum lindbergii 187
Leucobryum albidum 123
Leucobryum glaucum 123
Loeskeobryum brevirostre 311
Mnium hornum 133
Mnium marginatum 135
Mnium spinulosum 135
Oxyrrhynchium hians 241
Plagiomnium ciliare 141
Plagiomnium cuspidatum 139
Plagiomnium medium 141
Plagiothecium cavifolium 295
Plagiothecium laetum 297
Pleurozium schreberi 287
Pohlia nutans 89
Polytrichastrum alpinum 55
Polytrichastrum ohioense 59
Polytrichastrum pallidisetum 59
Polytrichum commune 57
Ptilium crista-castrensis 179
Rhodobryum ontariense 145
Rhynchostegium serrulatum 243
Rhytidiadelphus subpinnatus 309
Rhytidiadelphus triquetrus 259
Rosulabryum capillare 147
Sphagnum fimbriatum 339
Sphagnum girgensohnii 337
Sphagnum palustre 325
Sphagnum russowii 333
Sphagnum squarrosum 323
Sphagnum warnstorfii 333
Sphagnum wulfianum 321
Thuidium delicatulum 271
Thuidium recognitum 271
Timmia megapolitana 71
Weissia controversa 81

Rocks (boulders, cliffs, ledges)

Abietinella abietina 269
Andreaea rothii 121
Andreaea rupestris 155
Anomodon attenuatus 239
Anomodon minor 315
Anomodon rostratus 217
Anomodon rugelii 315
Anomodon viticulosus 191
Bartramia pomiformis 33
Bryhnia graminicolor 209
Bucklandiella microcarpa 117
Dicranum fulvum 45
Dicranum fuscescens 45
Dicranum montanum 41
Encalypta ciliata 159
Encalypta procera 159
Entodon cladorrhizans 293
Entodon seductrix 291
Grimmia pilifera 119
Gymnostomum aeruginosum 83
Hedwigia ciliata 275
Homalia trichomanoides 303
Hypnum imponens 181
Hypnum pallescens 183
Leskeella nervosa 215
Mnium marginatum 135
Myurella julacea 273
Myurella sibirica 273
Orthotrichum anomalum 107
Orthotrichum strangulatum 109
Paraleucobryum longifolium 43
Platydictya confervoides 229
Pseudotaxiphyllum distichaceum 299
Pseudotaxiphyllum elegans 299
Ptychomitrium incurvum 93
Pylaisiadelpha tenuirostris 227
Rhabdoweisia crispata 83
Rhytidium rugosum 175
Schistidium apocarpum 111
Schistidium rivulare 113
Syntrichia ruralis 157
Taxiphyllum deplanatum 299
Timmia megapolitana 71
Tortella humilis 79
Tortella tortuosa 77
Ulota hutchinsiae 95

Wet Rocks (in seepage, along streams, in spray of waterfalls, but plants generally not submerged)

Brachythecium rivulare 247
Bryhnia novae-angliae 249
Codriophorus acicularis 115
Fissidens bryoides 165
Hygroamblystegium varium 211
Hygrohypnum duriusculum 279
Hygrohypnum eugyrium 281
Hygrohypnum luridum 281
Hygrohypnum ochraceum 281
Loeskeobryum brevirostre 311
Myurella julacea 273
Myurella sibirica 273
Philonotis fontana 125
Plagiothecium denticulatum 297
Platylomella lescurii 253
Pohlia wahlenbergii 125
Rhizomnium appalachianum 143
Rhizomnium punctatum 143
Rhynchostegium aquaticum 251
Schistidium rivulare 113
Sciuro-hypnum plumosum 207
Sematophyllum demissum 219
Sematophyllum marylandicum 219
Sphagnum capillifolium 333
Sphagnum fallax 329
Sphagnum russowii 333
Thamnobryum alleghaniense 201

SWAMPS, MARSHES AND FENS (nutrient-rich wetlands)

Atrichum crispulum 69
Atrichum crispum 131
Aulacomnium palustre 73
Brachythecium rivulare 247
Bryhnia novae-angliae 249
Calliergon cordifolium 261
Calliergon giganteum 261
Calliergonella cuspidata 285
Campylium stellatum 195
Climacium americanum 203
Climacium dendroides 203
Cratoneuron filicinum 257
Drepanocladus aduncus 173
Drepanocladus polygamus 195
Helodium blandowii 197
Helodium paludosum 197
Hygroamblystegium varium 211

Hypnum lindbergii 187
Leptodictyum riparium 211
Philonotis fontana 125
Plagiothecium denticulatum 297
Pohlia wahlenbergii 125
Polytrichum commune 57
Ptychostomum pseudotriquetrum 127
Rhizomnium appalachianum 143
Rhizomnium punctatum 143
Scorpidium revolvens 173
Scorpidium scorpioides 283
Sphagnum fimbriatum 339
Sphagnum palustre 325
Sphagnum subsecundum 327
Sphagnum warnstorfii 333
Thuidium recognitum 271
Tomentypnum nitens 199

BOGS (nutrient-poor wetlands)

Aulacomnium palustre 73
Polytrichum strictum 63
Sphagnum capillifolium 333
Sphagnum cuspidatum 331

Sphagnum fallax 329
Sphagnum fuscum 335
Sphagnum magellanicum 325
Sphagnum palustre 325
Sphagnum papillosum 325

SUBMERGED IN WATER (of streams, ponds, and lakes)

Fissidens fontanus 213
Fontinalis antipyretica 233
Fontinalis dalecarlica 231
Fontinalis hypnoides 231

Fontinalis sphagnifolia 231
Hygroamblystegium varium 211
Platylomella lescurii 253
Rhynchostegium aquaticum 251

DISTURBED AREAS (lawns, gardens, sidewalks, roadsides, fallow fields)

Atrichum altecristatum 69
Atrichum angustatum 67
Barbula convoluta 161
Brachythecium oxycladon 205
Brachythecium salebrosum 205
Bryoandersonia illecebra 255
Bryum argenteum 149
Ceratodon purpureus 87
Dicranella heteromalla 37
Ditrichum pallidum 35

Funaria hygrometrica 153
Gemmabryum caespiticium 91
Physcomitrium pyriforme 151
Plagiomnium cuspidatum 139
Pogonatum pensilvanicum 319
Pohlia nutans 89
Polytrichum juniperinum 63
Polytrichum piliferum 65
Ptychostomum creberrimum 91
Weissia controversa 81

MOSS PUBLICATIONS AND RESOURCES

Crum, H. A. & L. E. Anderson. 1981. *Mosses of Eastern North America*. 2 vol. New York: Columbia University Press.

Cullina, W. 2008. *Native Ferns, Moss, and Grasses: From Emerald Carpet to Amber Wave, Serene and Sensuous Plants for the Garden*. New York: Houghton Mifflin Harcourt.

Flora of North America Editorial Committee, eds. 2007. *Flora of North America North of Mexico*. Vol. 27. New York: Oxford University Press.

Schenk, G. 1997. *Moss Gardening, Including Lichens, Liverworts, and Other Miniatures*. Portland: Timber Press.

Vanderpoorten, A. & B. Goffinet. 2009. *Introduction to Bryophytes*. New York: Cambridge University Press.

HELPFUL WEBSITES

American Bryological and Lichenological Society:
http://www.abls.org/

Bryophyte Flora of North America:
http://www.mobot.org/plantscience/bfna/bfnamenu.htm

Missouri Botanical Garden database:
http://www.tropicos.org

SUPPLIER OF GOOD QUALITY HAND LENSES

We have been very pleased with the Iwamoto Wide Lens Triplet Hand Lens, 20×, and the Bausch & Lomb Hastings Triplet Pocket Magnifiers, 7× and 10×, available from:

Miners Incorporated
P.O. Box 1301
Riggins, ID 83549-1301
800.824.7452
Minerox.com

FEEDBACK ON THIS FIELD GUIDE

Dr. McKnight and Dr. Rohrer welcome suggestions that might improve the next edition of this book:

Dr. Karl McKnight
Department of Biology
St. Lawrence University
Canton, NY 13617
kmcknight@stlawu.edu

Dr. Joseph Rohrer
Department of Biology
University of Wisconsin — Eau Claire
Eau Claire, WI 54701
jrohrer@uwec.edu

Moss Names

A NAME SERVES AS A MEANS OF REFERENCE FOR COMMUNICATION and information retrieval. To look up a friend's telephone number, you start with his name. Or to learn more about your favorite sports hero, you might type her name into Wikipedia and click search. So it is with a moss: knowing its name is the key to unlocking a vast amount of information about the species. In our book you will notice that we give both a scientific name and a common name for each moss. Common names can be very evocative and memorable, such as the Pincushion Moss, Knight's Plume, and Brocade Moss; however, common names have not been standardized for mosses, so using them to communicate can cause confusion when different people use different common names. To avoid such ambiguity, scientists employ scientific names that conform to the rules set forth in the *International Code of Nomenclature for algae, fungi, and plants*. We have used the scientific names accepted by authors of *Flora of North America*, the most recent definitive treatment on the plants of the continent. Although at first the scientific names may be difficult to pronounce and remember, they have the advantage of being understood worldwide. Even journal articles written in Chinese characters use *Leucobryum glaucum* for what we call Pincushion Moss in eastern North America.

SCIENTIFIC NAMES by their construction also convey our best scientific guess at genealogical relationships of the mosses, and thus convey more information than common names. The scientific names of species are binomials (e.g., *Climacium americanum*); that is, they are composed of two words, a genus name (*Climacium*) plus a specific epithet (*americanum*). Genera (the plural of genus) may include one or more species believed to be closely related to one another. Our field guide includes two species in the genus *Climacium*: *Climacium americanum* and *C. dendroides*. When the genus name is unambiguous from previous reference, it is often abbreviated using the initial letter. *Climacium* spp. is a shorthand way of referring to multiple species of that genus. An epithet, such as *americanum*, is never used alone as the name of a species, because it can be combined with many other generic names to specify other species. For instance, *Ribes americanum* is a species of currant.

INDEX

The scientific name of the main species for each description page is listed in *italic type* whereas its common name is in regular type.

Look-alike species that are so similar to a main species that they share a description page are listed in green below.